A MOTHER'S WORST NIGHTMARE

"It's okay," Mary said, trying to reassure her. "Now you can get away from Marcus, too. You'll be safe now."

But Elizabeth knew that no one would be safe, not with the whole group of them going toe-to-toe with Marcus.

"What have you done?" Elizabeth said, dropping the cordless phone to the floor and frantically searching through her purse for her keys. "Oh my God, no!"

In her own way, Elizabeth had spent most of her life trying to protect her children from her husband. Although she'd always accepted his claim that the beatings he regularly dealt out were necessary discipline, she tried to intervene when he went too far, begging him to stop before he killed them. Marcus wouldn't hand the children over to their mothers without a fight. She was the only one who could reason with him. God only knew what he would do without her there.

This title is also available as an eBook

D0039719

DEADLY DEVOTION

PREVIOUSLY PUBLISHED AS *WHERE HOPE BEGINS*

ALYSIA SOFIOS
WITH CAITLIN ROTHER

POCKET **STAR** BOOKS

New York   London   Toronto   Sydney

Pocket Star Books
A Division of Simon & Schuster, Inc.
1230 Avenue of the Americas
New York, NY 10020

Copyright © 2009 by Alysia Sofios

Originally published as *Where Hope Begins*.

All lyrics by permission of Marcus Wesson, the author.

All rights reserved, including the right to reproduce this book or portions thereof in any form whatsoever. For information address Pocket Books Subsidiary Rights Department, 1230 Avenue of the Americas, New York, NY 10020

First Pocket Star Books paperback edition August 2011

POCKET STAR BOOKS and colophon are registered trademarks of Simon & Schuster, Inc.

For information about special discounts for bulk purchases, please contact Simon & Schuster Special Sales at 1-866-506-1949 or business@simonandschuster.com.

The Simon & Schuster Speakers Bureau can bring authors to your live event. For more information or to book an event contact the Simon & Schuster Speakers Bureau at 1-866-248-3049 or visit our website at www.simonspeakers.com.

Cover image of house © Roger Hornback / Getty Images
Cover image of man © Getty Images

Manufactured in the United States of America

10   9   8   7   6   5   4   3   2   1

ISBN 978-1-4391-3151-0
ISBN 978-1-4391-5769-5 (ebook)

To Sebhrenah, Lise, Illabelle, Jonathan, Aviv, Ethan, Sedona, Marshey, and Jeva, who I never had a chance to meet, but who will live in my heart forever.

To my parents, Chuck and Sandy, who have always provided me with unconditional love and support.

And to little Alysia, for making us all realize the true meaning of hope.

Wesson Family Members

(as of July 26, 2011)

Marcus Wesson, 64—b. August 22, 1946

Elizabeth Wesson, 51 (only legal wife)—b. July 31, 1959

Dorian Wesson, 36 (son)—b. December 12, 1974

Adrian Wesson, 35 (son)—b. November 6, 1975

Kiani Wesson, 34 (daughter)—b. April 23, 1977

Sebhrenah "Bhrenah" Wesson, 25 (daughter) VICTIM— b. April 5, 1978

Stefan Wesson, stillborn (son)—b. May 11, 1979

Almae Wesson, 31 (son)—b. May 23, 1980

Donovan Wesson, died at six months (son)— b. October 11, 1981

Marcus Wesson Jr., 28 (son)—b. December 2, 1982

Gypsy Wesson, 27 (daughter)—b. December 28, 1983

Serafino "Fino" Wesson, 26 (son)—b. February 12, 1985

Elizabeth "Lise" Wesson, 17 (daughter) VICTIM— b. March 28, 1986

Sofina "Sofia" Solorio, 35 (niece)—b. October 24, 1975

Ruby Ortiz, 33 (niece)—b. November 7, 1977

Brandy Sanchez, 31 (niece)—b. November 15, 1979

Rosa "Rosie" Solorio, 29 (niece)——b. October 21, 1981

Illabelle Wesson, 8 (daughter with Kiani/granddaughter)
VICTIM——b. September 16, 1995

Jonathan Wesson, 7 (son with niece Sofia) VICTIM——
b. March 14, 1996

Aviv Wesson, 7 (daughter with niece Ruby) VICTIM——
b. June 16, 1996

Ethan Wesson, 4 (son with niece Rosie) VICTIM——
b. July 15, 1999

Marshey Wesson, 19 months (son with Sebhrenah/
grandson) VICTIM——b. August 8, 2002

Sedona Wesson, 18 months (daughter with niece Rosie)
VICTIM——b. September 9, 2002

Jeva Wesson, 13 months (daughter with Kiani/
granddaughter) VICTIM——b. February 22, 2003

Prologue

I'd really gone all out to make my first Christmas celebration with the Wessons perfect, but things weren't going as planned. The angel in her purple dress kept toppling off the tree, and our names had dribbled down the five stockings because we'd hung them before the glitter glue was dry. On top of that, the four-foot artificial tree that was supposed to light up and change colors every ten seconds had gone completely dark on one side.

And that wasn't all. Every year since I'd become a TV reporter, I'd worked on Christmas Eve, and this one was no different. As usual, I couldn't find a decent meal anywhere; this time my dinner had consisted of a convenience store hot dog that looked like it had been sitting under the warming lamp for weeks. Needless to say, I kept everyone in my apartment awake throwing up that night.

My stomach trauma had subsided by seven o'clock on Christmas morning, so I snuck into the living room to lay out the gifts I'd carefully chosen for Elizabeth, her niece Rosie, and her daughters Kiani and Gypsy. My parents had sent some soft, fluffy blankets from Michigan, and I had bought a bunch of bath gel, candles, makeup, and other stocking stuffers. I couldn't wait to surprise the girls on their first

Christmas without the patriarch who had never allowed them to celebrate the holiday with presents, decorations, or Santa Claus.

After I finished, I collapsed onto my couch, looking forward to watching their reactions when they came out of their bedroom.

Elizabeth emerged first, and for a moment her face was all lit up with the enthusiastic response I'd hoped for. But her gleeful expression soon faded. I knew she was thinking about the nine other children who would never be able to join the rest of the family on this or any other holiday.

I'd really wanted to get the girls' minds off the terrible loss they'd lived through earlier that year, even if it was just for a few hours; Elizabeth had assured me that this would be a happy day for all of us.

I should've known this was a promise she couldn't keep. I didn't think it was possible, but she looked even more down than usual.

"The kids would have loved this," she said, her voice cracking as she looked mournfully at the five stockings.

It wasn't just the kids, though. Elizabeth missed her husband, Marcus, and although they'd never admit it to me, I was sure Rosie and Kiani missed him, too. I knew them well enough by now to know.

"No crying," I said sympathetically, but firmly, to Elizabeth. "You promised."

"I know, Alysia, I'm sorry."

Rosie and Kiani wandered in next, their eyes practically popping out of their heads when they saw the presents stacked under the tree.

"These are for us?" Kiani asked in disbelief.

"Yes," I said, smiling. "Santa Claus came last night. We have to wait for Gypsy to get here before we can open them, though. Where is she, anyway?"

Like me, Gypsy liked to sleep in, so she was running late that morning. As Elizabeth called her daughter to hurry her along, I went into their bedroom to get Cosmo, my pet ferret. Although I used to think it was cruel to dress animals in costumes, I could have sworn Cosmo liked it when I bought him a new outfit. I dressed him in his tiny Santa suit and hat, then let the little critter run out to greet the Wessons.

Just then, Gypsy walked in.

"What in the world?" she asked, laughing at Cosmo's festive costume.

"Merry Christmas," I said, trying to hug her around the armful of gifts and the book of baby names she was carrying.

"I heard you were sick," Gypsy said.

"Let's not talk about it," I said, hoping to avoid another trip to the bathroom. "Let's start opening!"

I doled out the presents and watched as they cautiously peeled away the wrapping paper.

"Don't worry about ripping it, you guys," I said. "Tearing them open is half the fun."

Half an hour later, we had filled two garbage bags with shredded paper and scrunched boxes. Still glowing from receiving the gifts that surrounded them, the girls slipped off their usual high heels and replaced them with their new fuzzy slippers. I could tell how much Elizabeth loved the vanilla-scented perfume I got her because she kept spraying her arm and sniffing it. Marcus had never given her frivolous luxury items like that, nor had he allowed the kids to have any toys. The few times Elizabeth's family had given them toys at Christmas, Marcus had thrown them away.

Kiani, Rosie, and Gypsy went into the kitchen to start cooking the Christmas meal, while I stayed slumped on the couch. As much as I loved ham, mashed potatoes, and green beans, my stomach was in no condition to accept anything resembling food. Gypsy slathered the ham with honey glaze and stuck it in the oven with the rolls; Rosie strained the pot of potatoes she'd boiled.

As a single, twenty-eight-year-old workaholic, I wasn't very domestic and lacked many of the utensils necessary to cook a big feast—including a potato masher—so Rosie tried to use a fork to mash the potatoes. Realizing she hadn't cooked them long enough, she decided to finish the job in the blender.

"That's not going to work," Gypsy said, shaking her head.

Gypsy was right. When Rosie hit the button, the blender made a horrible noise, like a garbage disposal with a metal spoon stuck in it.

I chuckled to myself as I watched the drama unfold.

Growing up, Rosie and her family had been taught to make broken things work and to prepare meals with whatever food items they could afford, so she tried to fix the blender. But it was no use. I watched a cloud of smoke drift into the living room, bringing the odor of burned rubber along with it.

"I told you," Gypsy said, shaking her head again.

"I'm sorry," Rosie called out to me, turning red with embarrassment. I wasn't mad at her. I knew she'd been punished enough in her life already, and besides, I was more amused at the situation.

"It's okay. Open the window, please, before I get sick again," I replied.

Elizabeth jumped up and opened the front door, while an unattended Cosmo jumped into the trash bags and dragged out the boxes until they were all over the floor again.

In the midst of the commotion, the smoke alarm went off. This time it was the rolls that had burned. With each excruciatingly annoying beep, my headache got worse.

"This is more like it," I yelled, covering my ears and smiling at the stunned group. "Now you know what Christmas is like in most people's homes."

When dinner was finally served, the girls sat around the circular table, talking between bites of the salvaged meal; I contributed to the conversation from the couch. I could tell they were all happy to be together, but I could see on Rosie's and Kiani's faces that they couldn't shake the guilt over eating a holiday meal while Marcus was behind bars.

Gypsy didn't say much either, but I figured she was still feeling guilty about leaving her sister Lise and her other siblings behind when she ran away from home a year and a half earlier. She was also most likely reveling in the fact that their father was where he belonged. And Elizabeth, well, she was doing what she always did: trying unsuccessfully to hide her grief.

The girls had a long-standing coping mechanism of focusing on the brighter side of their lives, even when it seemed like there was little brightness to see.

Twenty-three-year-old Rosie bragged to the other girls that she had recently gotten her driver's license, although she admitted she was still scared to drive on the freeway.

"I'm so jealous," said Kiani, who was four years older and still couldn't drive.

Gypsy, who would turn twenty-one in three days, was jealous, too. She gazed at me with an unspoken plea.

"Don't look at me," I said, laughing. "Teaching Rosie to drive was scary enough for a lifetime."

Rosie sighed melodramatically, so I assured her I was only kidding.

"You should learn how to drive before the baby is born, though," I said to Gypsy, who was six months pregnant.

Gypsy's goals for the new year were to get a license, to earn a high school diploma, and to come up with a name for her baby girl, who was due in March. She opened up the book she'd brought and thumbed through it silently until Kiani took over and threw out a few suggestions.

Rosie was the only one who liked the name Emma.

"Taylor is good," Kiani said, looking around at us. When no one responded, she went on. "Okay, you don't like it. What about Arianna?"

"That's so cute," Gypsy said, smiling, and everyone agreed.

Whatever her name turned out to be, I knew this was going to be a very special little girl. She would be the first child in the Wesson family not to be named by Marcus. The first child who would grow up free from his abuse. And, more important, the first child not to be fathered by him.

One

E lizabeth knew something was wrong that Friday afternoon. There was tension in the air.

Yvette kept shooting her furtive glances while whispering into the cordless phone at Ruby's apartment. Elizabeth didn't know who her nephew's girlfriend was talking to, but it felt like she was the topic of conversation. She wanted to go home.

"I need to leave now," she said, walking toward Yvette on her way to the front door.

"Wait," Yvette called out. "Here, talk to her," she said, shoving the phone at Elizabeth.

"Hello?" she said in her soft, childlike voice.

"Aunt Lise, it's Mary."

"Oh," Elizabeth said cautiously. "What's wrong?"

Mary, the girlfriend of a different nephew, sounded anxious and jumpy, immediately confirming Elizabeth's suspicion that something *was* going on. Nonetheless, she wasn't prepared for Mary's answer.

"We're all at your house," Mary said. "The girls came back to get their kids."

Mary was referring to Elizabeth's nieces Ruby and Sofia, who had lived with the Wesson family but had left their two children behind several years ago, when Ruby ran away and Marcus kicked Sofia out of the house. A dozen nieces, nephews, cousins, and friends had gathered at Ruby's just an hour ago. What were they doing at Elizabeth's?

"They are talking to Marcus right now and—"

"What?" Elizabeth interrupted.

Sofia and Ruby had said they were going to the store to buy food for a barbecue, but it was clear now that they'd left Yvette behind to keep watch over Elizabeth while they snuck off to try to take their seven-year-olds, Jonathan and Aviv, away from Marcus.

"It's okay," Mary said, trying to reassure her. "Now you can get away from Marcus, too. You'll be safe now."

But Elizabeth knew that no one would be safe, not with the whole group of them going toe-to-toe with Marcus.

"What have you done?" Elizabeth said, dropping the cordless phone to the floor and frantically searching through her purse for her keys. "Oh my God, no!"

In her own way, Elizabeth had spent most of her life trying to protect her children from her husband. Although she'd always accepted his claim that the beatings he regularly dealt out were necessary discipline, she tried to intervene when he went too far, begging him to stop before he killed them. Marcus wouldn't hand the children over to their mothers without a fight. She was the only one who could reason with him. God only knew what he would do without her there.

Elizabeth ran out of the apartment. Her ears were ringing, and she could hear her blood pulsing as her heart pounded. In the parking lot, she finally got ahold of her keys and yanked them out of her purse, scattering tubes of lipstick and loose receipts onto the asphalt. Her hands were so shaky and slippery with sweat, she could barely get the key into her car door.

How could Ruby and Sofia do this? Please, God, let me get home in time.

Marcus hadn't allowed Elizabeth to get her license until she was thirty-one and he was in jail for welfare fraud, so she'd gotten into the driver's seat later than most. She had never speeded before; in fact, she habitually drove so slowly that motorists glared at her as they passed by.

But this was different. This was about saving the babies.

Never even glancing at the speedometer, she flew home on surface streets, blowing through several red lights. Ruby's place was only a few miles away, but the trip seemed to take forever.

She made a sharp left turn onto Hammond Avenue, where she could already see about twenty people gathered in front of her house on the corner. She gasped when she saw two patrol cars parked across the street. It was even worse than she'd thought.

The tires of her Toyota Echo squealed as she made another sharp turn into the driveway, pulling in next to the yellow school bus Marcus had retrofitted to drive their enormous family around.

When she'd left the house, two hours earlier, everything had seemed so normal. Marcus, Kiani, Sebhrenah, and Rosie had been repairing the bus and packing it up for a trip to Seattle, while seventeen-year-old Lise was inside home-schooling the seven little ones.

Their roughly one-thousand-square-foot house had formerly been occupied by a law firm, so it was zoned for commercial use in the middle of an otherwise residential, working-class neighborhood, and their driveway was actually a small parking lot in front of the building. The city had left repeated notices on the door about the Wessons' zoning violations, so Marcus had decided it was time to relocate the clan once again.

Elizabeth looked more closely at the group clustered in the front yard and realized there weren't any children.

Where are my babies?

The car was still rolling when she shoved the gearshift into park. Her hands shook as she turned off the ignition, the keys rattling against the steering column. She didn't take time to remove them before she pushed the door open and jumped out.

As she ran to the house, she could see the imposing bulk of Marcus's three-hundred-pound body blocking the doorway. Two of her children, Kiani and Serafino, were standing just behind him with Rosie, her sister Rosemary's daughter. Marcus had trained his sons, daughters, and nieces to be soldiers, warning them that this day would come.

Elizabeth ran over to Marcus to ask what was going on, but he spoke before she could get a word out.

"I need the keys, Bee," he told her calmly, using the pet name he'd given her when she was eight and he was twenty-one. His use of the endearment now struck her as odd, given the circumstances.

"Where are the keys?" he pressed. "I need the keys right now."

Elizabeth knew it was a bad sign when Marcus was calm in a stressful situation. But after having done his bidding for nearly four decades, she felt she was in no position to stand up to him. She ran back to the car to retrieve the keys and, clutching them against her chest, obediently delivered them.

Afterward, she wondered why he would need her car keys and why the house was so quiet inside, but she didn't dare ask. She didn't think anything bad had happened—at least not yet.

Rosie, Kiani, and Serafino stood tall behind Marcus, their shoulders back, on alert and at attention, their expressions stern.

A uniformed police officer stood silently off to the side of the house, a few feet away. There were two more officers across the street.

Elizabeth knew her whole family was in danger. The police presence only made the situation more volatile. Marcus had always said one day they would go to war with the government or Child Protective Services (CPS), but this was as close as they'd ever come.

Marcus remained calm while he made his case for keeping custody of his children. He'd been fooling the police and the social workers for years with that calm exterior of his, but Elizabeth knew what he was truly capable of. She knew the situation could blow up like a powder keg with just the slightest spark of provocation.

Elizabeth burned with anger. She wanted to yell at someone. She knew she couldn't scream at Marcus, so she decided to confront Ruby and Sofia. She wanted answers, and she knew she wasn't going to get them from her husband.

SOFIA AND RUBY had known that Marcus would put up resistance, but they were determined to keep their children from suffering any more of the abuse and incest that had been going on for years. So they brought along a posse of family and friends to surround Marcus while they grabbed Jonathan and Aviv.

But things didn't go as they'd hoped.

For the first fifteen minutes, the family members argued and called one another names inside and outside the one-story house as Sofia and Ruby demanded that Marcus give up the two children he'd fathered with them.

"I'm not leaving without my baby," Ruby declared.

When Marcus accused the mothers of trying to kidnap the children, Kiani jumped to her father's defense.

"You have no rights to these children. You are surrogate mothers," she said. Marcus had told his daughters and nieces that they should bear his children for the Lord because Elizabeth could no longer do so.

Marcus told Ruby and Sofia that they could come back and visit the children if they agreed to leave the house peacefully, but they knew the family was moving out of town, so they didn't believe him. If Marcus took the family away, the two women might never see their son and daughter again.

Around 2:15 P.M., about forty-five minutes after their arrival, Sofia was in the living room talking to Marcus when he whispered something to Rosie, Kiani, and Sebhrenah. Sofia grabbed her son's hand but started to panic when Rosie took him from her and walked him into the back bedroom, where the older girls had gathered the other children.

Sofia recalled the suicide pact that Marcus had made with them when they were growing up. If the police or CPS tried to bust up their family, the children had been given a plan "to go to the Lord." The plan changed over time, but essentially the older ones were to shoot their younger brothers and sisters, then turn the gun on themselves. Sofia had almost carried out the plan herself years before, when the family was living on a boat in Tomales Bay. She had loaded twelve bullets into a gun, but Marcus had stopped her just in time.

Sofia and Ruby hadn't planned to call the police today because they knew Marcus still kept that gun in the house; they didn't want to risk anyone getting hurt. But as soon as it became clear they needed outside intervention, Sofia desperately called out for someone in their group to get the police.

Mary called 911 and reported the incident as a domestic dispute. When the police didn't show up, she called again and again, trying to convey to the dispatch operator that this was no ordinary custody dispute; this was a matter of life and death.

IN FACT, THE police didn't seem to be taking it seriously. After about five of Mary's calls, the California Highway Patrol dispatcher transferred her to the Fresno Police Department, but not before warning the police dispatcher that Mary might be overreacting.

"We have transferred these out-of-control people on 761 West Hammond I don't know how many times," the CHP dispatcher said to the police counterpart.

"Mm-hmm," the police dispatcher said.

"And every time we transfer them, their story gets more embellished."

The police dispatcher laughed.

"Now they have guns," the CHP dispatcher said.

"Okay."

"It's a civil thing, supposedly, and now, I'm not sure if it's true or not, but I think it's embellished. But I'll let you try . . . Talk to her."

The police dispatcher sighed and said, "Okay," before the CHP transferred Mary over.

"I believe one of the guys in the house has a gun," Mary said.

"Why do you believe that?"

It was clear that the police dispatcher did not believe Mary knew what she was talking about, despite her increasingly urgent pleas for help.

At the end of the conversation, the dispatcher said, "Nobody's hurt or anything like that, right?"

"Not yet," Mary said, her voice shaky.

THE FIRST OFFICERS on the scene arrived around 2:30. Marcus stood in the doorway to block them from entering, explaining that he was the children's biological father. The officers sensed trouble and called for backup.

At first, Ruby and Sofia thought they had the upper hand. They presented the officers with birth certificates for Jonathan and Aviv, and the officers told Marcus he had to give the children back to their mothers or they would call CPS.

"A mom's a mom, and that's the way it stands," said Officer Frank Nelson.

But apparently this only fueled Marcus's need to prove he still controlled the situation. He tried to convince the officers that the women had abandoned their children, leaving them in his care. "They never had the children in their lives," he said.

The police weren't buying it.

"A handshake," Nelson retorted, dismissing the informal agreement. "That doesn't cut it."

Marcus must have known that the mothers were winning the dispute. As Ruby and Sofia continued to press their claim with the officers, he managed to slip away from his post, darting into the back bedroom around 3:30. No one saw him go, and by the time they noticed, it was too late.

ELIZABETH, WHO HAD been arguing with Sofia and Ruby, glanced over at the doorway and noticed that no one was there. No Marcus, no girls, no police.

Where did everyone go?

She walked slowly toward the front door, fully expecting an officer to stop her. Surprisingly, no one did, so she walked right into her home. At first, nothing looked out of place, but something definitely felt wrong. The house seemed eerie at the best of times, but the family was used to Marcus's unique taste in design: the rooms were crammed with heavy, ornate antiques, battlefield relics, and even coffins, on top of which some of the children slept. The home felt like a mausoleum now more than ever.

Before Elizabeth made her way to the rear of the house, she stopped in the kitchen for some water. Her mouth was unbearably dry, and she couldn't swallow. She gulped down a cupful with the faucet still running. Her hands were shaking so much, water spilled over the sides of the cup and into the sink. When she turned off the tap, she was startled by the silence.

I've never heard it so quiet in here. Oh, God, where are the babies?

Elizabeth began praying out loud. "O Lord, please help us!"

The seven little ones were often quiet, but not this quiet. As she headed for the door, she vowed that, if they were still safe, she would try to get them away from Marcus once and for all.

Someone had dragged one of the antique tables in front of the bedroom door. This wasn't a good sign. Elizabeth was still praying aloud when she pulled the table away from the door, just enough to let her squeeze by. She offered up a final prayer to God, cracked open the door, and warily peeked inside.

She couldn't see much of the dimly lit room, but what she could see stopped her cold: Marcus was kneeling on the forest green carpet, his head down as if he were praying, with one arm wrapped around their daughter Lise, his hand resting on the small of her back.

Lise stood facing Elizabeth, staring straight ahead, her eyes swollen with tears that were running down her face. The seventeen-year-old didn't call out or ask for help; it was as if she was passively accepting her fate, whatever that may be.

Marcus suddenly realized that his wife was in the doorway.

"Bee?" he said, as if she'd caught him doing something wrong. "Bee, come here."

To this day, Elizabeth doesn't know why, but she turned and ran as fast as she could. She was screaming and crying as she ran past the kitchen, out the front door, past the group of women, and past the school bus, down the long driveway, where she finally collapsed.

Witnessing Elizabeth's terror, all the family members outside thought the worst and started yelling.

But it turned out there was more to come. Marcus barricaded himself inside the bedroom, apparently backing a dresser or a coffin against the door.

"Nooooo," one of the women wailed as they realized he was in there with the kids.

"I told you, I told you!" another one said.

"Oh my God," Ruby and Sofia cried to police from behind a length of yellow crime scene tape. "You need to get him out of the room right now. He will kill them. He has a gun!"

If the officers had understood that this was no exaggeration, surely they would have known they had the necessary probable cause to break down the door. But they had already called the city attorney, who told them they didn't have enough information—or the right—to go inside.

"You guys don't care," Sofia said, sobbing.

THE POLICE CALLED for backup once Marcus had retreated inside. Seeing that the family dispute had escalated into a hostage situation, police officials agreed this was now a job for the SWAT team. The call went out at 3:46.

Officers spread out around the house, with at least one posted at the window of the back bedroom, trying to see what was going on inside. But Marcus had drawn the blinds, so all the officer could see was a pair of thick dark fingers pulling down one of the slats to peek out. The police yelled through the open front door for Marcus to come out but got no response.

Outside, the women felt powerless. With each passing minute, Ruby and Sofia knew the situation was growing more dire. They hoped and prayed that they were wrong about what was going on in that back bedroom.

The standoff lasted a little more than an hour while the SWAT team suited up and headed to the house. After they arrived, the officers rushed in, guns drawn.

About two minutes later, Marcus emerged from the back bedroom, his dark T-shirt wet with fresh blood, and allowed officers to escort him out without a struggle.

Although the entire family was still screaming in the front yard, Marcus remained uncannily calm as the officers hand-cuffed him. Saying nothing about what had just happened, he asked the police not to hurt him with the cuffs. Apparently, the chain connecting his two massive wrists was too short. The officers obliged and used two sets as they arrested him on suspicion of homicide.

MEANWHILE, ANOTHER SET of officers went inside to rescue the children from the back bedroom.

"Kids, kids, we're here to help you," one of them yelled as they made their way down the dark hallway. "You can come out now."

Officer Eloy Escareno shone his flashlight into the bed-room. With the blinds still drawn, it took a minute for his eyes to adjust to the darkness.

He looked down and saw what he thought was a pile of blankets. When a fellow officer reached in and turned on the light, Escareno got a full view of the horror he would never forget: a pile of bloody children, their bodies entangled with clothing. They spilled from the corner of the room toward the middle, sandwiched between a coffin and a dresser. Escareno dropped his shotgun and got down to check the bodies for signs of life. But it was too late. Although the bodies were still warm to the touch, none of them was breathing or had a pulse.

The former army medic broke down and cried.

OUTSIDE, ELIZABETH AND the rest of the Wesson family stood behind the yellow tape, fearing the worst but holding their breath for good news, not knowing who was alive and who was dead.

At 4:57 P.M., the paramedics arrived, and they entered the house two minutes later. When they came out, they confirmed Officer Escareno's findings. All of the children inside were dead.

Police, however, instructed them not to move the bodies. That was the coroner's job.

As word spread around the yard, the hopeful silence was overtaken by weeping and hysteria. Ruby fainted, and paramedics had to put her on a stretcher. Elizabeth was so upset she couldn't breathe and had to be hooked up to an oxygen tank.

"My babies," she kept saying. "They're gone."

ADRIAN WESSON HAD known this day was coming, ever since Marcus had abandoned him and his brother Dorian in the Santa Cruz Mountains six and a half years earlier.

The two oldest boys knew from the secret coffee dates they had periodically with Elizabeth that their father had been spiraling further out of control since they left. But they'd been taught to ignore his increasingly delusional and abusive behavior.

Over the years, whenever Adrian saw the Fresno area code, 559, on his cell phone's caller ID, he wondered if someone was going to tell him that Marcus had finally snapped. That afternoon, he got the call he'd been dreading.

"Adrian!" Serafino exclaimed between sobs. "Adrian!"

"Fino? What happened?" Adrian asked, panicked by the terror in his brother's voice.

"Get down here!" Serafino cried. "Just get down here."

At that moment, Adrian knew in his bones what had happened, but he asked anyway. "What did he do?" he yelled. "Did he kill them?"

Adrian thought he had prepared himself for this call, but he was sadly mistaken. Nothing could have prepared him for the real thing.

"Did he kill them, Fino?" he asked again. Somehow, he needed to hear his brother say it out loud before he'd accept it as truth. "He killed them, didn't he?"

But Serafino wouldn't—or couldn't—answer.

Instead, he told Adrian to get on the road. The 150-mile journey from his home in Santa Cruz would take him almost three hours, maybe longer given the rush-hour traffic. They would be three of the longest hours of his life.

As soon as Adrian hung up, he started gasping for air. It felt as if someone had punched him in the stomach. And just when he thought he could start walking to his car, someone punched him again. He inhaled deeply, pursed his quivering lips, and slowly exhaled until he felt like he could drive safely.

There was one call he needed to make before picking up Dorian and rushing to Fresno. He had a feeling that his father had killed at least one of his brothers or sisters, but he wanted specifics. He dialed the number for the prepaid cell phone Elizabeth usually carried.

She didn't have to say hello for him to recognize the sound of her crying.

"Mom?" Adrian asked. "Is that you?"

Elizabeth was wailing, but she managed to muster some type of affirmation.

"Did that motherfucker finally do it, Mom?" Adrian screamed.

Adrian was usually the picture of politeness—he didn't swear, rarely raised his voice, and had spoken out against Marcus only once before. But that day, he thought nothing of committing all three offenses simultaneously.

Adrian could hear the frenzied voices of police officers in the background, telling everyone to step away from the house.

"Mom?" he yelled.

"What?" Elizabeth finally answered, trying to be heard over the chaos.

"Did that motherfucker kill everyone?" Adrian asked again.

"Don't talk like that," she said defensively. "You need to calm down and get here."

His mother sounded too distracted to say anything more, so he hung up and drove to Dorian's.

He pulled up and ran toward the front door looking pale and sweaty, his eyes spilling over with tears.

"I think he finally did it," he said. "We need to get to Fresno."

Dorian dropped his head. He followed Adrian to the car and got in without a word.

* * *

ADRIAN WEAVED IN and out among the cars creeping south along the narrow coastal freeway. The brothers usually listened to loud house and trance music during road trips, but that day, the radio was off.

Dorian dealt with the stress by sitting silently, while Adrian spewed out rhetorical questions.

"How can he think he'll get away with this?" he asked. "Who does he think he is? Why now?"

After he'd vented for a while, Adrian's thoughts turned to a chilling conversation he'd had with his sister Sebhrenah two months earlier. He'd been silent on the topic of their father for years, but he couldn't bite his tongue any longer. He had to make Sebhrenah see that she could go further in life if she broke away from Marcus's manipulative clutches.

"Sebhrenah, what Dad is doing with you guys is wrong," he told her. "He's controlling you and not letting you amount to anything. You need to get out of the house."

He would always remember her robotic response: "Adrian, I don't want to be like everyone else out there," she said. "I am doing this by choice. It is what I really want to do and you need to accept it."

She sounded as if she were repeating a speech Marcus had dictated to her; Adrian was frustrated that he couldn't get through to her. This was the first real conversation he'd ever had with Sebhrenah, who, at twenty-five, was two and a half years his junior. Marcus had forbidden him and his brothers to talk to their sisters and female cousins, fearing they would develop sexual feelings for one another. After Adrian hung up the phone with her that day, he couldn't shake the feeling that Sebhrenah was on her way to a very bleak place.

Adrian had left the traffic far behind by now. He looked down at his speedometer and realized he was going a hundred miles an hour, but he didn't slow down. He desperately wanted some idea of what he was going to find once they arrived in Fresno, so he called Serafino for an update.

It was hard to hear anything over the commotion at the house, so he hung up and dialed every number in his cell phone until he could find someone to give him some answers. He was finally able to reach Marcus Jr.'s friend Michael, who was standing in the front yard, but even he was able to give Adrian only one- or two-sentence news bites before he'd hang up again.

"Your dad is barricaded inside and we don't know who's in there with him," Michael said.

The mini-briefings did little to comfort Adrian and Dorian, especially when the news seemed to be getting worse.

Finally, after dozens of these calls, Adrian heard what he'd been dreading all along.

"Your dad just came and surrendered to police, Adrian," Michael said somberly. "I think it's over."

"Okay, who else is coming out of the house?" Adrian asked. "Where is everyone else? Are the kids following behind Dad?"

"It's just him, Adrian. It's just your dad."

"Are you sure they're not coming out?"

"I don't see them."

"The kids aren't coming out, are they?" Adrian cried. Turning toward Dorian, he repeated, "The kids aren't coming out."

Adrian felt his mind slowly close down and his hands and

feet grow numb. It took every ounce of emotional strength he possessed not to pass out. He had to talk himself into staying conscious so he wouldn't lose control of his speeding car.

DEPUTY CORONERS JOSEPH Tiger and Kelly Wiefel got called to the Wesson house around 6:00—an hour after they'd finished working a ten-hour shift.

Earlier, police had blocked off half the neighborhood, but as soon as they opened the roads, the area became a swarm of people surrounded by the mess of TV satellite trucks that had arrived earlier.

Police chaplains were comforting family members, reporters were interviewing neighbors and new relatives as they arrived, and paramedics were treating those overcome by the trauma.

In the midst of all the hoopla, the Wessons' dog, a black Chihuahua mix named Betty, ran out the front door and raced down the street. Rosie loved that dog like a child, but her escape was the least of the family's problems that day.

ADRIAN AND DORIAN pulled up to their family's home around 7:30 P.M., two hours after the police had hauled Marcus away.

Adrian lifted the yellow tape so he could run toward his family; no one tried to stop him. He reached the group of women and wrapped his arms around them. Then, he took inventory of the faces.

Elizabeth, Rosie, Rosemary. Wait a minute, where's Kiani? Where's Sebhrenah? Where's Lise?

Adrian prayed they were standing somewhere else. He

breathed a sigh of relief when he saw Kiani in the back of a police car.

Thank God, she's alive.

He ran toward the car to greet her. This time, an officer grabbed his shoulder to restrain him.

"Who are you?" the cop asked.

"I'm Adrian Wesson. That's my sister back there."

Kiani stared out the window at her brother, her eyes red and glassy. She looked so lost.

Adrian searched around for the other girls but had a sinking feeling he wasn't going to find them. He stopped searching when he heard Ruby and Sofia's side of the family behind him, saying that, by process of elimination, there must be *nine* victims.

That meant Sebhrenah and Lise were dead, too.

How could Dad do this?

After that, the night was one long wait. He watched the police load his mother and sisters into two police cars, which he and Dorian followed to the police station. The boys sat outside numbly for more than five hours, hoping the police would finish questioning the women and release them.

Around 1:00 A.M., the brothers gave up and found a motel.

THE POLICE WERE finally able to get a search warrant allowing a small team of investigators to take a preliminary walk through the house at 8:30 P.M.

Forty-five minutes later, several police detectives, two CSI technicians, and four members of the coroner's office entered the three-bedroom house and walked single file past the three cannons and the half dozen or more Indo-nesian mahogany coffins that were stacked in the living room and on to the back bedroom. They wondered what the hell these people were doing with so many coffins—twelve in all.

The air was warm that night—77 degrees inside the house. But it seemed even hotter with all those people crammed into the back bedroom. And the smell was sicken-ing. It was going to be a long, grueling night.

Tiger and Wiefel were used to processing crime scenes and examining dead bodies. But they'd never seen anything like this. A pile of dead children. Babies.

The brunt of it didn't really hit them until they started to pull the bodies off the pile, one at a time, bagging them and moving them into the living room, where they could be examined further.

Sebhrenah was found facedown on top of the pile with a .22-caliber revolver under her right arm; presumably she'd been the last one to die. She was wearing a black and yellow flowered dress, zippered brown boots, and on her right hand two rings, one of which was a wedding band. A hunting knife lay on the floor nearby.

At the time, investigators didn't know the names of any of the victims. They all had black hair, and their faces looked so much alike. So, for the time being, they were identified simply as Jane Doe One or Baby Jane Doe Two, in the order they were pulled off the pile, which was assumed to be the reverse order in which they died.

As the investigators worked their way down, Lise was right under Sebhrenah, and under her, they discovered the bodies of three babies in diapers—tiny thirteen-month-old

Jeva, still wearing a bib labeled "Princess"; eighteen-month-old Sedona; and nineteen-month-old Marshey.

As they picked up little Sedona, they noticed that her white Onesie had turned a deep red, saturated with not just her blood but that of her brothers and sisters as well.

Four-year-old Ethan was next, the only one who was shot twice—once in the right eye and once in the right side of his abdomen.

Then came eight-year-old Illabelle. On the very bottom of the pile—apparently the first ones to be shot—were Aviv and Jonathan, the daughter and son of the women who had initiated the confrontation with Marcus. That made a total of nine victims.

EXCEPT FOR SEBHRENAH'S son, Marshey, who was shot in the left eye, all the other victims were shot in the right eye or just below it.

The investigators put the bigger bodies into white bags and wheeled them out to the van, but the babies were too small for the standard-size bags. Instead, the investigators draped them in white sheets and walked them out, cradled in their arms, an image that played repeatedly across the TV news that night.

Suspecting a cult angle or a bizarre ceremonial ritual, investigators initially wondered if the victims had been drugged, like the thirty-nine members of the Heaven's Gate cult who had committed suicide by eating applesauce laced with phenobarbital and vodka. But when the toxicology tests came back, the Wesson family members were found to be drug- and alcohol-free. Nothing had dulled their senses during their final terrifying moments.

Rigor mortis had already started to set in by the time investigators began the examinations. After taking Sebhrenah's liver temperature, they determined the approximate time of her death was 5:00 P.M.—two and a half hours after the police responded to the initial 911 call. The pathologist would later determine that the seven younger children were killed between 3:00 and 4:00 P.M., some possibly while Marcus was standing at the front door talking to police.

Marcus was the only one alive who knew what really happened in the back bedroom that afternoon, but his offspring—and everyone else—would speculate about this tragedy for years. Although neighbors and some family members would claim they heard one to three shots fired between 2:30 and 3:30 P.M., Fresno police insisted they never heard a single gunshot.

Elizabeth lost two of her own daughters, Sebhrenah and Lise, in the massacre, but she carried the heaviest burden of grief and guilt of all the Wesson women. Even though she had given birth to only two of the children, she felt as if she had been a mother to all nine. And she had been unable to stop the massacre.

Two

I was frantically typing to meet my noon deadline on March 12, 2004, when I saw that one of the other TV stations had scooped me on a story. They'd learned that the city councilman who had driven his car over a curb on election night had registered a blood alcohol level more than twice the legal limit. I'd been making calls all morning trying to get those test results.

A police lieutenant called to apologize a couple of hours after I left him a frustrated message. "Sorry about the miscommunication, Alysia," he said.

"You really owe me one," I countered, playing the guilt card to the hilt. "Give me the scoop about something else to make up for it."

"Well, I'm sending a SWAT team over to a house near Roeding Park," he said. "No one knows about that yet. Not even some of my officers."

I looked at the big round clock over the radio booth and perked up. I still had about twenty minutes before my first radio report at 4:00 P.M. "What's going on?"

"Sorry, looks like it's just a domestic. Custody issue or something, but it may turn into more, you never know.

Let me get that address. 7-6-1 West Hammond, in case you want to check it out."

"A domestic?" I asked, disappointed. I settled back down a bit. I couldn't sell that to my news director. "Got anything else going on?"

"Not at the moment," he said, chuckling. "I promise you'll be the first to know when something happens."

I was doing double-duty at KMPH's radio and TV stations for a couple of weeks, so I spent most of the day working on stories for six radio spots from 4:00 to 6:30 P.M., then a short one that would air on the TV news at 10:00 P.M.

The radio and TV stations were separated by a narrow parking lot, but the working environments couldn't have been more different. Although the radio deadlines came more frequently, the mood was more relaxed. Fewer radio workers were packed into closer quarters, so no one had to raise his voice to be heard. Even the police scanner's volume was set on low. It was a nice break.

Or so I thought.

For the third day in a row, I'd spent the day interviewing people at gas stations about skyrocketing prices at the pump. This time I was asking whether they had changed their driving habits. I was running out of new angles—and patience. What I really wanted was to dump the gas story and chase down something new.

"So," I said, turning toward Adam,* my radio boss. "There's a lot of SWAT action at a house in southwest

---

* The names of some individuals in this book have been changed. Such names are indicated by an asterisk (*) the first time they appear.

Fresno. Sounds like a pretty big deal," I embellished. "The lieutenant thinks it could be something."

I asked if we should call over to the TV side to see if they wanted to send someone to the scene—I was supposed to stay in the radio newsroom until 7:00 P.M.—or if I should head over there myself. I'd found the story, so I wanted to cover it, but I knew he would probably tell me to stay put.

I was right. He had me call TV and let them find out if it was a story worth pursuing. I told the TV assignment editor that the SWAT call hadn't hit the scanners yet, so we would have a head start on the other news outlets.

"I'll send someone right away," she told me. "We'll call you back and let you know what it is."

I started editing my gas story for my first two radio reports, hoping that I could use the SWAT story for my third hit. I walked across the parking lot to TV—as fast as my high heels would allow—to see if they'd heard anything yet, then I dashed back.

I made it into the booth just in time to pull the headset over my ears and yank the microphone toward my mouth, hoping it didn't pick up my panting.

"Alysia Sofios joins us now with more on the rising prices at the pump and reaction from valley drivers," the radio anchor said to introduce me, and off I went.

Shortly after my 5:00 P.M. report, the TV reporter called from the SWAT scene to say that the police chief was about to hold a news conference, and that he would go live afterward. A few minutes later, he called back with a breathless report that went something like this:

"What apparently began as a domestic dispute in this southwest Fresno neighborhood has turned into a massive crime scene. Officers have discovered the bodies of seven children inside a bedroom in a house on the seven-hundred block of Hammond Avenue. The SWAT team is still here, and Police Chief Jerry Dyer is expected to hold another news conference with more information any minute."

Turned out it was something after all.

Temporarily numb with shock, I quietly exited the booth while the anchor was still on the air and headed for my desk. Before I had a chance to fully process the gravity of what I'd heard, my phone line lit up.

I answered it on the first ring. "KMPH Newsradio, this is—"

"Alysia," my TV news director interrupted. "Get over here, *now*! We need—"

Max* hung up before he even finished his sentence, so I figured I'd better hop to it and get the hell over there. A Vietnam veteran and former national news reporter, Max could be pretty intimidating.

I ran across the parking lot and pulled open the heavy outer door that led into the newsroom. The temperature in there was always kept frigid so that the equipment functioned properly. But on this night, the wall of air that hit me seemed even colder than usual, sending goose bumps down my arms and legs.

Inside, nearly twenty people were swirling around, picking up phones and slamming them down. Arms were gesticulating wildly. The scanner was blaring. And the two anchors were shouting out orders to editors, reporters, and writers as everyone worked to throw together a series of newsbreaks that would cut into the regularly scheduled programming throughout the evening.

The square newsroom spanned two stories, with the executive producer's and the news director's glass offices upstairs and the rest of us downstairs. The two levels were connected by an open staircase covered with black rubber to prevent people from slipping while running up and down on deadline.

The on-air set was at one end of the room, where dozens of TV monitors sat on desks and hung from the walls and ceiling. The rest of the space was dedicated to edit bays and circular desks for the reporters and writers. Seen from above, the area was shaped like the Olympic logo, only the desks were separated by dividers like the spokes of a wheel. That meant everyone had several phones within reaching distance, a factor that was about to come in handy for me.

"What angle should I chase?" I yelled over the dull roar to no one in particular. No one responded.

As I listened to my producer talking with the anchors about the latest details of the story, I heard the words "incest," "polygamy," "occult," "suicide pact," and "vampires." I couldn't believe this crazy story was breaking in my town—and I was going to get to cover it.

Journalists live to work high-profile stories like these. It's not that we don't understand the seriousness of the event or are not sensitive to the victims' plight. We do and we are. In fact, that's what makes them such good stories. Everyone's emotions run high at such times, so we know that viewers will be glued to their TV sets, hungry for more information. But at the same time, we have to remain objective and detached while we gather the most gruesome details. Making dark jokes often helps us keep our sanity. And this story was getting more intriguing by the minute.

I looked upstairs and saw Max glaring down at me from behind the stacks of videotapes and résumés that cluttered his desk. I could tell he was frustrated that I wasn't doing anything yet.

I wished I could be at the scene, but with such a big story, everyone, including me, would get a piece of it. No one had given me a specific assignment; we were expected to wait for direction, which usually came after the editors and anchors finished discussing story strategy among themselves.

Max got halfway out of his chair and yelled at me through his open door. "Get on the phone with CNN and get some video of famous cult deaths, Alysia. And find out where they got those damn coffins!"

I immediately called CNN. Although we are a Fox station, we subscribe to a service that gives us quick access to CNN's old news footage.

"Yeah, give me all the file video you have of David Koresh," I said, running through a mental checklist as I watched my boss heading down the staircase with his eye fixed on me. He definitely had more orders but held off when he saw I was on the phone. "Ummmm, do you have any Jonestown video?"

"Hale-Bopp! Don't forget those Hale-Bopp folks!" he barked at me as he stormed past. "The ones with the tennis shoes!"

The woman working the CNN archive desk must have heard my boss screaming. "I think we have that Heaven's Gate shot with the shoes and the bunk beds," she told me. "I'll get it on a feed as soon as possible."

I felt we should be putting our attention on a more local angle—trying to track down the surviving members of this massacred family, not chasing cult stories that had happened in other cities—but I didn't have the time or the opportunity to protest. I'd been a TV reporter for seven years, most of the time in Michigan and the past five months in Fresno, and was still learning the ropes of being in a bigger market.

I leaned back into my squishy chair and tried to think of other ways to chase the story. Then, worried my boss would mistake my concentration for laziness, I sprang up and did hurried laps around the newsroom maze, trying to look busy while I racked my brain to come up with something different, something local.

Then, out of the corner of my eye, I saw something on one of the TV monitors that made me stop abruptly.

It's him.

The menacing figure was none other than Marcus Wesson, the man who had come out of his house covered in the fresh blood of his children. I stood there, paralyzed, my mouth wide open, as I watched another station run video of him being handcuffed that afternoon.

He was a heavy man, with an enormous belly that protruded over the top of his pants. He was wearing a black T-shirt, his frizzy, graying dreadlocks pulled back from his dark face into a low ponytail that hung in a matted mess to his waist.

I felt so disgusted by the basic details of the crime that had been revealed so far that I couldn't move.

"Oh my God!" a female coworker screamed. "Look at him."

"He's so scary," a writer to my left said, shaking her head.

My assignment editor called out to me, bringing me back to reality. "Yoo-hoo, Alysia," she said, pointing to the phones, which were ringing like crazy.

I pitched in and took some calls.

AFTER I'D SPENT a few hours talking to reporters in the field and relaying the updates to my producer, my assignment editor yelled out my name again.

"Alysia, you're going to want this phone call," she said. "I'll transfer it to your desk."

"KMPH Fox 26 newsroom," I said, picking up. "This is Alysia Sofios. May I help you?"

It was strict company policy to answer the phone with the station's call letters and our name, followed by a pleasant greeting. That night, it seemed like a waste of time.

"Hi. I'd like to remain anonymous," the female caller said.

Sometimes good tips came in like that, so she had my attention.

"Sure, what's going on?"

The woman talked fast.

"You know that man on TV who killed those kids? Well, I know him," she said.

"Okay. What do you know?"

"Well, my sister works at the thrift store. And those women came in and they had to walk behind that big man on TV with the dreadlocks. They wore all black and had long black hair. And he wouldn't let them talk. And they had their heads down and he ordered them around."

I looked down at the clock on my computer screen. My ultimate 10:00 P.M. deadline was still a couple of hours away.

"You know what? I'd love to talk to you about this in person. Can I come to where you are and you can tell me about it?"

"Oh no," she said, her nervousness escalating to panic. "I'm afraid of that man. I don't want him to come kill us if he sees us on TV."

"I'm pretty sure he will be in jail for quite a while, ma'am."

"No, he has sons. And they'll do whatever he tells them."

I felt like I was losing her.

Don't hang up.

"Okay," I said, trying to calm her down. "Forget the interview. Just tell me what else you know."

"Well, you know those coffins they found in that house? They got them at Dugovic's over there downtown."

Who was this lady?

I thumbed through the yellow pages as I listened to her story, picked up a phone on the next desk over with my other hand, and called Dugovic's, an antique furniture store.

No one answered. I figured; it was after business hours. I returned my full attention to the woman, who was rambling in midsentence. ". . . and he was really scary and my sister said he was like the Devil. But I just can't go on TV because it would be too dangerous and I shouldn't have even called you, but we watch your station, and I couldn't believe it when I saw what happened."

"Thank you so much for calling," I said, seeing that the cult video I had ordered from CNN was rolling in the edit bay.

I scrolled through the surreal images of the Branch Davidians, Jonestown, and the obligatory Heaven's Gate, wondering how people could be brainwashed like that.

It was approaching 9:30 when I started tapping out my script on the keyboard: "Tonight's mass murder is the largest in Fresno's history. Neighbors speculate the arrested Marcus Wesson was much like infamous cult leaders of the past."

I stared at the text on the screen but couldn't seem to draw any significant parallels between Wesson and the others. I felt uneasy about making the comparison without knowing more about the family dynamics. These weren't strangers. Wesson had brainwashed his *children*.

"I want to leave the cult video out of it," I said, testing my boss. "It doesn't seem to fit the mold."

"What else do you have?"

"I have enough," I said. "Oh, and I know where they got the coffins."

He smirked appreciatively, which for him was an unusual expression of praise.

"Well, go with it," he said.

I felt relieved. Heaven's Gate was officially on the cutting room floor.

Twenty-five minutes later, the newsroom was nearly empty. The on-air talent were in the greenroom getting ready. I suddenly realized I should be in there, too, putting on makeup, brushing my hair, and changing into my suit jacket. I had been so consumed by the story I hadn't left any time to do my usual preshow grooming routine.

Oh, God, it's been a fifteen-hour day already. I got ready for radio this morning, not TV. But I'm sure the audience isn't worried about my appearance.

The director's voice echoed over the station's intercom

at 9:58, eight minutes later than everyone was supposed to be in their spots. "Places, everyone! *Places!*"

I heard voices and footsteps scurrying toward the set. I'd only had time to type up a partial script that I would read off the teleprompter; the rest was in talking points. I shoved the script at my boss, and he glanced at it as he made one last sweep around the set, ensuring that everyone was ready.

"Okay, uh-huh, looks good," he said distractedly.

"I'm going to ad-lib here," I said, pointing at the script, "and I figure the anchors can ask me questions here."

He looked up at me. "Forget that," he said matter-of-factly as he put a hand on my shoulder. "You need some lipstick."

I pulled out a mirror and saw he was right. I knew I wasn't ready, but I hadn't realized I looked so frazzled. People at home would wonder why I was so pale.

I wish I worked for the newspaper.

I grabbed my makeup bag and dashed into position as I heard the beginning of the newscast through my earpiece. While another reporter was doing a live shot at the crime scene, I had barely enough time to brush on some blush and apply a layer of lipstick.

THE MINUTE OUR show was over, at 11:00 P.M., we huddled around the monitors to watch how the competition handled the story. One veteran reporter broke down in tears on the air, and after the frantic night I'd had, I wasn't surprised.

A coworker had scheduled a party at a friend's house and invited the other local TV crews to stop by. My colleagues and I considered not going, but it was midnight and we were all still hyped up.

"I need a drink," one of the reporters said. "Let's make a deal. We aren't allowed to talk about what happened the rest of the night. Anytime someone says 'Marcus Wesson,' 'dreadlocks,' 'incest,' 'coffins,' or 'worst mass murder in Fresno's history,' they have to do a shot."

Dozens of people showed up, and as much as we tried not to talk about the story, it was no use. Many of us had to take cabs home that night.

News of what had happened inside that house on Hammond Avenue spread around the globe in a matter of hours.

It was a story that would change my life forever.

Three

Elizabeth, Kiani, and Rosie had never been inside a police car before. It was 8:00 P.M., and an officer was taking them downtown for questioning.

Elizabeth sat in front, and Kiani, Rosie, and Elizabeth's sister Rosemary sat in back, all of them sobbing during the three-mile trip to police headquarters. The air-conditioning vents dried some of Elizabeth's tears before they had a chance to drip onto her dark, sleeveless turtleneck and her dark, striped, ankle-length skirt.

Another police car brought Elizabeth's sons Marcus Jr. and Serafino to the station. She knew Sofia and Ruby were there somewhere, too, but she didn't see them. Rosie and Kiani had been arguing with them, blaming them for what happened, so Elizabeth figured the police had decided to separate the dueling factions of the family.

Elizabeth blamed Sofia and Ruby, too. They knew how dangerous Marcus was, yet they'd tested him anyway. If they hadn't come to the house to try to take back their kids, those nine innocent children would still be alive.

An officer led Elizabeth's group into the middle of the bustling station and sat them around a gray laminate table, where they cried and whispered as they waited to be called into the interrogation room. Elizabeth tried to push away the angry thoughts about Sofia and Ruby, focusing instead on consoling Kiani and Rosie. The police, however, seemed to care more about protocol.

"Do not talk to each other," an officer instructed them as he passed by.

Officers stared curiously at them from their cubicles, but Elizabeth was too thirsty and upset to notice.

"Can I have some water, please?" she asked.

An officer handed her a plastic bottle. She immediately drank its contents, but it did nothing to quench her intense thirst. She asked for another one, then another. She could not seem to get enough.

Fresno Police Detectives Doug Reese and Michelle Ochoa were assigned to question the family. Reese, the lead investigator on the case, came out and took one family member at a time back to the room. It was going to be a long night.

By midnight, the police had talked to Sofia, Ruby, and Rosemary. It was Rosie's turn next.

"Rosa Solorio? We're ready for you," Reese said, beckoning for her to follow him.

When Rosie came out an hour later, her face was pale and her eyes were red from crying. Elizabeth felt her anxiety escalate, knowing that it was just a matter of time for her. She dropped her head and watched her tears form a miniature reflecting pool on the table below, wondering how she was going to make it through this.

For the past four decades, she had relied on Marcus to make her decisions. He had always dealt with the authorities, not her. He never let her question anything about their lives, but, for the moment, that was all she could do. Only he couldn't answer her now that he was in the jailhouse across the street. Though physically Marcus was nearby, to Elizabeth he was still a world away.

What had gone wrong? Marcus had always promised her that he would never hurt her or their children—and she had believed him. Sure, the "spankings" were bad, but she'd accepted his rationale for them. He'd pointed out that no one had disciplined Elizabeth's brothers and sisters until he came along, and look how they'd turned out.

He was right—some of them had become drug addicts or alcoholics and had gone to jail; she didn't want her children to turn out the same way. So she went along with his tactics, partly because the girls seemed so happy and partly because she suspected they would turn on her if she tried to intervene or break up the family. Besides, none of her children, except for Gypsy, had ever complained to her about Marcus or his beatings. At the time, she knew nothing of the suicide pact Marcus had made with the children when they were growing up.

What could have happened inside that back bedroom? She was sure he would have a reasonable explanation if she could only ask him. He always did.

Elizabeth crossed her arms on the wet table, laid her head on her hands, and replayed the day's events. Rosie and Rosemary followed her lead. They sat like that for hours, quietly weeping together.

Even though they hadn't eaten anything since lunch the day before, they weren't hungry. No one asked them if they wanted any food anyway.

* * *

IN THE INTERVIEW room, the detectives were discovering that Marcus had fathered children with his daughters and nieces, something Elizabeth didn't want to think about and would never admit to knowing.

After Kiani told Reese she'd heard a gunshot in the back bedroom and assumed Marcus was the one shooting the children, the detective asked if she'd had any problems with her father growing up. Kiani didn't seem to understand where he was going with his questions.

"Like what kind of problems?" she asked.

"Well, um, did your dad do anything with you that made you uncomfortable at all?"

"No, no."

"Did he ever do anything that he shouldn't have done with you?"

"No."

"Did he ever, um, have any sexual contact with you?"

"Yeah."

"Okay, but you didn't think that was unusual?"

"No."

"Was that okay with you?"

"Yeah, because I, I agreed with it. That's okay with me."

"What kind of sexual contact would he have?"

"Well, um, the children. That's how I got my babies."

"So he'd have sexual intercourse with you?"

"Yeah."

REESE CAME OUT to get Elizabeth just after 4:00 A.M.

"Elizabeth?" he said in a commanding tone, waiting for her to look up. "We need you now."

She picked herself up and followed the detective

apprehensively down the hall, growing more scared with each step. Scared of what they were going to ask her. Scared of what they might think about her family. And scared that they might arrest her or her children.

REESE WAS A tall, athletic-looking man who looked to be in his mid-forties. In his hard-nosed, matter-of-fact style, he started asking Elizabeth questions about her childhood—when Marcus came into her life, and when their relationship became romantic. Then he shifted gears to more sensitive subjects as Elizabeth squirmed in her chair, watching him mouth the words under his thick brown mustache.

"What happened to the kids inside the house?" he asked.

"I didn't see the kids," she said.

"Is Marcus the father of them?"

"I said no."

"You didn't ask the girls. How do you know he's not?"

"Why would I want to ask them a question like that for?"

"Well, you don't know who the father is, so how do you know that Marcus isn't the father? Do you understand my question? You know that Marcus was having sex with your daughters and that he gave birth to these children. Is that not true?"

Reese ordered Elizabeth to hold her head up so he could see her eyes. As he hammered at her, she grew so upset she couldn't answer him anymore. She was so tired she could barely stay awake. All she wanted was for him to stop asking questions so she could sleep, escape from this nightmare. But he just kept on with the questions.

"Elizabeth, why don't you tell me what happened tonight?" Reese said. "Just spit it out; you can tell me. I know it's a traumatic night for you, okay, but you need to be honest with me. So tell me what happened tonight. Elizabeth, I need you to keep your eyes open so I know you're awake. Can you tell me what happened?"

"I can't tell you," she said. "I don't know what happened."

"Well, you were there and you do know. Just like you know about Marcus and your daughters. Were you involved in the killings? How do you know if you don't remember anything?"

Elizabeth couldn't believe Reese could even think such a thing.

"How can you say something like that?" she asked.

"I'm trying to get you to talk to me."

Reese asked if she knew that Marcus had been molesting her nieces and daughters, having children with them.

"No," she answered. "No."

Elizabeth hadn't wanted to believe all the children were Marcus's, so she'd never asked. And because Marcus had allowed the girls to have only casual conversation with her in recent years, they'd never told her. At first, she'd thought the girls had boyfriends at work who had gotten them pregnant. One time, Marcus told Elizabeth he was taking the girls to the sperm bank to be artificially inseminated. She didn't think they could afford that, but she didn't question it. Frankly, she wasn't sure what to think about the new babies' paternity.

Elizabeth shut down emotionally, but that only seemed to make Reese more aggressive.

"You helped your husband do this to your children, didn't you?"

"No."

"You knew he was planning to do this, didn't you?"

"No."

As the grilling continued, Elizabeth stopped talking altogether. She was crying and thirsty again, and she wanted to go home.

"You're just going to hide everything, huh?" Reese barked at her. "You're just going to cover it up and make it go away, is that what you want to do? Or do you want to fix it, so you can move on? Elizabeth, talk to me. It's not going to do you any good to hide it. You see, we already know all that stuff."

Elizabeth sat quietly, sniffling, as Reese went on.

"And all it does is make you look bad," he said. "Do you condone that, is that okay with you?"

Sensing that he wasn't getting anywhere, the detective got up and left the room. A few minutes later, his female counterpart came in and took over.

Ochoa, a short, muscular woman in her mid-forties, her graying dark hair styled in a boyish cut, spoke to Elizabeth in a quiet, gentle voice.

"It's going to be okay," Ochoa said comfortingly. "It's going to be okay."

If only she were right, Elizabeth thought.

"You know why this happened," Ochoa said. "And it's not your fault. You keep wanting to blame yourself, deep down. Do you think you could have prevented these deaths?"

"Probably, if I was there," Elizabeth said.

"Well, you were. He had Elizabeth [Lise] in his hands."

Elizabeth started crying again, remembering the sorrow she saw in her daughter's eyes before Elizabeth ran from the house.

"And you survived."

"I shouldn't have run." Elizabeth couldn't believe that her babies were dead. "It can't be real," she said, still crying.

"Well, I'm here to tell you it's real. 'Cause I saw those bodies and I . . . I can't get it out of my head. You're trying to get it out of your head, and I understand that. But I saw those dead bodies, and it was the worst thing I ever saw. And telling those parents, Ruby and Sofia, that their children are dead. And me telling you that your two daughters are dead. No, it's real. Elizabeth, it's very real."

Elizabeth could barely talk, she was crying so hard. "I got to see them, I got to hold them, I want to hold them."

"There's no more holding them," Ochoa said. "They're gone."

THE REST OF the night was a blur for Elizabeth. By the time the detectives let her go, it was 7:30 in the morning.

Dorian and Adrian came to the station to pick up what was left of their family and took them back to the Econo Lodge. Cramped and musty, their room had a king-size bed with a burgundy and blue bedspread, a long dresser, and not much else. No one could figure out how to turn on all the lights, so it was dark, too.

Although there were eight of them in that room, it felt empty without the little ones.

"You should get some sleep, Mom," Adrian said. "I love you."

Elizabeth nodded. Her head was throbbing. She couldn't see straight. She couldn't think straight. She felt dizzy and knew she needed to lie down for a while, so she let Adrian help her onto the bed, where Rosemary, Rosie, and Kiani joined her. They were used to close quarters, but on that March morning, they couldn't quiet their minds enough to fall asleep.

THE NEXT MORNING, a man from the coroner's office called Elizabeth on her cell phone and told her that a local funeral home had offered to donate services for her children. She felt the bottom of her stomach drop as his words struck her. She was going to her children's funerals. Parents weren't supposed to bury their children.

She copied down the funeral home's name and number, then asked when she could come down to the morgue to see her children.

The man told her to call the mortuary to make the arrangements, then to call back and set up a time to view the bodies.

When she called the coroner's office back an hour later, the woman who answered the phone was short of helpful. In fact, she was downright rude.

"You'll need several forms of identification, and you need all of the children's birth certificates," she said curtly.

"But I don't have any of that," Elizabeth said. "The police took everything I had, even my purse. I can't get any of my documents back yet."

"I'm sorry, there's nothing I can do for you, then."

Elizabeth was so frustrated and angry, the tears began streaming down her face before she could even hang up the phone. Why was everyone being so mean to her? She'd just lost her family, yet they were treating her like she was to blame. It wasn't fair.

Ultimately, Detective Reese took one of Elizabeth's

nephews to the morgue to identify the bodies. Elizabeth didn't see them until the funeral, lying in their coffins.

STILL TRYING TO decide who was to blame for the murders, Reese came to the motel to collect the keys to the family's bus and house. Gypsy, who was closer to her brother Almae than to any of her remaining siblings, had been living with his girlfriend, Janet,* for the past few months. The only one of Elizabeth's daughters police had yet to question, Gypsy happened to be at the motel, visiting, when Reese arrived that day.

"My son has the keys with him," Elizabeth told him.

"Well, we need them right now or else we'll break down your door," he said, straight-faced.

Elizabeth grew angry again, but she called Adrian and asked him to bring her the keys.

Reese looked at Gypsy as if he were noticing her for the first time, his eyes widening and the corners of his mouth twitching. He looked almost happy for once.

"I'm going to need to speak with you," he said. "I'd like to bring you into the station and talk to you there."

Gypsy wished she'd hidden in the bathroom when she heard him knock on the door. She didn't want to talk about her father. She hated him and wanted to forget everything he'd done to her. But when she looked over at her mother, Elizabeth was nodding in approval.

"I guess that will be okay," Gypsy said hesitantly.

"How about tomorrow?" Reese asked.

"That's fine."

REESE AND OCHOA not only interviewed Gypsy but also insisted on doing a second round of questioning with

Elizabeth, Kiani, and Rosie a week later. This round lasted a total of six hours and was much more grueling than the first. The investigation into the Wesson family had progressed, and not even Ochoa was nice this time.

Elizabeth was growing increasingly defensive about the life she and her husband had led and the way he had raised their family. Marcus had always told them that the world was cruel and that no one would treat them as nicely as they would treat one another. As far as Elizabeth was concerned, his words were proving to be prophetic.

"You were in the room when it happened, weren't you?" Reese said accusingly to Elizabeth, referring to the murders.

"No."

"People saw you go in the back room. What did you see?"

"Eyes. I just see Lise's eyes."

"And you saw your children lying there, didn't you?"

"No. I didn't see them."

"You saw them."

"No, I didn't."

Reese had a crime scene photo on the table, which he said depicted the bloody stack of her dead children. He threatened to show it to her to jog her memory.

Elizabeth was getting sick of his threats and provocation. "Fine," she snapped. "Show me."

But for some reason, Reese didn't follow through.

Elizabeth shut down nonetheless. "I want to go home," she said wearily. "I'm tired. I just want to go home."

The problem was, she didn't have a home to go to. She and the girls had moved from the Econo Lodge to the cheaper Super 8 on Motel Row, a strip of low-budget motels where prostitutes worked the corners and police had made numerous drug arrests.

The boys had scraped together enough money for the family to stay there a week, but they didn't know where they were going to go after that. Moving from place to place was nothing new for the Wesson family; they'd always found a way to manage in the past. Only this time, Marcus wasn't there to take care of things.

As if everything else wasn't bad enough, the police wouldn't leave them alone. First they wanted Elizabeth, Kiani, and Rosie to come in for DNA tests. The women didn't understand why that was necessary, but they grudgingly let the detectives swab the insides of their cheeks. A couple of days later, Reese called with another request. This time, he wanted blood samples from the girls, threatening to arrest them if they didn't comply.

The girls already felt violated and now the police wanted their *blood*?

"Do what you have to do," Elizabeth said. "Go ahead and arrest us. We don't care anymore."

WHEN REESE SHOWED up at a relative's house a couple of weeks later, Elizabeth thought he'd come for the blood. The detective tried to hand her an envelope, but Elizabeth wasn't going to take anything more from this man.

"I don't want that," she said.

"You have to take it," he replied.

Reese threatened again to arrest her, so she took the envelope. The detective handed one to each of the girls as well. After opening them, they were surprised to see that they'd been subpoenaed by the district attorney's office to testify against Marcus. *Against* Marcus? As his staunch supporters, they'd thought they would be testifying for the defense, not helping the prosecutor send their husband and father to prison. They also didn't know that spousal privilege didn't apply to felony crimes against a couple's children.

The women thought Marcus was being unfairly targeted. He'd trained them to defend him to the death, and that was what they intended to do. They didn't want to help the police, especially when they felt Detective Reese had been so insensitive to them through all of this.

Then, to make matters worse, Elizabeth looked closer at the name on her subpoena. Someone had typed in "Elizabeth Breani Kina Wesson"—the name of her dead daughter.

It felt like a cruel taunt.

THE DIVIDED WESSON family wanted separate ceremonies at separate funeral homes for their loved ones. So Ruby and Sofia organized a funeral for Jonathan and Aviv, while Elizabeth handled arrangements for the seven other children. Both funerals were on March 24, but the two factions did not attend each other's services.

A few days beforehand, Elizabeth went to buy new clothes for the children. She still hadn't seen their bodies, but she had decided on an open-casket ceremony nonetheless. The women decided to do their shopping at Ross, a discount department store that offered a change from their usual practice of buying used clothes at thrift stores or sewing their own.

Elizabeth, Kiani, Rosie, and Gypsy wept and hugged as they made their way up and down the aisles, searching for just the right outfits. They started in the baby section and slowly worked their way up to the adult sizes.

Kiani chose dresses for her two daughters, Illabelle and Jeva; Rosie found a dress for her toddler daughter, Sedona, and a shirt and tie for her son, Ethan. Elizabeth was too emotional to make decisions for any of the children. She couldn't escape the image of Lise's tearful eyes in that bedroom.

"Gypsy, baby, can you pick Lise's dress for me?" Elizabeth choked out. "She would have wanted it this way."

Lise had been Gypsy's best friend in the house, and Gypsy knew her mother was right—Lise *would* have wanted Gypsy to pick out her dress. She searched through the end-less racks until she spotted a calf-length blue number with a white floral print.

"I think she would love this one," Gypsy said, holding it up for the others to see. Blue had been Lise's favorite color and, well, the dress just looked like her.

It had been eight months since she'd run away, and during that time Gypsy had developed a clothing bug. She'd always dreamed that someday she and Lise could go on a carefree day of shopping. And now here she was, picking out a dress for Lise's funeral.

The sorrow was too much for her to take. Gypsy's knees gave way, and she collapsed on the cold linoleum floor, still clutching the dress. She broke into a wail, her body shaking as she sobbed. Her family rushed to console her.

"I shouldn't have left Lise behind," Gypsy said. "I feel so guilty."

"It's not your fault," they said. "It's not your fault."

After the crying subsided, Gypsy sat on the floor with

her hands over her eyes, taking deep breaths until she could compose herself enough to stand up. She had to be strong; she needed to pick out a skirt for herself, too. She'd thrown all of hers away. Marcus had never let them wear pants, so that was all she wore these days.

But as much as she wanted to defy her father, Gypsy would wear a skirt to her sister's funeral. She knew Lise would have wanted that, too.

Four

S aturday was my day off and I tried to sleep in, but I kept jumping up with the startling feeling that I was late for something. The biggest story of my life was playing out a few miles away, and I couldn't stop replaying the image of the coroner's investigators carrying the Wesson children out of the house.

How could their father have done this?

Why didn't the children scream?

I grabbed my cell phone from the floor next to my bed and saw that I had nine messages, far more than usual. I'd turned off my ringer when I got home so no one would wake me up. One of the messages was from the sports guy at my last TV station, in Lansing, Michigan, who was known for his sarcastic humor.

"Alysia, what kind of scary town did you move to? Just making sure you're still alive. If you are, call me back. If not, I call dibs on your CD collection."

The rest were pretty similar—friends and family nationwide who had seen the Wesson story and wanted to know if I had been at the scene. My reporter friends who were stuck in smaller markets peppered their messages with jealous comments about the magnitude of the story I was getting to cover.

"I can't believe you move and this happens right away," one said.

"You better get the exclusive on this one, Alysia. Do it for the little people," another one said, laughing.

Fresno, three hours southeast of San Francisco and three and a half hours north of Los Angeles, had been my home for the past five months. I'd always wanted to live in California, but I hadn't always wanted to be a TV reporter. While I was studying journalism at Michigan State University, my professors said newspapers were dying and there was no money in radio, so I chose to go into television. It didn't take long before I knew I'd made the right choice. I loved it.

I dug into my career with fervor, toiling long hours and putting my job before everything else—family, boyfriends, even the chance for a vacation. I spent three years at the Fox affiliate in Lansing, then jumped to the station in Fresno, a bigger market, where I'd been since October 2003.

Getting the big story often involved working on my days off, even if I didn't get paid for them, and I knew this was going to be one of those stories. So I jumped into the shower to get ready for my "day off" at the Wesson crime scene.

THE ONLY TIME I'd taken the Olive Avenue exit on Highway 99 was for a trip to the Chaffee Zoo shortly after I'd moved to town. The Wessons' house, less than a mile from the zoo, was surrounded by a dozen live satellite trucks. I couldn't park anywhere near the house because of all the media and spectators, so I promised myself to bring a marked news van next time for better access.

Families were lined up as if it were a haunted house on Halloween, peering in through the mail slot to see the coffins stacked in the living room, and taking photos of the blood-stained carpet through the cracked windows. After sufficient titillation, they ran away squealing. I couldn't believe that the yellow police tape was down already.

I walked over to a group of reporters gathered near a makeshift memorial that was growing on the sidewalk.

"I didn't know you were working this weekend, Alysia," said one of the TV reporters who had been at the party the night before.

"I'm not," I said, laughing.

"Me neither," he responded with a wink. "Couldn't stay away, huh?"

The memorial must have had more than a hundred mementos already—smiling teddy bears; yellow daisies, red roses, and pink carnations; homemade cards with hand-written poems, held in place with rocks; and nine prayer candles, their flames quivering in the wind. A constant flow of community members moved like a conveyor belt down the sidewalk, stopping every few inches to read the heartfelt messages.

My phone rang as I was reading one of the poems.

"What's all that noise?" Max asked. "Where are you?"

Worried he would make me stick around and work through the night, I ran out to the nearest clearing so he wouldn't hear the crowd noise anymore and asked him what he needed.

"We need you to come in tomorrow to cover the Wesson story," he said. "I'd like an extra reporter on the scene."

I panned across the crowd and nodded. "I'll be here—I mean, *there*—tomorrow."

I'm pretty sure he already knew where I was, but that confirmed it.

"Very good," he said.

Realizing I'd have to spend the entire day at the creepy house on Sunday, I got back into my car and took one last look before I drove home.

I WOKE UP at 7:30 on Sunday, way before my alarm was set to go off. Most people don't need an alarm to wake up at 10:00 A.M., but I never went to sleep before three or four in the morning. Since I was already awake, I decided to go to work early.

This time, I drove a marked news vehicle and was able to pull right up to the action. The crowd was much larger than the day before, but far more subdued now that the police tape was back up and blocking off a large perimeter around the house. Apparently, photos of the scene had been posted on the Internet and, after realizing that the hundreds of people stomping around the area could put their homicide investigation in jeopardy, the police had strung the tape up again.

Hundreds of onlookers were just staring at the house, almost as if waiting for a bloody Marcus Wesson to walk out all over again. I understood why. Thinking about what must have happened inside was mesmerizing.

The memorial had doubled in size overnight and was now about ten feet across and ten teddy bears deep. I walked over to a woman who was kneeling in front of it, hands folded, praying. Hoping she was a family member, I waited until she stood up before I asked if she knew the victims.

"No," she said, shrugging, tears welling up in her eyes. "But I feel like I do. I haven't stopped praying for them since I heard."

Someone had tied several "Happy Birthday" balloons to the prayer candles, commemorating what would have been Jonathan's eighth birthday that day. I sat on the hot sidewalk, put down my reporter notebook, and thought about *my* eighth birthday. My parents had taken me to Toys "R" Us and told me to pick out any one thing I wanted. I'd searched the aisles until I saw a shiny red bouncing ball.

"This is what I want," I'd said, my grin fading as I wondered why they seemed so disappointed by my choice.

"Okay, Alysia," my mom said. "You can have the ball. Now pick out your big present."

I didn't understand what they meant, so they picked out one for me: a pink Huffy bicycle with a wide padded seat and long streamers. It was nice, but I quite liked the hand-me-down bike my sister had given me; it still had a perfectly good seat that was long enough to fit me and my best friend. But my parents insisted on buying me the ball *and* the bike. The car ride home was strained, and I never rode the Huffy.

I was jolted out of my memories by an elbow to my ribs from the newspaper reporter sitting next to me. "Hey, I think some family members just showed up," he said, excited.

I jumped to my feet before he finished his sentence. I'd always prided myself on being able to get exclusive interviews for big stories, and I was even more determined on this one.

"See that blue car driving around the corner? I think that's them."

As if someone had shot the starting pistol at the Kentucky Derby, we all dashed toward the car. But the story stopped being just a game the moment I saw the sad brown eyes of the two young men inside that Chevy Cavalier. I was struck by the deep sense of loss and helplessness reflected there.

Unlike their father, the boys looked innocent, vulnerable, and genuinely devastated. And in sharp contrast to Marcus's nasty dreadlocks, their hair was clean and cut short, their clothing pressed. I recognized Serafino, in the passenger seat, from TV, but I hadn't seen the driver with the goatee before.

How could they be related to that monster?

We surrounded the car, and Serafino rolled down his window. After the dozen of us shoved our microphones in his face, he rolled it down a bit farther.

My adrenaline surged, and I jockeyed for an opening as everyone began yelling out questions.

"How is your family doing?" I kept repeating, hoping he would answer eventually.

The national reporter from CBS was louder than the rest of us and wasn't afraid to throw an elbow to try to force us to back up, but I didn't budge.

"How is your family doing?" I tried again.

This time, the driver answered.

"This is very hard on our family," he said, looking up toward me, unsure of where the question had come from. "We're having a very hard time."

The car began rolling forward as the media, myself included, scattered to get out of the way. I vowed to elicit longer answers the next time, when there weren't so many of my competitors around.

MARCUS'S ARRAIGNMENT WAS that Wednesday, a morning assignment that required me to set my alarm for the ungodly hour of 6:30. For a city of a half million, downtown Fresno rarely had much street activity, but that day was an exception: news vans, cameras, and journalists lined every street around the courthouse.

I had made the hundred-mile trip to Modesto a few times to cover community reaction and a couple of pretrial hearings in the Scott Peterson case, but outside of that, I had never seen anything quite like this—especially not in Fresno.

One thing I'd learned from the Peterson story—seating was everything. I wanted to be able to look into Wesson's eyes when they led him into the courtroom so I could convey my impressions to our viewers. I wondered where the family was going to sit and who else would show up. I was particularly eager to catch a glimpse of his wife on what might be the first time they'd seen each other since the murders.

The media queue to get into Judge Brant Bramer's courtroom wound down the first-floor hallway, where reporters and photographers sat shoulder to shoulder on the wooden bench that stretched the length of the wall under a tinted window. I was in the front third of the line, sandwiched between an Associated Press photographer who admired my wide-eyed enthusiasm and a newspaper veteran annoyed by how much I was talking first thing in the morning.

When the bailiff opened the double doors leading into the courtroom, the media mob nearly ran him over. I slipped into an aisle seat in the third row of wooden pews on the left, waiting with anticipation for the show to begin.

I searched the room for family members but, seeing none, I focused on the clear plastic divider that separated us from the enclosed area where Marcus would stand. The monster and I were about to be in the same room. I didn't know what to expect—how he would act, how I would feel when I saw him, or if he'd turn around and roar at the gallery. I just had a feeling this wasn't going to be your typical arraignment.

"Excuse me," a young man's shaky voice said. "Can we sit here?"

I looked up and saw the two Wesson sons I had chased down the day before.

"Sure," I said.

I couldn't help but think how much sitting next to them could enhance my story for that night. I stood up so the two of them could squeeze past. They seemed very nervous; they kept sliding around and bumping into me.

"How are you guys doing?" I asked, immediately realizing it was a stupid question.

How do you think they're doing, Alysia?

"We're okay," they said, avoiding eye contact.

They were clearly distracted by the rolling and clicking of the twenty or so video and still cameras from the national networks and local stations that were pointing at the three of us.

"All rise," the bailiff said, silencing conversation as we stood up.

The judge walked to his seat on the podium, visibly upset, and immediately reprimanded the media for taking pictures and video before he'd even made a ruling on whether to allow cameras in the courtroom. He ordered the photogs to discard every image they'd taken so far and prohibited them from photographing anyone sitting in the gallery. It was the media's first collective defeat.

"What just happened?" Serafino's brother, who I would soon learn was named Almae, leaned over and whispered to me.

I whispered back, noticing the expressions on some of the other reporters' faces. I could hear them thinking, *I can't believe the family is talking to her. It's not fair.*

Then, like an icy winter wind, I felt Marcus Wesson enter the room from a door to the right of the judge. He was walking straight toward us when he saw the boys and looked right at me, sitting next to them. He shocked me by smiling at us. Shuddering at his gaze, I didn't smile back, but the boys were visibly happy to see him.

The room was completely silent now. The accused mass murderer shuffling through in his yellow jumpsuit and shackles still seemed dangerous, like a wild beast that could break free from his chains and turn on his captors at any time.

I was on the edge of my seat. From what I knew about him so far, it seemed impossible that anyone could contain Wesson. His dominating and dangerous reputation was already larger than life—and two of his obedient offspring were at my side. I wondered if they might try to help him escape. What if they grabbed me, held a gun to my head, and said, "Let our dad go or we'll kill the girl"? I scooted to my right until my hip was snug against the armrest at the end of the bench.

Before the judge could formally charge Marcus with nine counts of first-degree murder, there was an issue with legal counsel. Marcus was no stranger to the law, thanks to a welfare fraud conviction more than a decade ago.

"I don't want a public defender. I beg thee," he said to the judge, insisting he already had a private lawyer.

"Is anyone here to represent Mr. Wesson?" the judge asked.

No one responded. After an uncomfortable silence, Almae sprang up next to me. I waited for him to put me in a headlock and draw his weapon.

"I am," he called out to the judge.

All eyes spun around to our row. The bailiff turned and said, "You need to sit down."

"I love you, Dad!" Almae yelled, making the most of his public moment.

Two bailiffs converged on us and, sensing he was about to be thrown out, Almae met them in the middle and started walking toward the door.

"Dad, I love you!" he screamed, repeating it two more times on his way out.

My adrenaline surged. Marcus looked unfazed and somewhat annoyed. I had two choices. I could stay there and take notes like the rest of the media pack, or I could go after the story that had just left the room.

I darted out of my seat and pushed through the wooden door into the hallway. I felt everyone's eyes follow me and could hear them thinking, *Is Alysia going to get the story out there? That bitch! Maybe I should go, too.*

I also knew what they were whispering to each other: *I can't believe Alysia is out there with the family. That is so unprofessional. The real story is in here. I mean, how will she know what happens?* But I knew I'd be fine—a verbatim transcript of the court proceedings would be available on the Associated Press wire in about fifteen minutes, and it would be hours before I had to go on the air.

I watched the bailiffs lead Almae into the courtroom next door, then saw Serafino come out of the first courtroom and follow his brother into the other one. I sat in the empty hallway, wondering if I had done the right thing.

"Excuse me, miss?" a female court employee said, peeking out of the second courtroom. "The young man in here is asking for you."

I walked in and saw the two young men sitting in the back row, looking traumatized.

"Hey," I said, joining them.

"I shouldn't have yelled out like that," Almae said without looking up.

"How many cameras are out there?" Serafino asked.

"None when I was out there, but there will probably be about fifteen soon," I said, lowballing the number to make them feel more at ease.

They looked at me directly for the first time. I would never forget their disillusioned expressions when they asked why people were saying such mean things about their father.

Then it hit me.

They actually don't know their father has done anything wrong.

I didn't have the heart to tell them the truth. The DNA evidence was back, and Marcus was the father of all nine dead kids—two by his wife, three by his daughters, and four by his nieces.

At this time, everyone assumed he had pulled the trigger, but I still remembered the first lesson of my Journalism 101 course: There are two sides to every story.

"Is there anything you guys want the public to know about your dad?" I asked.

That got them talking. I didn't want this to feel like an interview, so I never pulled out my notebook, taking a mental log of their dialogue instead. I could tell they still weren't quite ready for a taped interview, and I didn't want to spook them.

They gave me plenty of good stuff. I would own the story that night.

After eliciting a promise to talk exclusively to me in the future, I handed them my cell number and shook their hands. The boys were wearing two layers of shirts, so they pulled the top ones up to hide their faces, and the three of us left the room together.

I searched the sea of flashbulbs and microphones in the hallway for my photographer.

"How did you score that one, Alysia?" he yelled over the crowd.

I shook my head to signal that we could talk about that later, saying, "That was a quick arraignment."

"Not really. It never happened," he said. "The judge postponed it until tomorrow."

So, I hadn't missed a thing. Ultimately, the arraignment was delayed another week, at which time Marcus pleaded not guilty to the nine first-degree murder charges. Bail was set at $9 million, $1 million for each murdered child.

I had twisted my ankle running in high heels that Sunday, so today I'd worn flats. But this time, it proved unnecessary. The boys were soon driving away in their blue car—without talking to anyone else—so the other reporters gathered in a semicircle around me.

"What did they say?" one of them asked.

"Did they talk to you?"

I was vague. A newspaper reporter asked if he could paraphrase what the boys said to me if he mentioned they'd spoken to our station exclusively. I knew my boss would like the plug, so I agreed.

It wouldn't be published until the next morning, so I would still have the information out there first. The national reporters would read the article after they checked out of their hotels. They were done here in Fresno, but for me, the story was just beginning.

WITH ONE MORE week of filling in at the radio station to go, I got my first phone call from the Wesson boys.

"Is this Al-iss-ah?" the nervous boy said, mispronouncing my name. "It's Serafino Wesson."

"Hi, Serafino. Thanks for calling," I said, getting the attention of Adam, my radio boss, who was sitting nearby. "How are you guys doing?"

The question sounded just as stupid this time as the last, and I was mad at myself for making the same mistake.

Ignoring my question, Serafino began asking me about the charges against his father. He was still confused about the legal proceedings, not to mention the details about Marcus trickling out in the media. He and his brothers needed to talk to someone, and I had landed the job.

A few minutes into the conversation, I noticed my co-workers inching toward me.

"She's talking to the family," one of them said.

"No way. They called you?" another said loudly, standing uncomfortably close to me.

I had to shush them and turn to face the corner of the cramped radio newsroom for some privacy. It sounded like Serafino was finally ready for an interview.

"So, can I meet you guys somewhere?" I asked, crossing my fingers.

"We'll call you back," he said before hanging up abruptly.

Maybe I pushed too hard.

"What did they say?" my coworkers asked.

"They're going to call me back," I answered, only half-believing it.

My phone rang again. It was them.

"We'll meet you behind the house. Please don't bring anyone else."

"See you then," I said without thinking.

Wait a minute. I'm meeting a mass murderer's sons in a secluded area by myself?

I announced my rendezvous, and my coworkers thought I was crazy, too, but this wasn't the time to play it safe. I had a chance to get an exclusive story with the survivors of a family torn apart by incest, polygamy, and murder. I grabbed my tape recorder and went to tell Adam the good news.

"I'm not so sure about this, Alysia," he said. "But if you insist on going, I can't stop you."

I smiled at him. We both knew he was only saying that because he was my boss and he was supposed to put my safety before a story. But we both felt the story was more important. It was all part of the job.

"If I'm not back in an hour, come after me," I said, laughing.

But I wasn't kidding.

I SPED TOWARD the Hammond Avenue house, pulled into the burger joint behind it, and waited in the parking lot for them. I could see other reporters' news vans parked in front of the house. If only they knew they were in the wrong place to get the story.

The Wesson crew pulled up beside me in a gold Saturn. This time, they had several girls in the car with them.

Are those Marcus's daughters? Oh my God.

There was an SUV parked between us, and I couldn't get a good look at the girls without blatantly staring, so I didn't. Almae and Serafino got out and met me near my car.

"I'm glad you guys called," I said, trying to sound reassuring, my recorder tucked under my arm.

I didn't see any evidence that they planned to kidnap me, and I felt silly for having worried. In fact, they seemed more nervous than I was.

"We want people to know some things about our dad," Almae said.

"I think that's a good idea. What do you want them to know?"

I glanced down at my watch and realized it was very close to my 4:00 P.M. deadline. I needed to move this along. I pulled out the recorder while they were talking and hoped they wouldn't clam up. They didn't react, so I turned it on and held it up near their faces.

"My dad is a good father," Serafino said. "He taught us many things and took us many places."

Marcus's two sons proceeded to paint a portrait of a loving father who would do anything for his children, a stark contrast to the mental image I—and probably most every other citizen in Fresno—had of him.

I'd already learned from the police about the physical and sexual abuse he'd inflicted on his daughters, sons, and nieces. I had also observed his overweight and sloppy appearance for myself. Suffice it to say the man repulsed me. And yet, I would be on the air in twenty minutes with a story saying what a great guy he was.

I consoled myself with the thought that at least his children, not I, would be putting that message out on the airwaves. Unbelievable but true, this was the other side to the Marcus Wesson story.

Five

Elizabeth, Rosie, and Kiani hadn't gotten a good night's sleep since the murders, and the night before their children's funerals was even worse. Kiani and Rosie had never been to a funeral before, so they were apprehensive about the ceremony.

On the morning of March 24, the three women dressed in what was a common outfit for them—black blouses and skirts with heels—then waited for the rest of the Wessons to meet them at their motel so they could ride together in the black Lincoln Town Cars the mortuary sent to pick them up. Elizabeth's sister Rosemary and Marcus's sister Cheryl came along, too.

Elizabeth fell apart as soon as they arrived. She couldn't walk through the double doors between the hallway and the chapel because she could see all seven caskets lined up—their lids open for viewing—near the front of the room. It was too much for her to take, so she backed into the hallway until the coffins were out of her line of sight.

"You're going to be okay," Adrian said. "We're all here for you."

He and Cheryl each took one of Elizabeth's trembling

arms and guided her through the doors. She'd been weeping in the car, and she hadn't stopped yet.

The family filled the chapel's front row of pews and waited for the pastor to begin. He had never met the seven victims but, like many people living in the Fresno community, felt as if he knew them from the media coverage.

The pastor needed a list to keep track of the victims. As he began calling out the names of each child, Elizabeth could no longer control her loud sobbing.

"You shouldn't be acting like this," Rosemary scolded her. "You know the babies are okay. They're in heaven now."

Elizabeth thought her sister had no right to talk to her like that. After all, if Rosemary hadn't asked Elizabeth and Marcus to raise her four daughters, the children might still be alive.

"Leave me alone," Elizabeth said, looking her sister in the eye. "Just leave me alone."

Nonetheless, she cried more quietly through the rest of the hour-long service of prayers and songs that seemed to blur together for the grieving family.

Elizabeth was the first in line to say good-bye to the children. She walked up to the smallest casket, which held little Jeva, and stopped. The baby had been so small for her age that she looked like a dress-up doll, lying in the padded ornate casket in her new outfit.

"I love you," Elizabeth said quietly as she knelt down to kiss her granddaughter's forehead. The cold, dense texture of the baby's skin caught Elizabeth off guard. She had never touched a dead body and was surprised at how unnatural it felt to her lips. Jeva had always had such bright eyes, rosy cheeks, and warm skin.

Elizabeth repeated the gesture down the line, and Kiani and Rosie followed her lead, saying good-bye to their four children, Ethan, Sedona, Jeva, and Illabelle. The other family members did the same, each lingering at certain caskets.

Gypsy stayed the longest at Lise's side. The figure in the casket didn't look like Lise, even though she was wearing the blue dress Gypsy had picked out. The person at the funeral home who had done Lise's hair must have straightened it first, then added tight, stiff curls with a curling iron. But Lise had never done it that way. Her hair was naturally curly, and that was how she'd worn it. Gypsy wished they'd done it right. But then again, she wished that everything about Lise's life could have been different.

About ten members of the media and a few neighbors waited on the sidewalk outside the funeral home for the family to emerge. It was hot that afternoon, and the reporters, myself included, had taken off their suit jackets to stay cool. A thick black iron fence stood between us and the chapel's parking lot. After about an hour, we heard voices coming out and figured it was the Wesson family, so one reporter peeked through the spaces between the rods of the gate to confirm it.

"It's them," he said. "They're standing in a circle, but I can't really tell what they're doing."

I had been sitting on the curb with a notebook, scribbling out a radio script. I was covering the story for radio and TV that night, and my cameraman was sitting next to me, ready to fall asleep from boredom. The sound of wings in flight made me jump to my feet.

"Get up. Start rolling," I yelled, nudging my coworker harder than I should have.

Before I could get out my next sentence, the sight overhead took my breath away. A white dove rose above the fence and flew up into the cloudless sky. When I realized that the grieving family members were probably going to release more doves, I pushed my photog out of the way and stuck my face deep into the viewfinder.

"I *need* this shot," I said.

Right on cue, eight more doves followed the same path. Through the lens, I slowly trailed them into the blinding sunlight. Even though I couldn't see them as they flew into the brightness, I could still hear the nine birds fluttering their way to freedom, so I kept rolling.

THE FUNERALS WERE over, but life wasn't going to get much easier for the family. We'd found out that Marcus was going to be formally charged with the nine murders the next morning.

Shortly after Marcus's arrest, an "anonymous family member"—who I later learned was Gypsy—had called police and begged them not to let Elizabeth, Kiani, or Rosie visit Marcus in jail. She was afraid Marcus would instruct the women to kill themselves or others, and she was convinced they would obey. Although his visits were monitored, she said Marcus might send a message by using code words or phrases such as "go to the Lord" or send others "to the Lord." The Fresno County Sheriff's Department took the warning seriously and prohibited their most notorious inmate from getting any visitors other than his lawyers.

A hearing on the matter was set for a week after the

funerals. I had another story to go to earlier in the day, so I arrived just in time, but I didn't get a great seat. I had to lean around several other people to see the family sitting in the pew on the left side of the room.

My heart began beating a little faster when I saw two girls sitting next to Almae and Serafino.

They couldn't be his daughters, could they? They're so pretty.

The low hiss of whispering filled the courtroom. Had the mysterious Wesson girls shown their faces at last?

They both looked to be in their early twenties, maybe younger. One had porcelain skin and wore her long black hair pulled into a bun. She wore a royal blue button-down shirt and a below-the-knee black skirt with high heels. The other girl, who had darker skin, straight shoulder-length hair, and full lips, looked more like Marcus. She was dressed in a black V-neck shirt and a black skirt, and was wearing even higher heels.

My suspicion that they were related was confirmed when Marcus was led into the room. As he walked by the girls, he stopped and smiled at them. I was so busy watching him, I didn't get a chance to see their reactions.

The judge saw no need for a hearing, determining that the prosecution could work something out with the defense, so it was over, just like that. Everyone but the reporters jumped up and flooded through the door, but we didn't budge. We wanted to interview the newly available family members.

When the girls stood up, so did we, following them into the hallway like a row of ducks.

"Will you guys answer a few questions for us?" a reporter yelled out from the back of the line.

"We have a letter to read to you," the girl wearing all black responded.

We eagerly guided the girls out to the front of the courthouse and surrounded them with a half circle of microphones.

I secured the closest spot but still had to stretch my arm as far as it would go, holding a TV microphone and my handheld tape recorder in that hand. I asked the question we all wanted to know: "Can you tell us your names and your relation to Marcus?"

"Yes, my name is Kiani Wesson," the girl in black said confidently. "I am Marcus's daughter."

"And I'm Rosie Solorio," the other girl said shyly. "I'm his niece."

Kiani began reading her letter aloud without much emotion. I felt sorry for them. They sounded like windup dolls. Kiani was saying that Marcus was a good man and a good father and that the other side of the family was spreading lies about him.

I was so consumed by her comments, I didn't realize that my outstretched arm had fallen asleep until it started hurting under the weight of the recorder and microphone. I switched the mike to the other hand and discreetly pumped my fist at my side to get the blood moving.

As soon as Kiani was done with the letter, the reporters began shouting questions. "Do you think your father is innocent?"

"Who do you think killed the kids?"

"Why do you think this happened?"

Kiani did most of the talking, but she didn't give us any real answers. She just kept repeating what a great man

Marcus was. It struck me as odd that she kept calling him by his first name rather than "my father."

"So you want to visit him?" I asked. "What would you say to him if you could?"

"I hope to visit him," she answered, looking directly at me. "What would I say? I don't know what to say. I love him. I can say that."

Hearing that made me want to shake my head in sadness. Instead, I nodded with an empathetic half smile, to make her feel as if she had given us a good answer. I was amazed at how brainwashed they were. Surely someone out there watching the news that night would do something. Maybe a psychiatrist would come forward to start the girls on an intensive therapy regime. Weren't there cult rehabs? Deprogramming facilities, maybe? It was obvious these people needed to go through a Marcus Wesson detoxification.

THAT NIGHT, I studied the Wesson family tree the *Fresno Bee* had published. I needed to print a new copy, because mine was crumpled from so much use. I dragged my finger down the oddly shaped diagram and found Kiani and Rosie. My stomach dropped. Together, the two of them had lost *four* children in the murders, all fathered by Marcus, yet they were still defending him.

I felt sick the rest of the night, and I didn't get much sleep, tossing and turning. I couldn't believe how much Marcus's daughter and niece were like Stepford Wives. I had expected them to be upset, but they weren't. Marcus was still controlling and manipulating them, even from jail.

* * *

I WAS AWAKENED by my cell phone ringing early the next morning.

"Did you see the paper yet?" one of my coworkers asked.

"No, why?"

"I can tell I woke you up, sorry," she said. "You should look at the paper, though."

"I'll go get it. Thanks."

I hung up, stumbled to the door, and opened it to retrieve the paper from my front doorstep, where the wind was blowing the top fold up. I focused my tired eyes and jumped back. Kiani, Rosie, and I were featured on the front page in full color. The picture of me standing next to them with my microphone loomed large.

Why was I making such an ugly face? I look so mean.

When I got to work that day, someone had tacked up the photo and accompanying article on the bulletin board like a prize ribbon. Clearly, we owned the story.

ONE WEEK LATER, on April 7, the DA's office slapped Marcus with thirty-three sex abuse charges on top of the nine counts of first-degree murder he already faced. The new charges were for raping and molesting six of his children and nieces. Five of the six victims had been under the age of fourteen when the alleged sexual abuse occurred.

The announcement was a disappointing and surprising setback for the defense attorneys, Pete Jones and Ralph Torres, who had come to court that day to ask the judge to dismiss the entire case against Marcus, contending that Sebhrenah was the one who pulled the trigger.

But the judge rejected the defense's motion without batting an eye. I actually felt sorry for the defense team.

Jones, a middle-aged man with a full head of gray hair, a bushy mustache, and big blue eyes, talked to the reporters afterward, lamenting his situation as "impossible." Jones said Wesson had rejected his right to ask for a delay, and he complained that he hadn't received any transcripts of interviews with witnesses. I could almost see the gravity of the case pressing down on his shoulders.

WHEN I INTERVIEWED Serafino and Almae that night, they seemed even more somber than before. I figured out that it would have been Sebhrenah's twenty-sixth birthday that week. Now that the defense was pinning the murders on her, the boys felt protective of her, although they didn't want to place the blame on their father either.

Given my exclusive stories and the picture of me with the girls in the paper, people started thinking of me as *the* authoritative Wesson reporter in town. I began seeing myself that way, too. The longer I covered the story, the harder I strove to uncover new details about the case. Elizabeth had done an interview with another TV station, and I desperately wanted to talk to her myself. During the first broadcast, she told them to disguise her identity, so the station showed only her hands to accompany the sound of her soft, wavering voice. All that did was add to the mystery surrounding "the wife," one I wanted to solve more than ever.

Other reporters at my station had her phone number, but none was able to get her to go on camera again. I asked one of them to give Elizabeth my phone number and have her call me. The following Sunday afternoon, two hours before I had to be at work, she did.

"Alysia? This is Elizabeth Wesson. I know you've talked to my sons several times."

"Yes, thanks for calling. How are you doing?"

There I go again, asking the same stupid question.

I was taken aback when she began crying uncontrollably. After having watched the other women act like automatons, I found Elizabeth's breakdown oddly refreshing. *Finally, some emotion.*

I had decided not to ask her any probing questions, and she opened up to me right away. She obviously had a lot to get off her chest, so I just listened to her cry, defend her husband, and blame Ruby and Sofia, while I interjected an "mm-hmm" every so often.

As I sat on my bed listening to her, I leaned back against the stack of pillows I'd propped against my wall while Cosmo rustled through the hula bed skirt underneath me, then jumped up onto the faux palm tree in the corner near the sandbox. The newest reporter at my station, I knew I was last in line for vacation time, so I had turned my bedroom into a makeshift Hawaiian vacation. I stared at the life-size hula girl cutout on the wall in front of me. It occurred to me that she looked like Elizabeth's niece Rosie, only happier. I had yet to see Rosie smile.

Elizabeth told me that the county was taking good care of Ruby and Sofia, the prosecution's star witnesses, but not Elizabeth's side of the family. I understood how it worked, but she didn't get it. She wondered why her kids were left homeless while the women she blamed for the murders were in protective custody. I knew if she and her children shifted their allegiance away from Marcus, they, too, would benefit, but I could tell from our conversation that that wasn't going to happen. Still, I thought, they needed more help than Ruby and Sofia.

"I don't know what we're going to do," Elizabeth cried. "We have nowhere to go. I just don't know how we're going to make it."

"There has to be someone who can help you guys," I said. "Let me look into it and call you back."

But Elizabeth wasn't ready to hang up yet. She kept talking about the babies who were gone, and I felt it would be cruel to cut her off, so I continued to listen.

I ended up being half an hour late for work.

IT WAS MID-APRIL, and I couldn't believe it was 90 degrees outside. Understandably, I didn't mind sitting with the other reporters for hours in the air-conditioned courtroom during Marcus's preliminary hearing, baking in the heat only when I did quick radio reports during breaks.

The testimony was intense as four Fresno police officers recounted what they'd seen in that back bedroom a month earlier. One of them talked about the intertwined stack of bodies and how he couldn't tell which bloody arm or leg belonged to whom. He said he stuck his hand deep into the tangled pile past Lise, but all he felt was blood. No life, no pulses. When he realized he wasn't going to be able to help any of the children, he started to cry.

Some testified that they'd taken time off and gotten counseling to deal with the trauma of that day. I only wished that the family would undergo similar therapy, but I figured they weren't ready to delve into their troubled past.

Watching veteran officers grow visibly saddened as they recalled details of that day upset me, too. Shortly after the murders, Police Chief Dyer had said of his officers, "If someone wasn't emotional, I'd have to question if they have a heart." Now I understood what he meant.

Given that Sebhrenah's body was found on top of the pile with the gun under her, "The evidence is woefully slim that points to Mr. Wesson as the shooter," Pete Jones said during the hearing. "All the circumstantial evidence points away from Marcus Wesson." Marcus's attorneys also argued that the sex abuse charges were "vague" and had "jurisdiction" problems.

But at the close of the prelim, Judge Lawrence Jones decided there was sufficient evidence for Marcus Wesson to stand trial for the murder of his nine children. Without much explanation, he also granted the prosecution's request to drop nineteen of the thirty-three sex charges, by combining some of them and dismissing some altogether. If this was a preview of things to come, the main trial was going to be emotionally draining for everyone.

Although Elizabeth and her children were subpoenaed for the prelim, none was called to testify. I was glad they didn't have to endure being questioned, but I was also a bit disappointed that I didn't get to see what Elizabeth looked like. I kept hearing her hopeless voice in my head, telling me her family had nowhere to go. I kept thinking there had to be something I could do to help.

I HAD THAT Friday off, so I devoted the afternoon to finding an answer to the Wessons' housing problem. They couldn't have stayed in the house on Hammond Avenue even if they'd wanted to because of the zoning violations. After the family's money ran out, the county had put them up in a motel for nearly two weeks, but that stint was up, too. The boys were staying with friends, but Elizabeth, Kiani, and Rosie considered themselves homeless. They had been staying with a relative, but Elizabeth told me she felt like they had overstayed their welcome and needed to find another place quickly.

I opened the phone book but didn't know where to look.

Temporary housing? But they don't have any money.

Red Cross? But they weren't victims of a fire or natural disaster.

Shelters? Maybe that could work.

I called a local women's shelter that catered to domestic abuse victims but didn't identify myself as a reporter, so the lady thought I was interested in staying there myself. She was nice but informed me the beds were full and there was a long waiting list. She suggested I try another shelter and read me the number. Deep down, I knew the girls wouldn't be able to handle sleeping under the same roof with a bunch of strangers, so I didn't make the other call.

Instead, I searched the Internet for something, anything that would lead me in the right direction, but came up empty. I called Elizabeth to break the bad news, and she said she was grateful I had looked into it for them.

"I wish I could help my family," she cried. "I really do. We need somewhere to go."

I wondered if I'd given up my search too easily. Fresno was full of nice people and dozens of charities. There had to be somewhere they could stay.

My apartment was big enough for three more women. I joked to myself that they could always sleep there a night or two.

Yeah, right, as if I could get involved like that! I pushed the thought out of my mind.

Six

I threw a party that Saturday night to distract me from the case. Being a huge fan of the Rat Pack, I made them the theme for the evening and went shopping for all of the essentials, including decks of cards and poker chips, gin, vodka, vermouth, and big green olives for martinis. I invited about twenty local media types, many of whom had never been to my apartment before.

"Wow, it's pretty big in here, Alysia. It's just you who lives here?" one of the newbies asked.

My second-floor apartment was more than a thousand square feet, with two bedrooms, one and a half bathrooms, and a wooden deck overlooking a parking lot. I hadn't brought much with me when I'd moved from Lansing, so the apartment appeared larger than it really was. Rent in Fresno was less expensive, and I was earning more money, so I could afford luxuries like parties.

"It's just me and Cosmo," I replied.

I'd brought Cosmo with me when I moved, only to find out that ferrets were illegal in California.

Oops.

Everyone at my station referred to him as the "illegal alien." He was somewhat of a local celebrity and deservedly had his own bedroom, with a mini-closet where I kept his dress-up outfits.

My guests and I played poker and blackjack, sipped dirty martinis, and listened to Frank, Sammy, and Dean until the wee hours of the morning. After saying my last good-bye on the doorstep, I looked around at the empty martini glasses and the sea of poker chips spilled all over the floor and tables. The crooner music was still playing, but all I could hear was Elizabeth's trembling voice and her persistent mournful crying in my head.

We have nowhere to go, Alysia.

As my martini buzz wore off, I couldn't help wondering where the Wesson women were staying that night. The sad possibility that they might be sleeping in their car kept me awake. I knew I wouldn't be able to rest until I figured out somewhere safe for them to go, so I tossed off my covers and headed toward Cosmo's room. Meanwhile, the thoughts I'd been pushing away kept coming back.

If I weren't a reporter, they could just crash here for a couple of weeks.

But I *was* a reporter, so ethically, that was out of the question. A journalist's ethical standards are higher than most people might realize. One of my college professors had practically made us memorize the Society of Professional Journalists' strict ethics code, which stated that journalists should "remain free of associations and activities that may compromise integrity or damage credibility."

Which meant I couldn't help the Wessons.

Then again, the code also said that journalists should "show compassion for those who may be affected adversely by news coverage. Use special sensitivity when dealing with children and inexperienced sources or subjects."

However, I knew they didn't mean the kind of compassion I was feeling.

I walked back into my bedroom, sat on the bed, and flashed on a photo that had haunted me since I'd seen it in my journalism ethics class at Michigan State. It pictured two dueling images: a little Sudanese girl, shriveled by starvation and crawling weakly to a food camp, and a vulture patiently waiting for the girl to die so he could devour her flesh.

Turned out that the photojournalist Kevin Carter had been patiently waiting there, too, and snapped the shot.

A little more than a year later, in April 1994, he won the coveted Pulitzer Prize for the image, which had been published in the *New York Times* and other newspapers around the world. Carter's ethical dilemma became a volatile topic of debate in my class that semester: Should he have saved the little girl from the vulture or taken the award-winning photo?

A majority of my classmates said Carter should have taken the picture and never looked back. As journalists, after all, we were supposed to observe and record events, not change or get involved in them. Still, I was shocked at my classmates' callousness. It was a little girl, for God's sake. If the picture was so important, why not take it and then rescue her?

I was appalled that my professor seemed to agree with the students who said Carter did the right thing.

"So, this Carter guy," I said. "Does *he* think he did the right thing?"

"I don't know," my teacher answered. "He killed himself three months after getting the Pulitzer."

The classroom echoed with the gasps of my fellow students—as well as my own. That answered my question.

I promised myself I would never be like Kevin Carter.

HERE I WAS, a decade later, facing what I saw as a similar dilemma. Every instinct I had told me I needed to help the Wessons. But I'd always put my professional ethics before my human urges. I had separated myself from emotion on every story I'd worked so far—from car accidents with dead babies lying in the road to murder scenes with hysterical parents screaming and hovering over their children's bloody bodies.

Up until this point, I'd always been good at compartmentalizing work from the rest of my life. But the Wesson case had changed all that.

We have nowhere to go, Alysia.

As a journalist, I knew I would be committing an enormous ethical violation, but as a regular citizen, I felt that I ought to be able to be a reporter and a human being *at the same time*. I felt I could still be objective about the story even if I helped the Wesson family. It wasn't as if I were sleeping with a politician or something. They would feel more comfortable with me during interviews. Their family had been murdered, and no one was taking care of them. They needed to feel safe.

I started wondering, What would be so bad if I let them stay with me for just a few nights and see how it went? No one would even have to know. I'd keep helping them search for a place to stay, and if I felt it was affecting my journalistic judgment, I'd move them out. What was the harm in that?

IT WAS 6:00 A.M. when I made the decision, and for a minute, I felt as if a weight had been lifted. Then I thought about what my friends and family would think, and the heaviness came back.

My worry-prone and protective parents weren't going to like this at all. Although I was 99 percent sure I would move the Wessons in with me, I still wanted to run it by my mom, dad, and boyfriend. Maybe they could reason with me. The three of them lived in Michigan, where it was already 9:00 A.M.

Here goes nothing.

The phone rang longer than usual before my mom picked up.

"Hi, Mom," I said assertively.

"What are you doing up so early, Alysia? Is everything okay?"

"Mom, I've made a decision. Please don't interrupt me or give me advice because I'm calling to tell you what I've *decided*. I'm not calling for advice."

"Alysia, you're scaring me."

"You know the man with the dreadlocks who killed his family here in Fresno?"

"Yes," she said cautiously.

My parents had seen the national coverage early on. It terrified them that I lived in the same state as Marcus Wesson, let alone the same city. I hadn't told them how closely I'd been pursuing the story because I knew they'd be too worried.

"Well, there are some family members who are still brainwashed, and they still support the father."

"Those poor kids."

"Well, it's his wife, too."

"It's such a tragedy."

"I know. And it's worse because these people have no place to go."

"Aren't the police taking care of them?"

"It's complicated. They don't want to testify for the prosecution, so—"

"Because they are so brainwashed."

"Anyway, they need help, and I don't think they're going to get it anywhere else," I said, walking into the kitchen with the phone to get a drink of water. "Mom?"

"What, honey?"

"I've decided to move them in with me."

Silence.

"Mom?"

More silence.

I knew her big green eyes were growing larger by the second. I could see her with one hand on the high kitchen countertop, bracing herself so she wouldn't fall over from shock.

"Mom, are you there?"

"Dear God, please tell me you're not serious," she finally responded, her voice shaky.

"I have to do it," I said. "I have to."

"It's not safe. Oh my God." Her voice was louder now, and she was rushing through her sentences, asking me how I knew it would be safe to bring them home.

"I just have a feeling about this," I said, trying to reassure her. "It's the right thing to do."

But that wasn't enough for my mom. "It is not your responsibility," she said. "That's why we pay taxes. That's why *you* pay taxes. Can't the government help these people?"

"It will only be temporary. Just until I figure out *who* can help them. These people lost everything. Hell, Cosmo has his own room and they have nowhere to go. I just feel bad."

"Alysia, I admire what you're saying and how you're feeling. But this just cannot happen. What about your job?"

"Reporters have personal relationships with sources all the time, whether they admit it or not. It will help my stories. I'll have more perspective about the case. Anyway, this is larger than my job. I want to do this. I'm going to do this."

"Do you need us to fly out there?"

"Mom, it will be fine. Trust me."

"We're flying out there."

"No you're not."

"But you don't have enough room."

"They had, like, twenty people living in that house where it happened," I said, trying to lighten the mood. My mom called in my dad for backup.

"Chuck, your daughter wants to live with the family of that serial killer from TV," she yelled.

"He's a *mass murderer,* Mom, not a serial killer," I said.

"Oh, *excuse me,*" she said sarcastically. "Chuck, your daughter wants to live with a *mass murderer's* family. And they are still brainwashed."

My dad grabbed the phone. "Who are you talking about?" he asked worriedly. "That man with the dreadlocks who had kids with his daughters?"

"Dad, the family has nowhere to go. And I thought they could stay with me until they find a place. Listen, I'm not asking you guys for permission. I didn't even have to tell you. I'm doing it."

My mom took the phone back, and I could tell she'd calmed down. "Alysia, we just want to make sure you're safe."

"Mom, once you meet them, you'll understand. I promise."

I hung up, thinking it had gone pretty well. The fact that my parents weren't on the first flight to Fresno told me that they didn't think I was completely insane. My boyfriend, Juan, would be another story.

Juan and I had been dating for about a year. He was a week away from finishing his master's degree at Michigan State—in social work, ironically. After that, he was moving to California to be closer to me. I shuddered at the thought of a serious commitment; I loved the freedom that came with a long-distance relationship. He hoped I would change my mind once he moved, but I knew differently. Although it was in his nature to help everyone and he often told me I was "too insensitive," I knew even he would think I was going too far by doing this.

My conversation with him was a lot like the one with my parents. He was worried about my safety and wished I would reconsider. But after ten minutes of listening to my rationale, he said he supported my decision and told me I was being uncharacteristically sensitive.

No one had talked me out of it.

I felt like a giddy child whose parents had given her permission to have a slumber party, so I called Elizabeth on her cell phone, barely able to keep the excitement out of my voice.

"I found a place for you, Kiani, and Rosie to stay," I said proudly.

Her sad voice perked up. She almost sounded cheerful. "Oh, thank you, Alysia," she said breathlessly. "Thank you so much. Where?"

"At my place," I said. "You guys can stay with me until we figure out a permanent solution. Okay?"

Elizabeth started crying with relief. "Oh, thank you, Alysia," she said. Then, pausing for a moment, she asked hesitantly, "Are you sure? I mean, can you do that?"

For a minute, I questioned my decision. Even Elizabeth could tell the situation was a bit sketchy. But I held to my resolve. Kind of.

"Of course I'm sure," I said half-truthfully. "Just let me worry about it."

"Thank you, Alysia," she said again. She said she would tell the girls the good news and call back to arrange a time to come over later that day.

By the time I hung up, I felt sure once again that I was doing the right thing.

I walked around my apartment, surveying the space like a real estate agent. I stopped inside Cosmo's room, which would soon be the Wessons', and took stock of its minimal contents: Cosmo's four-story cage, his mini-closet, and toy chest. There was plenty of room for the inflatable mattress I had stowed in the closet for visitors. It slept only two people, though, so I realized I needed to buy another one for my third roommate.

Luckily, Target was just a few blocks away. I jumped in my car and, moments later, was pulling into the parking lot. As I was walking into the crowded store, Elizabeth called.

I assumed she was ready to come over, so I almost turned around and headed back toward my car, but I kept going. I really needed that second mattress.

"Would it be okay if we came over now?" Elizabeth asked.

"Sure," I said, rushing through Target's automatic doors. "I live in northwest Fresno. I'm at the store, but I can be home in two minutes. Where are you coming from? I'll give you directions."

"We're at Target right now on Shaw Avenue."

I couldn't believe the coincidence. I chalked it up as another sign that supported my decision.

"Are you serious?" I asked, looking around for them. "I'm here, too."

They probably thought I was stalking them.

Elizabeth explained that they were in the women's clothing section at the front, left side of the store. I saw them immediately and started walking toward them.

Elizabeth caught my eye first. She was Latina and appeared to be about forty, with light brown skin; wavy, shoulder-length black hair; a heart-shaped face; and full lips, painted with burgundy lipstick. She had on a long-sleeved black blouse and a long, flowing black skirt, with strappy black heels. She looked so much younger than I imagined and *so normal*. I must have been staring because her face turned red and she looked down.

I held out my hand to greet her. "Hi, I'm Alysia."

She reached out with a hand with painted nails that matched her lips and laid four fingers loosely in my palm. I lifted the deadweight of her hand twice, then turned my attention to the two girls, who were each standing with one hand on a rack of T-shirts.

"Nice to see you again, Kiani and Rosie," I said.

Both of them gave me half smiles. Rosie, who was unable to look me in the eye, seemed more shy than her cousin.

We stood there awkwardly, wondering what to do next. It had been so much easier when I was chasing them down after court and yelling questions at them. Now that we were face-to-face, I had no clue what to say.

"Well, I was just picking up a few things," I said finally. "Do you want to wait here and I'll go grab them?"

I didn't want them to feel like they were imposing on me, so I didn't tell them I was there to buy them a new bed. I found the right section, yanked a box off the shelf, then covered it with a greeting card and package of magnets so they couldn't tell what was inside.

I found them again, standing empty-handed between the women's clothes and the mini–food court. They seemed surprised when I pulled a personal pizza from the Pizza Hut heated display case and headed toward the checkout line.

"Oh, did you guys want one?"

They answered quickly and in unison. "No, no, we're fine."

I could see by the way they looked at the pizza that they hadn't eaten, but I didn't push.

The checkout girl looked first at me, then at the three women in black, then back at me again. She didn't say anything as she rang up my items, but it seemed as if she was about to. I wondered if she recognized Kiani or Rosie from the news—or me, for that matter. I didn't want to stick around to find out.

As we approached the parking lot, I realized the trio was walking three or four steps behind me, exactly the way I pictured them following Marcus all those years. I slowed down and waited for them to catch up so we could walk in a horizontal line together.

ON THE SHORT trek back to my apartment, I kept glancing in my rearview mirror at their small silver car following me. I could see them talking and wished I could hear their conversation.

I slowed down once we got to my parking lot and rolled down my window.

"You can park right in there," I said, motioning toward my stall. I wanted them to feel like they belonged here, so I drove on and searched for an empty visitor spot.

They followed me slowly up the concrete stairs to my apartment, their three pairs of high heels clicking on each step like a drum line.

I unlocked the front door and walked in, waving them inside, where we stood, looking at one another uncomfortably.

"This is it," I said, smiling. "Make yourselves at home."

Cosmo trotted over and gazed up at the new faces.

"This is my ferret, Cosmo," I said, swooping him up, which broke the ice. "Cosmo, these are your new roommates."

Cosmo inspected Elizabeth first, then Rosie, then Kiani. You could tell he didn't know what to think. He wasn't the only one.

THE WESSONS STAYED for about an hour, until I had to leave for work. They were able to stay with a relative two more nights, so they showed up at my place with their bags that Tuesday.

At first, they huddled together between my small kitchen and dining area, whispering among themselves. I felt like a stranger in my own apartment, as if I were at a party where I didn't know anyone. I tried to make everyone feel more at ease by striking up a conversation, but Kiani was the only one who would respond. Rosie wouldn't say a word to me—she would whisper to Kiani, and Kiani would speak for her. Elizabeth said a few words here and there, but her voice was so quiet I couldn't understand her.

Elizabeth and Rosie hid in their room that night, while Kiani and I sat on the living room floor, talking about music. She told me how her father would spend hours mixing house and trance tracks together on tapes, to which the family would dance until 3:00 or 4:00 A.M. every Friday night, each girl competing to be the last one standing.

In turn, I told her about my experiences at raves in London and Athens during college. Kiani and I were less than a year apart in age, but our experiences couldn't have been more different. That night, we traded stories about anything but the murders that had brought us together.

I DIDN'T SLEEP well and woke up around 8:00 the next morning to the soft hum of voices on the other side of the door. It was strange to hear other people moving around in my apartment. I got up and searched for something civilized to put on for company.

I can't walk around naked anymore.

I looked for some conservative pajamas at the bottom of my drawer but, finding none, settled for a pair of nylon running pants and a cotton T-shirt.

They would never wear something like this.

It was my birthday, and I had planned to have a Cinco de Mayo party that night but had canceled it because of my new living situation. Of course, I couldn't tell my friends why.

The bag of balloons, sombreros, and colorful leis I'd bought for the occasion were still in a box in a corner of my room so, laughing, I wrapped a red lei around my neck.

"Happy birthday," I whispered to myself.

I took off the lei, inhaled deeply, and opened my bedroom door to see what my houseguests were up to.

Elizabeth, Kiani, and Rosie were all showered and dressed, sporting their usual dark shirts, skirts, and high heels, and sitting side by side on my long red couch in front of the TV. Only the screen was black.

"Good morning," I said, looking down the line.

Kiani grinned as she handed me a birthday card.

"Thank you," I said, surprised.

I tore open the envelope, which read "Happy Birthday" in beautiful gold and silver embossed letters. Inside was a handwritten note, signed by all three of them.

```
With everything that has happened
to our family, you have been our only
blessing through this. Thank you so
much for taking us into your home. God
Bless You and we wish you the happiest
of birthdays.
```

They must have bought it after I mentioned my birthday would be the day after they moved in. "That was so nice of you," I said, genuinely moved by the thoughtful gesture.

Pointing toward the television, I said, "You can turn on the TV, you know."

I snatched up the remote and sat down on a chair. I always sat on the red couch; the black and silver armchairs, which I'd bought for style over comfort, normally were for guests. I hit the power button and glanced over at the girls. Despite their brave faces, they looked so sad. Their eyes were red from crying.

I wonder if I've ever seen anyone so sad before.

I heard a strange rustling noise coming from outside. It was growing louder.

"What is that?" I asked.

"I think it's just those birds," Elizabeth said.

"Birds?" I asked in disbelief. "There aren't any birds over here."

The only birds I'd ever seen flocked to the trees with the red berries on the other side of the apartment complex.

"Yeah, right there," Kiani said, pointing to my patio.

I stood up and was amazed to see a group of mourning doves gathered outside my floor-to-ceiling window.

"They're nice, Alysia," Rosie said, uttering her first words to me since she'd moved in.

I peered out the window and counted them.

One, two, three, four, five, six, seven, eight, and, oh my God, nine. No way!

Nine mourning doves were at my window, one for each dead child. I knew it had to mean something.

THE FOUR OF US quickly fell into a routine. The three Wessons would wake up around 7:00 A.M., get dressed in their skirts and high heels—the only shoes the girls owned—then

Elizabeth would begin her crying jag in the living room while Kiani and Rosie read and wrote in their diaries in the bedroom. I would get up around 10:00 and join Elizabeth on the couch, where she would tell me stories about her children and how much she missed them for a couple of hours before I got ready for work. She'd spend the rest of the day sitting on the couch, with her heels on, weeping.

"My babies are gone," she'd say. "My babies are gone."

There was nothing I could say to console her.

Meanwhile, the doves returned to my deck each morning. They were building a nest now in the wooden rafters overhead. The red roses Juan had sent me for my birthday were wilting, so I pulled back the sliding glass door and placed the vase outside for the birds to use as nesting material. I put the vase of wildflowers from my friend Jon out there, too.

"Oh, that's a good idea," Elizabeth said, taking a break from crying to gaze out the window.

"I'm telling you, they only started coming around when you guys moved in," I said.

"You know, Sebhrenah loved doves," Elizabeth said quietly. "She drew them all the time."

Did Sebhrenah send the doves to comfort her loved ones?

"Yeah, Bhrenah made me a birdhouse not too long ago," she said. "She painted doves just like that all over it."

After a couple of weeks, Elizabeth opened up more and more, revealing details about her life with Marcus. I had so many questions about what he was like and how he controlled them, but I held back. Oftentimes, I was too nauseated by the information to say a word anyway, so at the beginning, I just sat there and listened.

Seven

Elizabeth's family life with Marcus grew out of her own unstable beginnings.

Her mother, Rosa "Rose" Maytorena, dropped out of school after the sixth grade to work the fields around Brawley, a small California town just north of the Mexican border. Rose was nineteen when she began dating Mike Solorio, who was working at the Pepsi factory there.

The couple had four children before they got married in July 1959, two weeks before their fifth child, Elizabeth, was born in Baja California. The family subsequently returned to California, where Elizabeth grew up thinking she was born in the United States—only to find out that Baja California was actually part of Mexico.

Rose and Mike Solorio had four more children, but their marriage didn't last long. When Elizabeth was seven, Mike told the kids he was going on a trip and drove away.

Twenty-one-year-old Marcus Wesson moved into Elizabeth's neighborhood in San Jose in 1968, after having been stationed for almost two years in the U.S. Army's 695th Medical Ambulance Company in Europe. His mother lived two doors down from Elizabeth.

One summer night, Marcus and his sister came over to

Elizabeth's house so he could protect Rose and her family from a violent neighbor. Marcus was the first black adult Elizabeth had ever talked to, and she was fascinated by the darkness of his skin. He endeared himself to her by saying hello and smiling at her.

Rose had long since quit her job at a cannery to take care of the kids. And now that her family had no man at its helm, Marcus was soon able to work his way in. Before long, he'd struck up a romantic relationship with Rose, thirteen years his senior.

When his own mother learned about this, she warned Rose to leave Marcus alone.

"You're too old for my Marcus," Carrie Wesson, a nurse and a devout Seventh-day Adventist, told her. "What do you think you're doing with my son?"

Rose cried all day after the confrontation, but nothing changed. Marcus wasn't going anywhere.

Marcus, who was taking courses at the local community college, helped Rose get on welfare, and he encouraged her to take a more active role in raising and disciplining her children. Before Marcus came along, Rose used to yell at her children when she was angry, and sometimes she would just throw rocks or shoes at them. But under his influence, Rose began using more consistent, structured discipline on Elizabeth's older siblings, taking them into a room and hitting them with a belt when they misbehaved. When Elizabeth later looked back on this period, she saw that her family had never seemed happier or functioned better as a cohesive unit.

For his part, Marcus made sure all the kids ate dinner together and also started "family nights," when they would watch movies at home or at the drive-in. Marcus would pile them into his green Volkswagen bus, which they called the *Jolly Green Giant,* and have them hide under blankets so they wouldn't get charged admission.

ALTHOUGH ELIZABETH ENJOYED having Marcus around, any outside observer would have questioned the playtime activities Marcus shared with her and her two sisters.

One night, Marcus asked his brother to officiate at a wedding ceremony between him and nine-year-old Elizabeth. Pretending the driveway was a chapel, Marcus took a Bible, placed Elizabeth's hand on it, and covered hers with his own.

"Marcus," his brother said. "Do you take Elizabeth to be your lawfully wedded wife?"

"I do," he said.

"And Elizabeth, do you take Marcus to have and to hold till death do you part?"

The wide-eyed fourth-grader looked up and said, "I do."

"I now pronounce you husband and wife. You may kiss the bride."

Marcus bent down and kissed Elizabeth's cheek, so she rose up on her tippy toes and did the same to him.

Playing house was fun, but Marcus looked so serious.

"You know, we swore over the Bible," he said, staring at her intensely. "In God's eyes, we are really married, Elizabeth. Don't forget, you are my wife now."

She was a little scared because he made it seem so real, but she was flattered, too. She knew Marcus was her mother's boyfriend, but he also had become the only man who had any consistent fatherly role in her life. And she liked the way he made her feel that she was *his.*

* * *

A FEW MONTHS later, Rose and Marcus took Elizabeth to the pharmacy at the Pink Elephant market to get her some cold medicine. On the way back to their car, Elizabeth saw her real father waiting for them in the parking lot. She was excited to see Mike, but he looked angry and barely seemed to notice her. He was too busy grabbing Rose's arm and confronting her about her new boyfriend.

"Stop it, Dad," Elizabeth pleaded, crying. "Don't do that to Mom. Please stop."

Marcus pulled out a shiny silver knife and threatened Mike with it.

"Don't, Marcus!" Rose screamed. "Run, just run away!"

Marcus took off, sprinting down the street, and didn't look back. Elizabeth, scared and confused about the volatile situation, stood next to her mother, sobbing.

After her father calmed down, he drove Rose and Elizabeth home, then disappeared into Rose's bedroom. Elizabeth hoped he was moving back in, but when she woke up the next morning, he was gone again.

AFTER THAT, MARCUS spent even more nights at the house, and Rose was soon pregnant with his child. Their son, Adair, was born in 1971.

That didn't change anything for Elizabeth, however, who knew in her heart that Marcus would never marry Rose. He was going to marry *her* someday.

"You are mine, Elizabeth," he'd remind her at least once a month.

Elizabeth's house had four bedrooms, one for Rose and three for the nine kids, for whom Marcus had constructed queen-size bunk beds. Elizabeth shared one of them with her younger sister Deanna; Elizabeth had the lower bunk, and their older sister, Rosemary, had a single bed in the corner. In a separate room, Marcus shared a bunk bed with her two little brothers, with him sleeping in the bottom bunk and them above.

Elizabeth would often wait until her little brothers were asleep, then crawl into Marcus's bed with him. Other times, Marcus would come to her bed, which made her feel special. He would reach under her T-shirt and shorts to touch her breasts and rub her genital area, but because they were "married," it didn't seem wrong.

Marcus even started getting jealous when she didn't act like his wife.

Elizabeth and her siblings ran wild, spending days and sometimes weeks at friends' houses without checking in with Rose, coming and going as they pleased.

When Elizabeth was ten, she came home from a neighbor's house to find an agitated Marcus.

"Where have you been?" he demanded.

"At the neighbors'," she said. "What's wrong?"

"You know what? You ignored me and you're not my wife anymore," Marcus said, pouting.

"Yes I am," she cried. "Please don't say that."

"Nope, you're not my wife."

Elizabeth couldn't stand to lose Marcus. "I'll never leave again," she said. "We *are* married."

After about twenty minutes, Marcus caved in and embraced the young girl.

"Okay," he said. "We *are* married. I forgive you."

Elizabeth was still crying, but she felt safe.

* * *

BY THE TIME Elizabeth was twelve, she was sneaking into Marcus's bed nearly every night. He was going through a black magic phase, and she noticed he had been collecting witchcraft paraphernalia and spell books. She was startled awake one night to hear Marcus groaning as if he were in pain, with his hand firmly on her bare breast.

"What's wrong, Marcus?" Elizabeth whispered, trying not to wake her brothers in the top bunk.

"The Devil reached inside me and was trying to pull out my organs."

"What do you mean?" she asked, frightened.

"I was putting a spell on you and God got upset. So the Devil took over. I'm praying to God now to forgive me. I'm never going to perform spells again."

Elizabeth was almost afraid to ask. "What kind of spell did you put on me?"

"The spell was so you would be mine forever."

When she saw him later that night, he told her he had burned all of his voodoo medallions and books.

IT WASN'T LONG before Marcus made good on his promise to legally marry Elizabeth. Two days before Christmas in 1973, the fourteen-year-old was washing the family's dinner dishes and turned to find twenty-seven-year-old Marcus down on one knee. His dark skin was flushed with a red hue. She'd never seen him bashful before.

"Elizabeth, I've always loved you," he said, smiling as he held out a thin gold band, engraved with sunflowers. "Will you marry me?"

"Yes, Marcus. I'll marry you," she said, overjoyed.

Marcus slipped the ring on her finger and kissed her.

"I told you," he said. "You are mine forever."

THREE MONTHS LATER, Elizabeth was pregnant. At five feet four inches, and only one hundred pounds, her protruding stomach became obvious almost immediately. Elizabeth knew that everyone, including her mother, noticed, but no one said a word about it.

Still, things weren't as easy as Marcus had anticipated. When he went downtown to apply for a marriage license, he learned he had to overcome two obstacles before he could marry his child bride. Not only did he need one of her parents' formal permission but he and Elizabeth had to get the consent of a court-appointed counselor, too.

Surprisingly, Rose's approval came rather easily. She even bought a girdle for Elizabeth so she could conceal her pregnancy from the counselor. Elizabeth tried it on right before her eighth-grade graduation ceremony when she was only a couple of months along. Rose helped her squeeze into it again for the couple's first counseling session. Although Elizabeth was very nervous, Marcus was cool and collected.

The counselor spent most of the first session speaking to Marcus. Elizabeth simply nodded periodically and let Marcus do the talking.

Everything seemed to go well until the third session, which took an unexpected turn. Halfway through, the counselor started pacing the room, shaking his head. Then he launched into her.

"That's it," he declared, looking straight at Elizabeth. "You never say anything! You don't ever tell me how you feel. I don't think you're ready to get married."

Elizabeth sat up, startled and angry. This time, she had no trouble speaking up.

"I want to marry him," she said in an uncharacteristically assertive voice. "I don't understand why you are doing this to me. I love him very much. This is what I want, and I don't understand how you can stop it. It's my life!"

"Finally!" the counselor exclaimed. "*That* is what I was waiting for. Why didn't you say so? I just wanted to make sure that nobody was forcing you into this decision."

A WEEK LATER, Elizabeth's estranged father got wind of her engagement and pregnancy and came back to try to prevent the marriage.

"I don't want her marrying no nigger," Mike screamed at Rose, ignoring his daughter crying next to them. "She's too young. How could you have let this happen? I'm going to call the police."

But Mike never followed through. He simply got in his car and drove home to his new family.

Once he was gone, Marcus pulled his fiancée aside. "We have to get married quick before someone stops us," he said. Elizabeth agreed.

A few days later, on August 19, Marcus and Elizabeth were watching TV at home and he jumped up impulsively.

"Come on, let's go," he said.

"Where are we going?"

"We're going to get married."

"Like this?" she asked, looking down at her yellow cotton shorts and gingham maternity shirt and at his black T-shirt and jeans.

"Yes, let's go."

The two raced to San Jose City Hall, where Elizabeth saw a woman wearing a beautiful white wedding gown with lace and silk flowers and her fiancé sporting a crisp black tuxedo. It was exactly how she had pictured her wedding.

But no matter what they were wearing, Elizabeth still thought Marcus was the most handsome man she'd ever seen.

So, five months pregnant, the fifteen-year-old Elizabeth stood before a judge and became Mrs. Marcus Wesson.

THE COUPLE WANTED to live on their own, but because neither Marcus nor Elizabeth had a job, they didn't have enough money. Marcus was going to college on the G.I. Bill, and Elizabeth was busy with high school.

So Carrie Wesson offered to help the newlyweds by letting them stay at her house—after demanding to see their marriage license.

Marcus had never gotten along very well with his father. Ben Wesson had spent a lot of nights away from home drinking when Marcus was growing up. Marcus would often pick up his father from a bar or a cheap motel after he had passed out or lay injured after a drunken brawl. Ben later moved to Los Angeles, where he had a sexual relationship with a nephew and only limited contact with his wife and their four children.

Marcus resented his father and the way his behavior disrespected his mother, but Carrie was so deep into her Seventh-day Adventist beliefs that she never acknowledged her husband's indiscretions. Nor did she consider divorcing him. She believed God would bring her husband back to her someday.

While Ben was gone, Marcus, the eldest child, took on many of the paternal duties of the household, such as making sure his siblings got off to school safely. Carrie treated him like the man of the house and often called him her "pride and joy."

Carrie had a full-time nursing job to support their family, and she spent her free time writing a book about the Bible, hoping to share her knowledge of the Revelation with others.

Elizabeth hadn't been to church much, so she was struck by the Wesson family's strong faith in the Lord. Carrie and Marcus took her to church regularly and lectured Elizabeth each day about the Bible and the Second Coming of Christ. Eager to learn more about her husband's religion, Elizabeth enthusiastically explored its teachings. Being from a broken home, she'd never felt like she had anything stable to hold on to. The church made her feel more secure. As if she belonged to something.

Despite the bad memories of his father, Marcus had a soft spot for Ben. And so, when Ben called and said he was dying, Marcus decided to take his new bride to L.A. to see if it was true. Ben had always been known to stretch the truth, and this time was no exception. When the couple showed up at his small apartment, Ben was in perfect health.

Although Elizabeth couldn't put her finger on it, something about Ben made her feel uncomfortable. She didn't want to be alone with him, so she stuck close to Marcus during their visit. Ben said he was working as a big-time writer at Universal Studios, but by the looks of his shabby apartment, Elizabeth doubted his claims. He also told her he had published many books, but when she pressed him about their titles, he said he wrote under a pen name and didn't want to disclose his identity.

"You know," he said, eyeing Elizabeth up and down and focusing on her pregnant belly, "I think I'm going to go out and marry myself a younger woman like Marcus did. Maybe have some kids with her."

Elizabeth didn't know how to respond, so she stayed mum. She didn't understand why Ben was talking about women other than his wife.

ON DECEMBER 12, 1974, Elizabeth gave birth to her first child at a hospital in San Jose. Marcus named him Dorian. Elizabeth couldn't believe how lucky she was to have such a wonderful husband and a healthy newborn son.

The fledgling family stayed at Carrie's house for the first few months of Dorian's life, then moved into a small cottage nearby. Marcus's behavior changed almost immediately.

Elizabeth was a sophomore in high school now, and she was having a hard time caring for Dorian and getting her homework done, too. But Marcus was less than sympathetic. He did little to help with Dorian other than handling the discipline. From the time Dorian was born, Marcus would spank him hard with his large palm.

Elizabeth hated it, but when she tried to protest, Marcus convinced her the spankings were necessary. "He needs to learn," he declared. "If a child is fed and changed, he has no reason to cry, and we must teach him that now."

She figured her husband knew best and tried to get used to it. Marcus also seemed to be disciplining Elizabeth, grilling her each day when she returned from class.

"Who did you talk to?" he would ask accusingly. "Did any boys try to talk to you? What did you do?"

"I didn't talk to nobody, Marcus," she'd say, trying to reassure him. "I promise."

It rarely worked. He would give her the silent treatment for days at a time while she constantly pleaded with him.

"Please talk to me," she'd say. "I didn't do nothing wrong."

When Dorian was only a month old, Marcus took his jealousy to a whole new level. Elizabeth was sitting on the couch as Marcus stared at her with disgust.

"What's wrong?" she asked, confused.

"I can't believe you," he said, shaking his head. "You are thinking adulterous thoughts."

"What are you talking about?"

"You are disrespecting me and thinking about other men."

Elizabeth didn't have time to defend herself before Marcus stood up and pointed toward the door. "Just get out of here," he demanded. "Go on. Get out right now."

She didn't know what to do. She wasn't old enough to drive, and she didn't have anywhere to go. Seeing how serious Marcus was, though, she figured she had to do something. So she walked over to get her newborn baby, but Marcus stopped her. "You're not taking him or anything else," he barked, blocking her from picking up Dorian. "Get out, now."

Elizabeth cried and begged him to let her stay, but he didn't budge, so she slowly walked out the front door.

It was raining hard on the coast that night, and the raindrops washed away her tears. She had nowhere to go but her mother's house, so she began the long walk over there. At the time, the five-mile journey seemed much longer.

She was sure Marcus would realize he'd made a huge mistake and would chase her down any second to apologize. He had to know she would never even *think* about another man.

Instead, she made it all the way to her mother's doorstep—wet, cold, and alone.

"What's wrong, *mi hija?*" Rose asked her daughter, who was still weeping.

Elizabeth didn't want to admit there was anything wrong with her burgeoning marriage, so she walked past her mother and into the kitchen to dry off.

Twenty minutes later, Marcus drove up and walked into the house carrying Dorian. He looked down at Elizabeth, whose eyes were red and puffy and her hair still damp.

"Let's go home," he said in a low voice.

Even though Marcus never raised his voice when he was angry, Elizabeth knew she needed to do what he said—not just because she wanted to be with him but also because she knew no other way to live than to follow Marcus's orders, just as she'd been doing since she was eight years old. In fact, she felt quite comfortable not having to think for herself or take action on her own.

So, Elizabeth stood up and followed him to the car. They never talked about it again.

Eight

The Wessons had been staying in my apartment for a month now, and we hadn't even discussed the possibility of them moving out. What was supposed to have been a temporary living arrangement certainly wasn't panning out that way. I considered warning my boss about my situation but decided to put it off until I knew how long they'd be with me.

The Marcus Wesson saga had died down in the media and his trial was nearly a year away, so I wasn't doing stories about the family for the time being and, frankly, I liked having the girls with me. It was nice not to come home to an empty apartment, and Cosmo loved having an all-day playmate in Rosie. I wasn't sure how long it would take them to get on their feet, and I wasn't in a rush to see them go.

As much as it was becoming the norm in my life, though, I knew other people wouldn't understand. I couldn't take a chance that we'd be seen by reporters from other TV stations who lived in my apartment complex, so the girls and I never walked outside together during the day. When my friends came to pick me up, I ran downstairs to meet them rather than letting them come in and hang out for a while like I used to.

After the third time I did this to my friend Michelle, she got suspicious. It was June, and we were on our way to the pool in my complex.

"Okay, girl," she said in her sassy Latina accent. "What are you hiding up there? You have a gimp in the basement or something?" she joked. *Pulp Fiction* was one of our favorite movies.

"Yeah, something like that," I said, laughing.

Michelle was one of those women who knew all the gossip before anyone else. She always knew who was dating who, who was fighting, and who was breaking up.

"You *are* hiding something, aren't you? I knew it!"

"Come on," I said, dodging the question as I started walking ahead of her. "Let's go."

"Oh, this is going to be good," she said, following me with her oversize duffel bag filled with beach towels, snacks, and a four-pack of bottled margaritas from the corner liquor store.

"I'll need one of these first," I said, grabbing one of the bottles. I unscrewed the top and took a big sip. "Okay, but you have to *swear* you won't tell anybody. I mean *anybody*, Michelle."

"I promise," she said.

"I sort of have some new roommates."

"New roommates? Who?"

I walked over to the edge of the pool at the deep end, then looked at her.

"Marcus Wesson's family," I said quickly, just before I dove in. I stayed underwater until I couldn't hold my breath any longer, swam to the surface to get some air, then went back under to give Michelle time to process my news. When I came up again, she was kneeling over the side, yelling at me.

"Oh no you didn't!" Michelle screamed, wagging her index finger at me.

"They didn't have anywhere to go! They're really nice. You'll love them."

Michelle gulped the rest of her drink, set it down, then raised both hands, palms out.

"Okay, I'm over it," she said. "Now, tell me everything!"

I laughed and told her all the positive changes I'd been noticing in the women who were living with me. How the once-silent Rosie was coming out of her shell, how Kiani was showing interest in learning new things, and how Elizabeth was opening up to me more and more about Marcus. Elizabeth and the girls didn't tell Gypsy where they were living for the first month, but once they did, she started coming over for visits, too, although we usually missed each other because I was at work.

It felt good to share my secret with a trusted friend. Even though she was a big gossip, this time I was confident that Michelle would keep her vow of silence.

WHAT I DIDN'T tell Michelle was that the good times with the Wessons were few and far between. I felt guilty seeing them get dressed and ready each morning, having nowhere to go. I'd leave to go to work or lunch with a friend, but their only outings were weekly trips to their old house to dust or vacuum. Even though they couldn't move back in, they still took pride in keeping the place clean because they knew they would have to sell it one day.

Kiani and Rosie had stopped working a couple of years

ago because they were too busy taking care of their children. Elizabeth had never held a job and was far too traumatized to start looking for one now. So their only social outlet was an occasional visit with one of the boys.

Since the murders, their sole source of income was Sebhrenah's tax refund check. But because it was only a few hundred dollars, they used it just for gas money.

It wasn't costing me much more for them to live with me because they weren't adding to my basic rent or utility costs. I didn't mind subsidizing our daily trips to McDonald's, In-N-Out Burger, or the Chinese place nearby. Knowing it was unhealthy for them to be cooped up in the apartment, I usually took them on a quick food or gas run before I left for work at 2:00 P.M. Sometimes, when Kiani and Rosie got out of the car, other patrons who recognized them from the news coverage would point, stare, and make comments about Marcus.

"I'm sorry for what happened and I'm praying for your family," the nice ones would say.

But the less tactful people would ask, "How can you support your father after what he's done to you guys?"

The girls would drop their heads and walk solemnly back to my car, feeling increasingly self-conscious with every outburst.

"Just ignore them," I'd say.

One 90-degree day in mid-May, I watched a middle-aged man bundled up in a long-sleeved sweatshirt take a picture of the girls with his camera phone. I wanted to jump out and ask the pudgy, balding homunculus what the hell he was doing, but I refrained, not wanting to out myself as the girls' benefactor.

As he walked proudly past my car, he looked as if he had just captured an image of the elusive Bigfoot and couldn't wait to show his friends. When he glanced over at me, I flashed him a dirty look. He stuffed the phone into his pocket and kept on walking.

Rosie's face was flushed as she and Kiani got back in the car.

"Alysia," Kiani said, closing the door. "I think that short man just took a picture of us."

"Are you serious?" I said, feigning surprise. I didn't want to make the girls even more upset by saying I'd noticed. "What a weirdo."

APART FROM MARCUS, Elizabeth was the Wesson family member who drew the most public scrutiny. I would sit and watch her suffer through the pain of her family's loss each morning, then overhear strangers at the grocery store blame her for everything.

"I can't believe the mother let that monster rape her children."

"She's just as bad as he is."

"How could she defend the man who killed her children?"

The truth was, before I met Elizabeth, I, too, had blamed her for not protecting her children from Marcus, but I was beginning to understand her behavior. He had groomed her to be submissive, and she didn't know how to challenge him. She and the girls were unaware of the extent to which he had controlled their minds for so many years, and the whole topic made them defensive.

"Alysia," Elizabeth said. "We are not a cult. Do you realize that people think we are actually *brainwashed*?"

I bit my tongue. I'd learned from watching them get angry and hurt when they saw these criticisms play out on the television news. I'd also seen how silent they would become when challenged on the most minor point concerning Marcus.

Kiani and Rosie were especially sensitive when reporters mentioned that the family members had speech impediments.

"Why does everyone say we have a lisp, Alysia?" Kiani asked.

The question caught me off guard, and as I frantically searched for a polite answer, Rosie spoke up, embarrassed.

"I think we do have a lisp," she said.

"No, this is just how we all talk," Kiani replied. "Alysia, we all talk the same, don't we?"

"You certainly do," I said.

Elizabeth spoke in a little-girl voice, two of the boys stuttered, and all of them had a lisp. Elizabeth told me that Marcus had stuttered until he was a teenager, but he'd managed to grow out of it somehow.

I saw a TV special once about the few documented cases of feral children who had lived for years without human contact. When they were reintroduced to society, they couldn't speak because that part of their brain had atrophied. I wondered if being so detached from society had something to do with the Wessons' speech abnormalities. I also wondered if their speech would improve as they became assimilated into the outside world. Only time would tell.

I DIDN'T REALIZE just how detached they had been until one Saturday night about six weeks into their stay, when we were sitting in the living room and they described some of the activities they'd always wanted, but weren't allowed, to try.

A couple of months earlier, staying home on a Saturday night would have been out of the question for me. Before the Wessons moved in, I spent my weekends going to dinner with my reporter buddies, dancing at clubs, and then heading to parties until three or four in the morning. But these days, I was just as comfortable spending quiet evenings talking with Elizabeth, Kiani, and Rosie. Little by little, Gypsy started coming over to hang out with us when I was home. We'd pass the time watching DVDs and playing games.

Although by then Gypsy had started adult education to earn her high school diploma, Rosie and Kiani had never set foot in a classroom or gotten their driver's licenses, and none of the women had ever been to the dentist. But I soon learned Rosie and Kiani had been deprived of the chance to meet many other typical childhood milestones as well: they didn't know how to swim or ride a bike, and they'd never been to the circus, the zoo, a concert, or out on a date. They'd never even been to a movie theater.

Knowing the three of us were so close in age, I was shocked to learn what drastically different lives we'd led. But of everything they hadn't done, school was the one experience they were most curious about.

"What is school like, Alysia?" Kiani asked. "I mean, it seems like it would be fun to have friends and boyfriends."

"It *is* fun," I said, looking compassionately at my twenty-seven-year-old roommate. "You would have really liked high school, especially."

"Oh yeah? Did you have dances and things like you see in the movies?"

That question prompted an entire night of stories—and more questions—about my high school adventures, from the prom and corsages to homecoming, pep rallies, football games, teachers, and final exams. They were rapt as I described how I used to stay out past curfew and sneak out my bedroom window to hang out with friends after my parents went to sleep.

Learning about their sheltered existence shook me to the core and altered nearly every paradigm I held true. My views on religion had previously been pretty neutral, but that all changed after I'd witnessed the result of the Wessons' restrictive rules, constant prayer, and Bible study. Also, I had always been the person in my group of friends who defended the police and the government, but now I was the one questioning them.

The more I heard about the Wessons' life, the angrier I became. Where was Child Protective Services while the Wessons were being abused and molested by their father? Where were the police? Where was *everyone*? How could something like this happen in the twenty-first century?

When I asked the girls some of these questions, they reminded me that the family did their best to hide, not just from the authorities but from their neighbors, too.

"We didn't trust anyone," Elizabeth said. "We still don't. Marcus made sure of that."

Just when I was about to celebrate the first acknowledgment of her husband's faults, Elizabeth finished her thought. "Alysia, you would be surprised at how many bad people there are in the government."

Again, I held back my biting response, choosing to focus on the positive. Rather than tear down Marcus with words, I wanted to give the girls healthy new experiences to illustrate how wrong he'd been.

Marcus hadn't allowed any of his children to drive, to limit their independence and maintain his hold over them. Taking on one project at a time, I figured that helping the girls get their learners' permits was a good place to start bringing them into their own.

Kiani liked the idea, but I could tell she wasn't ready to take on the challenge quite yet. Rosie, on the other hand, was eager to learn. So Elizabeth took Rosie to the closest Department of Motor Vehicles office to get a driver's ed handbook, and she began reading it on the way home. She was studying it each day when I left for work and still had her nose in it when I got home each night. I'd never seen someone so determined.

Then it dawned on me—this would be the first real test she'd ever taken. Of course, "real" was a subjective term. Marcus had constantly tested her faith, her will, and her devotion, and she'd always given him the answers he wanted.

At twenty-two, Rosie passed the written test and proudly walked out of the DMV with her permit in hand. Now she just needed some time behind the wheel.

"Have you ever driven before?" I asked her.

"Yes," she said confidently, then paused. "Well, not really, I guess."

"What does that mean?"

"Marcus let me drive sometimes at night," Rosie said. "When we would drive back to Fresno from Marshall, he would teach me."

"Really?" I asked, surprised. Marcus didn't strike me as a patient, understanding teacher. "So, would you say you're comfortable behind the wheel then or . . ."

I saw Kiani behind Rosie, waving her hands and mouthing the word "no." I couldn't help but chuckle, which prompted Rosie to turn around and catch Kiani in the act.

"Stop being ignorant," Rosie said, trying to keep a straight face. "I can drive, Alysia. Don't listen to her."

"Okay, whatever you say. Let's find out. Here," I said, handing her my keys. "Elizabeth, Kiani? Sure you don't want to come with us?"

Hearing no takers, Rosie and I walked out the door and headed for my car. After a few steps, I noticed her shoes and stopped walking.

"Uh, Rosie?" I said. "The high heels? I don't think that's such a good idea."

"But . . . ," she said, beginning to protest.

"I know you don't have any flat shoes. You can wear mine."

Although my tennis shoes were a couple of sizes too big for Rosie, I still felt they would be safer than the heels. I had never been more terrified than when she climbed into the driver's seat and I took the passenger's.

Sporting a huge grin, Rosie adjusted the mirrors, stuck the key in the ignition, then looked over at me.

"Go ahead," I said.

She turned the key, pushed down the brake pedal with my red-and-white tennis shoe, and pulled the gear stick into reverse. We inched back ever so slightly as she cranked the wheel to the right. Everything seemed to be going in slow motion, but that was likely because she was driving so slowly.

Once we got onto the main street, where the speed limit was forty miles an hour, she still crept along at twenty. That was good, though, because she didn't brake around corners. I envied driving instructors who had the special cars with the additional brakes on the passenger side. I found myself pushing an imaginary pedal at each turn and stoplight, but I tried not to let Rosie see my fear.

"Good job," I said reassuringly whenever I could catch my breath.

"Who taught you how to drive?" she asked.

"I'll tell you when we get back," I said.

I had purposely turned off the radio so Rosie could concentrate on the road, and I didn't want to begin a conversation to distract her now. Plus, I wasn't so sure I wanted to tell her the truth. I had gone to a private driving school where we learned to drive in new Mustangs. It was half as long as the free course at the high school, and they didn't plaster those embarrassing Student Driver signs all over the car.

After five trips around the square-mile block, Rosie and I pulled safely into my parking spot at the apartment complex. I patted her on the back; she blushed and smiled.

"Did I do okay, Alysia?"

"You were great," I said. "Do you want to hear a funny story?"

I told her about the time I decided to take my parents' white Pontiac Grand Prix out for a joyride. I was still two years away from driving legally, but my parents had let me drive a few times on dirt roads, so I knew the basics.

I was rounding the corner when I saw my parents un-loading shopping bags in the driveway. I panicked, spun the wheel to the left, and hit the gas. The Pontiac flew over the curb of my next-door neighbor's house, crushing their mailbox, and stopped on the front lawn just shy of their living room. My parents just stood there, watching the damage unfold.

As Rosie listened to the story, her eyes were huge and her mouth was open. "What did they do?" she asked, horrified.

"They tried to yell at me," I said, "but they were so shocked by my stupidity that they laughed in utter disbelief."

I could tell she couldn't comprehend their reaction. "Did you get in trouble?" she asked.

"They tried to ground me, but it didn't stick. I did have to use my allowance to buy a new mailbox for the neighbor, though."

Although we were laughing, I knew Rosie was thinking about the beating she would have gotten for pulling such a stunt. I felt good knowing Marcus could never lay a hand on them again.

"Let's go upstairs and tell them how well you did, Rosie."

As IT WAS becoming painfully clear to me how much life the girls had missed, they were apparently having some parallel thoughts about my woeful inadequacies, which were stacking up, too. Until recently, their definition of a successful woman had hinged on her domestic talents and strong religious convictions. I came up short in both departments.

"I can't believe you don't know how to cook, Alysia," Kiani said, her tone tinged with a mix of disbelief and pity.

I smiled before speaking up in my defense. "That's not true, I can *kind of* cook. I just never have time."

"Don't you cook for your boyfriend?"

I bit my lip and lowered my eyebrows in mock shame. A wave of guilt swept through me as I developed a sudden urge to fly to Michigan to do Juan's laundry, clean his house, and cook him a hearty meal of meat and potatoes. And then I was over it.

"It's okay, Alysia," Kiani said comfortingly. "I'll teach you how."

She walked into the kitchen and pulled out the flour the girls had asked me to buy them. "Let's start with tortillas," she said.

And so began my first formal cooking lesson.

Twenty minutes later, I was wrist deep in dough and being highly entertained by Kiani's stories of preparing meals for her large family. Her tales of cooking from scratch over an open fire reminded me of the time I went to an Amish camp for a week when I was nine: getting up before dawn to milk cows, clean horse stalls, and fetch eggs from the chicken coop, with no electricity, no TV, and no phone. I could hardly wait to get home. It wasn't for me, but Kiani seemed to romanticize the minimalist lifestyle, which her family had lived for a time.

I looked down at her perfect flat circle of dough and then over at my sad attempt, which was a lopsided mess. Kiani tried to contain her amusement, but she was soon doubled over, laughing hysterically, with tears flowing down her cheeks.

"It looks like Texas," she gasped in between breaths. "It's okay, Alysia. We used to make tortillas that looked like states, too."

"I give up," I said, walking into the living room, shaking my head.

"You did a good job," Kiani said, offering her sincere encouragement. "I like Texas."

After that, I left the cooking to the Wessons.

Nine

Elizabeth could tell that something wasn't quite right with her son Dorian. He had started talking earlier than some children do and was speaking in complete sentences by the time he was two. But about six months later, he stopped talking altogether, choosing instead to cry and point at things he wanted, and screaming when he didn't get them. Marcus got upset with Elizabeth for giving Dorian things when he wouldn't use words to ask for them and told her to ignore his pleas until Dorian asked properly. But nothing seemed to work.

One afternoon in the spring of 1978, Elizabeth heard three-year-old Dorian start to cry while Marcus was combing the boy's hair in the kitchen.

"Quit moving!" Marcus snapped.

Hearing the child's cries turn to screams, Elizabeth rushed into the kitchen to see what was wrong.

"What happened?" she asked Marcus. "What did you do?"

Elizabeth could see four bleeding puncture wounds on the outside of Dorian's left knee, a pattern that matched the long metal prongs on the cake slicer Marcus had been using to get the knots out of Dorian's hair.

"Bee, I didn't mean to do it, but he moved and I hit him," Marcus said.

Elizabeth didn't have a regular pediatrician for her children, so she insisted that they take Dorian to the emergency room for treatment. During the two hours Dorian had to wait to be seen, bacteria from the comb had seeped deep into the wounds, causing his knee to become red and swollen.

"What happened to him?" the nurse asked.

Marcus didn't say anything, so Elizabeth did all the talking. "I don't know," she lied. "He was just playing and he got hurt."

The nurse must have recognized that the injury was suspicious because she called in the doctor to take a look.

"How did he get hurt?" he asked.

"I really don't know," Elizabeth repeated. "Is it bad?"

"Yes, it's infected," the doctor said. "We'll have to drain it and keep him here for a while."

Pregnant with Sebhrenah, Elizabeth had her two other toddlers, one-and-a-half-year-old Adrian and one-year-old Kiani, in tow. Elizabeth didn't want to tell the truth because she was scared they would take all her children away from her. She was even more scared when she overheard the doctor telling the nurse that they should call Social Services.

They told her they were going to admit Dorian to the hospital for a few days, and she didn't argue when they wouldn't let her stay by his side overnight.

As much as Marcus hated hospitals, he ended up being admitted to the same facility a day or two later. Marcus, who loved eating cheesecake and Häagen-Dazs ice cream, had been fasting for the past month—a common practice when his weight reached two hundred pounds. The only substances he'd been ingesting were grape and apple juice—one half cup of each, three times a day.

Problems arose when some friends came over with a bag of potato chips and Marcus broke his diet. He doubled over in pain as his digestive system cramped up with the shock of the greasy chips, so his friends took him to the hospital, where he was hooked up to an intravenous line and his system slowly reoriented to solid food.

Dorian was released a day or so before Marcus, and the doctor warned Elizabeth that someone from Social Services would be coming to their house to talk to them.

About a week later, a social worker knocked on their door, but Marcus wouldn't let her come inside to check on Dorian and the rest of the children. Marcus calmly informed her that she couldn't enter the house without a search warrant, so she left and came back with two police officers.

Marcus remained calm and rational as he discussed the situation with the officers at his front door.

"What are you trying to hide?" one of the officers asked.

Marcus said he didn't want them violating his rights by barging in without a warrant. Elizabeth hid behind Marcus like a child listening to the adults' conversation. She feared what would happen if they didn't cooperate with the authorities. She didn't want to lose her children.

"Marcus," she pleaded. "Just let them in."

Marcus finally relented and stepped aside to allow the social worker and the two officers to search the house. After checking the bedrooms and bathroom, the officers seemed satisfied that the kids were playing happily, with no visible signs of abuse or neglect.

Bruises didn't really show up on the Wessons' light brown skin. Besides, Marcus was always careful to hit them on their bottoms. He said they couldn't get hurt by spankings there but, conveniently, any bruises he left there couldn't be seen.

Afterward, the officers chatted with Marcus in a much less confrontational manner. One said they needed to ensure that none of the children was chained to the toilet as they'd found in one home they'd searched.

"We just have to do our job," the social worker said.

"I understand," Marcus replied. "We have nothing to hide."

For the next six months, the social worker came back every two weeks, chatting with Marcus before she left.

Dorian still wasn't talking, so the social worker took him and Elizabeth to a special clinic for some tests. The diagnosis, which came back when Dorian was almost four years old, was a mild case of autism. The county placed him in a school for children with special needs, sending a bus to pick him up and bring him home each day.

The social worker's visits finally came to an end. Charmed by Marcus, she figured the children were in good hands.

Marcus pulled Dorian out of the classroom a few months later. Dorian was the first, but not the last, Wesson child to be kept out of public school. Marcus had different plans for his children. He would teach them *his* way.

MARCUS, A SURVIVALIST who believed the world was going to end, also spent most of the family's welfare checks *his way*——on buses he converted into motor homes and, later, the boats on which the family lived at various times. And because he controlled the household finances, Elizabeth was often left scrambling to find ways to buy——or to beg relatives for——the real necessities: food, gas, diapers, shampoo, and medication.

They were down to their last seven dollars, with two whole weeks before the next government check would arrive, but Marcus didn't seem the least bit worried about it as they made their habitual weekend jaunt to the flea market. Elizabeth knew they couldn't afford to buy anything there, so she assumed her usual spot at the picnic table out front to wait for Marcus to finish browsing and mingling with the vendors.

About an hour later, she saw him lugging an oddly shaped dark gray chunk of metal toward her.

"What is that?" she asked, hoping he hadn't bought it.

"It's an antique book press," Marcus said enthusiastically.

"But why did you . . . We can't afford . . . Marcus, how much was it?"

"Seven dollars."

Elizabeth began to cry. She had no idea what a book press was, only that he'd spent their final cent on it. The last thing they needed was another piece of junk to clutter up their small house.

"Bee, it's a good investment," Marcus said, shoving the press into the car.

"But we needed that money for food."

"The Lord will provide for us."

Elizabeth didn't even know how to respond. She couldn't believe he thought this oversize toy was more important than feeding his family.

Once they got home, Elizabeth remained visibly upset as Marcus disappeared out the front door.

Half an hour later, he came back with a sly grin. "This is for you," he said, grabbing her hand and placing a dainty object into her palm. "I love you."

Elizabeth looked down to see a beautiful cream, gold, and orange seashell, no more than an inch big, its coils shiny and opalescent. She had no idea where he'd gotten it—the ocean was at least half an hour away—but she knew it had to have been free. Elizabeth was so touched by the gesture that she didn't much care.

"Thank you, oh, thank you," she cooed. "I love it."

Marcus didn't believe in celebrating birthdays or anniversaries, so other than her wedding band, this was the only gift he'd ever given her. She would treasure the spiral shell for the rest of her life.

EVERY SATURDAY, ELIZABETH and Marcus dropped off his maternal grandmother at the Ephesus Community Seventh-day Adventist Church in San Jose.

One of the church deaconesses started coming by the house in the months before Sebhrenah was born. Sister Harris, a black woman in her seventies who wore white tennis shoes with her long black skirts and colored long-sleeved blouses, would talk for hours with Marcus about God and the Bible while Elizabeth dozed on the couch. Sister Harris slowly started taking the kids to church, led them in Bible study, and finally managed to get Elizabeth to come to church, too. Marcus got into the act as well.

One Saturday after church, Marcus introduced his wife to a girl he'd met at choir rehearsal.

"This is Illabelle," he said, explaining that she had just moved to San Jose from Tennessee.

Elizabeth smiled at Illabelle, a beautiful blonde with blue eyes and the sweetest southern accent, who stuck out at the predominantly black church. Not only were the two of them the same age—nearly nineteen—but Illabelle was pregnant, too.

After they dropped Illabelle at her apartment, Marcus explained that she'd left home after becoming pregnant by a black college student of whom her racist parents had not approved.

"She needs a friend," he said. "She's all alone."

That was something else the two girls had in common. The only person Marcus would allow Elizabeth to spend time alone with was her mother. He didn't even want Elizabeth to chum around with her sister Rosemary, whom he saw as a "bad influence." Elizabeth often had to beg and plead with him, pointing out that Rosemary could help them get food, before he would let Elizabeth visit with her sister.

In the same vein, Marcus didn't like Elizabeth talking to his male friends, a subject on which most of their fights centered. If she walked into the same room, or if one of them talked to her, Marcus would ignore her for up to a week.

"You have an adulterous mind," he'd finally tell her. "You were thinking nasty thoughts about other men."

"No I wasn't, Marcus. I swear."

Elizabeth couldn't even imagine leaving him for another man. At times, she wished she could get her kids away from his discipline, but she never gave it any serious thought, particularly after Marcus told her what he would do if she left him.

"You know, there are ways you can kill a woman without people knowing it," he said in the middle of an otherwise casual conversation.

"What are you talking about, Marcus?" she asked apprehensively. She knew he'd been reading spy novels lately; he'd also been talking about undercover assassins.

"Trust me, there are ways. If you were to ever leave me, Elizabeth, I would make sure you never had sex with another man."

"Marcus!" she yelled, turning red. "Don't talk like that."

"I would hunt you down and come to where you were," he said as she stared at him in disbelief. "First, I would cut off your legs with my hunting knife, so you couldn't run away."

Marcus always wore a hunting knife in a sheath around his ankle. She knew he had it on that very minute.

"Then, I would cut off your arms, so you couldn't touch anyone again," he continued, leaning in closer to his wife. "Next would come your tits. I would cut off your tits and then mutilate your pussy, so you couldn't have sex. I would leave you alive, though. I want you alive, but disfigured so no one would ever want you."

"That is so gross, Marcus."

He smiled mischievously. "That is what I would do to *any* woman who tried to leave me," he said.

Elizabeth had no doubt he was telling the truth.

A COUPLE OF days after Marcus introduced Elizabeth to Illabelle, the church was putting on a revival with the evangelist George H. Rainey. Illabelle didn't have a ride, so Elizabeth suggested they bring her along. At the time, Elizabeth had no idea what she was getting herself into.

Marcus had dated the daughter of a prostitute while he'd lived in Europe, and he'd come home with some strange ideas about sex and polygamy. He'd been talking about wanting to have more than one wife ever since Elizabeth was twelve or thirteen—he'd also tried to sell her on wife swapping after Adrian was born, so it didn't come as a huge shock when Marcus brought up the idea of a second wife again.

"I was thinking about Illabelle," he said. "What do you think about her?"

Elizabeth said what she always said when this conversation came up. "It's wrong," she said. "You're not supposed to have second wives."

She was so sure polygamy was a sin that Marcus dared her to find a prohibition against it in the Bible.

"Okay," she said, accepting his challenge. "I'll prove it to you."

The problem was, she searched through the whole book but couldn't find a single problem with second wives. So, when they talked about it again, Marcus was able to persuade her that it wasn't a sin. In fact, he said, Elizabeth was going to enjoy having the other woman around.

"Illabelle can be your friend," he told her. "You'll have someone to help you with the kids and the cooking."

Elizabeth really liked Illabelle. The two of them enjoyed each other's company, so she agreed—on one condition.

"The only way this is going to happen is that you cannot

have sex with her and she cannot have any children. I can't handle that," she told Marcus. "Will you still love me?"

Marcus put her fears to rest. "I will always love you," he said. "You will always come first."

Elizabeth felt even better once Marcus explained how it would work: Illabelle would have to prove that she could be a good, loyal wife for seven years before it was a done deal. Meanwhile, he promised Elizabeth that he wouldn't have sex with Illabelle, and Elizabeth naïvely believed him. In her childlike mind, Marcus loved her too much to cross that line.

After Sebhrenah was born, Elizabeth and Marcus were well on their way to having the twelve children he wanted, at a rate of one per year. Elizabeth got pregnant again, and two days before Mother's Day in 1979, she had her fifth child. But unlike her other pregnancies, this one ended in tragedy. The boy's umbilical cord had wrapped itself three times around his tiny neck, choking him every time Elizabeth had a contraction. Even though they didn't get a chance to know each other, Elizabeth would never stop grieving for the son Marcus had already named Stefan.

Wasting no time, Elizabeth got pregnant again and had another son, Almae, a year later.

Marcus and Elizabeth often brought their five children to play with Illabelle's daughter, one of the few children with whom Marcus would allow his kids to spend time. Meanwhile, Illabelle would teach Elizabeth how to make little pizzas on hamburger buns, how to bake fresh bread from scratch, and how to make crust for banana cream pie. Illabelle, who had grown up on a farm, also showed Elizabeth how to can the fresh tomatoes, peas, corn, and cabbage she grew in the garden.

Sometimes, Marcus would leave Elizabeth and the children at their house while he went over to Illabelle's for "Bible study."

It never even occurred to Elizabeth to be jealous.

THE WESSON FAMILY was living on welfare even after Marcus started working part-time as a teller at Wells Fargo in 1977. Marcus took full advantage of his military benefits, applying for a G.I. loan so they could buy some rural property they'd been eyeing in the Santa Cruz Mountains.

After Marcus got the loan in 1980, they bought ten acres for ten thousand dollars. They cleared the land to lay a foundation for a three-bedroom home, and lived on the property in an old city bus, which Marcus converted into a motor home while they developed the land. Illabelle rented a cottage in nearby Aptos.

In September 1981, Elizabeth was about a month away from having her seventh child, Donovan. The family was over at Illabelle's when it came time for Elizabeth to go to her prenatal checkup. Marcus didn't feel like driving her to the doctor's and told her to take the bus.

Elizabeth did what she was told, so she was tired and irritated when she returned to Illabelle's cottage. She saw the children playing in the kitchen of the small studio, so she went searching for the adults in the other room. She pulled aside the curtain that Illabelle had strung across the doorway and stopped, aghast at what she saw.

Illabelle was standing bare-backed in a skirt behind Marcus, who was seated at a small desk, enjoying the sensation of Illabelle's naked breasts pressing against him. Realizing that Elizabeth was in the doorway, Illabelle whirled around with surprise, covered her breasts, and ran, embarrassed, into the bathroom.

Marcus turned around nonchalantly and looked at Elizabeth as if she was the one to blame for coming in at the wrong time. Elizabeth was so shocked, angry, and hurt that she stormed out and headed straight for their friend Melissa's* house next door, where she poured out her troubles for the next two hours. Melissa, Illabelle's college roommate, and a woman named Linda, whom they'd met at Illabelle's, were the only two women with whom Marcus would allow Elizabeth to be friends. He especially liked Melissa, who was a free spirit and bisexual.

When Marcus finally came over to get his wife, Melissa wouldn't let him in.

"She doesn't want to talk to you right now," Melissa told him. "She's upset. You can't come in."

"Mind your own business," he said. "I want to talk to my wife."

But Melissa wasn't moving. "If you come in here, I'll call the police," she said.

Elizabeth didn't want to talk about it anymore; she just wanted to go home. "It's okay," she said.

So she and Marcus gathered up their children and drove home. Once a month, Marcus allowed Elizabeth to ask him anything she wanted, with the promise of full disclosure, so when they got back, she questioned him about his extracurricular activities with Illabelle. He confessed that they'd been hugging, kissing, and touching each other naked. She'd also been giving him oral sex.

The following month, on October 11, Donovan was born.

* * *

OVER THE NEXT few months, Elizabeth grew increasingly despondent. How could she stay with Marcus now that she knew what he'd done with Illabelle? He was her husband, and they had six children together, but she couldn't be happy if this was how things were going to be.

Elizabeth not only felt distant from her husband but also had started to become suspicious about the motives of the woman she'd once considered a close friend. In January 1982, Illabelle asked if Elizabeth wanted to go for a walk so they could talk, and for the first time, the hair stood up on the back of Elizabeth's neck. She was sure Illabelle wanted to take her into the woods and kill her, so she refused.

That night, Elizabeth had to tell Marcus how she felt. "If you want Illabelle, that's okay, but I don't want this anymore."

Elizabeth, who had been sure Marcus would choose the beautiful blonde over her, was quite surprised when he said he'd never been planning to leave her. "Bee, I'd never do that to you," he said. "I love you."

With that, Elizabeth felt it was safe to tell Marcus what else was on her mind.

"I'm afraid of Illabelle," she said. "I think she wants to hurt me."

When Elizabeth explained what had happened earlier that day, Marcus surprised her again, saying that he, too, had become scared of Illabelle because he'd been dreaming that she wanted to kill him.

It rained for the next four days, washing out the mountain's dirt roads and leaving them stranded for three weeks. But even after the roads were cleared, Elizabeth never visited Illabelle in Aptos again.

* * *

MARCUS BELIEVED THAT children shouldn't be given medications, even Tylenol, because their immune systems needed to build up resistance to illness. He and Elizabeth argued constantly about this, especially when one of the children had a fever. She was often forced to go to her mother for aspirin or Tylenol.

But even then, Elizabeth knew she was in for a fight.

"They don't need that stuff," Marcus said.

"But the fever isn't going down. It's only aspirin, Marcus."

"Not yet," he said.

If the child's fever wasn't gone in a day or two, he usually gave in. "Fine, give it to them," he would say, rolling his eyes.

If a child fell severely ill, Elizabeth fought with Marcus even harder, sometimes for days, until he let her take the child to the hospital.

That April, Elizabeth took Donovan to get his immunizations at a free clinic, used mostly by migrant workers, down in Watsonville. The doctor examined him and, seeing that Donovan had a cold, told her she'd have to bring him back after he got over the virus.

Two nights later, Donovan would not stop crying. Elizabeth was worried and wanted to take him back to the doctor, but Marcus refused. It was already 11:30 P.M., and it was snowing outside; everyone was too tired to make the forty-five-minute trip down the mountain, he said.

When they woke the next morning around six, Donovan's eyes were glazed over and his breathing was shallow. Elizabeth insisted that they take him to the hospital, so they packed the kids into their white Volkswagen Bug and drove to the ER.

They waited about half an hour to see a doctor, who immediately recognized that something was terribly wrong. He ordered a spinal tap, and Elizabeth held her baby for the hour or so it took to get results: Donovan had spinal meningitis, an inflammation of the brain and spinal cord.

"We got it just in time," the doctor told them. "Your son is going to be fine."

Donovan was moved to a baby bed in the ICU, where he was administered antibiotics through an IV. His little eyes looked so tired.

Marcus told Elizabeth the kids were hungry, so he was going to take them home for a while. Elizabeth wanted to stay, but because the doctor said Donovan was going to be okay, she let Marcus talk her into coming with them.

When they came back a few hours later, the nurse wouldn't let her see her son. "You can't go in there," she said. "The doctor wants to talk to you."

After speaking to the doctors, Elizabeth cried and cried. Her baby had died, alone, shortly after they'd left.

The doctor wanted to know what had gone wrong, so they got Elizabeth's permission to do an autopsy. A day or so later, she and Marcus went to the hospital morgue to see their son's body.

"We should ask the Lord to bring him back," Marcus said.

So they knelt on the linoleum floor and prayed for half an hour, then went home and prayed some more. Elizabeth cried herself to sleep.

The next day, Marcus decided they should visit the funeral home, where they were preparing Donovan for his wake.

"He's going to wake up," he said.

Elizabeth, beside herself with grief, was willing to believe anything at that point. They stood at the top of the stairs that led to the basement, where the bodies were readied for viewing, and heard a baby crying. One of the morticians came up and took Marcus downstairs, leaving Elizabeth frightened and uncertain of what to think. Her rational mind knew that her son was dead, but she couldn't help believing that her baby was alive in that room.

On the drive home, Marcus told her that he *had* brought Donovan back to life. But then he got scared, he said, and told God to take him back.

Elizabeth was too upset to know what was going on. She wanted Marcus to take her to the cemetery so she could watch Donovan being buried, but Marcus refused.

"He's already in heaven," he said. "We don't need to go down there."

"I want to go," she said.

"If you want to go, you can go," he said, but Elizabeth knew Marcus's tone all too well. This was his way of telling her that she *couldn't* go to the cemetery. After all, he was the only one with a driver's license.

A week after the burial, Elizabeth insisted that Marcus take her to the cemetery, only to find Illabelle there, too. Illabelle gave Elizabeth her condolences; she left town shortly thereafter.

Years later, Illabelle said she left Marcus after he told her she would always be his mistress and would come second to Elizabeth. However, Marcus still sent her letters occasionally, one of which was addressed to "Ilovebelle."

* * *

ELIZABETH HAD MARCUS Jr. in December 1982, bringing the number of her births to eight and living children to six, and she was still going strong. Since the children were home-schooled and the family was still receiving government assistance, a welfare worker was supposed to check in with them periodically.

Marcus, who handled the appointments, met a female social worker at the bottom of the mountain and told her to follow him back to the house in her car. Twenty minutes into the windy ride, the woman pulled over to the side of the road, so Marcus stopped, too, and asked what was wrong.

The woman told him she wasn't comfortable following him any farther, so she would report that the family had checked out. Marcus laughed when he got home and relayed the story to Elizabeth.

"She was too afraid to follow a big black man down a long dirt road," he told her. "You should have seen her face."

The social worker never came back.

Ten

The average high temperature in Fresno during July 2004 was a sizzling 98.9 degrees, so the air conditioner in my apartment ran almost constantly. The Wessons weren't used to the frigid air, and although Elizabeth welcomed the change, Kiani and Rosie had to wear sweaters and wrap themselves in blankets to stay comfortable.

Aside from the temperature, I could tell the three of them were more comfortable all around. The most dramatic changes over the past two months were evident in Rosie, who was now initiating conversations, making eye contact, and laughing. Even her appearance was evolving, although that wasn't completely her own doing.

Seeing their lack of clothing options, I went through my two closets, made a pile of items I didn't wear much, then told the girls to take whatever they wanted. Rosie chose several button-down shirts in bright solid colors that I had worn with my work suits. Kiani, meanwhile, went for the trendier, tight, short-sleeved shirts I usually wore to go out on the weekends. The girls completely avoided my stack of pants, however, stubbornly holding on to their below-the-knee skirts.

I also got to work on Rosie's heavy makeup. Every day

since she'd moved in, she'd painted harsh black lines on her eyelids, extending them far beyond the outer corners of her dark brown eyes.

Marcus had started letting the girls wear makeup in their teenage years and early twenties, when they went to work, saying he wanted them to blend in so no one would ask questions about the family's lifestyle. However, he also took the girls on trips—without Elizabeth—to San Francisco, where he had them dress in heels and provocative outfits as they walked together through crowded public places such as Fisherman's Wharf. When Elizabeth was pregnant with Adrian, he'd sexualized her in the same way, buying her a pair of denim shorts and cutting them even shorter.

I thought Rosie would look softer and prettier without the black eyeliner, so I asked her about it.

"I was going to get eyeliner tattooed on before everything happened," she told me. "I still want to."

"Please don't," I said. "You'll regret it. I promise."

"Then I won't have to put it on all the time and it will never smudge."

"But Rosie, when you get older, your skin will sag and it will look uneven and it will fade. Plus, you may not always want to have black eyeliner on like that."

"Yes, I will. Trust me."

I, like every other TV reporter, had collected a stockpile of foundation, powder, lipstick, mascara, blush—all the essentials for putting on the best face. After Rosie accepted my offer to do her makeup, I went through my three drawers and two large makeup cases to find soft shades of beige and brown for her eyes, a soft pinky brown for her cheeks, and a golden brown gloss for her full lips.

"What do you think?" I said, spinning her chair around so she could see herself in my large bedroom mirror.

"Wow," she said, surprised to see her new look. "I actually like it. I really like it."

Rosie slowly phased out the black liner.

ROSIE AND I were both animal lovers, so we had a lot to talk about. She was amazed that I had had a pony growing up and wanted to hear all about him. She also played with Cosmo constantly, loving to touch his little pink nose.

She was cuddling up with my affectionate ferret one day when she said, "I miss Betty," her black Chihuahua, which had run away the day of the murders.

"Aaaw, I'm sorry, Rosie," I said, seeing her sad expression. "You love animals so much, have you ever thought about becoming a veterinarian?"

Rosie's face lit up as if it was something she'd never considered. "Oh, Alysia, I would love that," she said. "But I don't have a diploma."

"Maybe it's something for you to work toward," I said. "You could start as a veterinary assistant, or you could work at a pet store while you're going to school."

"That would be nice," she said.

When I got home from work the next night, Rosie ushered me into their bedroom.

"Close your eyes," she said with a nervous smile. "Okay, open them."

I could see she was cupping something in her hands. As I leaned in to take a closer look, I heard a faint chirping noise. It was a scrawny, almost featherless baby chick that was barely moving.

"I think one of the stray cats got it out of its nest," she said. "Would you mind if I tried to save it? I can keep it in the room with us."

"Sure, Rosie," I said, not having the heart to tell her it wasn't going to make it. "I think that would be fine." I did caution her, however, to keep Cosmo away from the chick.

I walked into my closet, grabbed a shoe box, and handed it to her. She stuffed the box with tissue and grass to make a nest for her little patient.

At least it will keep her mind off her kids. God, please let that bird live.

As I watched her nurse the fragile bird back to health, I wondered how Rosie could have been the toughest woman in the Wesson clan. For at least five years leading up to the murders, Marcus had considered Rosie his "strong soldier." He had trained her to do whatever he said, even if it meant putting herself in danger, so the other children were all afraid of her and knew better than to get in her way.

For the first week she was at my apartment, she had seemed ridiculously shy, but as she grew more comfortable with me, I found it increasingly difficult to imagine her being Marcus's merciless watchdog. The Rosie I knew was amazingly gentle and kind and only grew more so as time went on.

Somehow, she managed to save the helpless little creature. For days, she woke up every hour on the hour to feed him a special formula by eyedropper. Before long, he had grown a mane of soft feathers and developed a loud chirp that never stopped. We named him Seinfeld after the sitcom the four of us watched together each night. I knew every episode by heart, but I enjoyed watching reruns with my roommates, who were hearing the jokes for the first time.

Then came the day for Seinfeld to fly our coop. Rosie coached him through the air in the apartment and caught him before he crashed onto the carpet. Soon, he was ready for the outdoors. Although she knew it was for the best, Rosie wasn't ready to say good-bye. She'd become attached to the little fellow.

We had a small good-bye ceremony on my balcony and wished him well, but Seinfeld stayed perched on Rosie's palm.

"It's time to start your new life," she told him proudly. "Go ahead. Fly away."

With that, Seinfeld took to the sky, circled above us a few times, then disappeared into the clouds. While I recalled the image of the doves being released outside the funeral home, I looked at Rosie's sad eyes and wondered if she was thinking about Ethan and Sedona.

"It's okay, Rosie," I said, hoping to comfort her. "He's in a better place now."

I was referring to the bird, but we both knew that my comment was also meant for her two children, who were free and somewhere good, too.

THE MORE I got to know the Wesson family, the more I liked them. It was obvious to my parents and the few friends who knew about my situation that Elizabeth, Kiani, and Rosie weren't moving out anytime soon. I didn't come to that realization myself, though, until my mom brought it up.

"It's been a couple months, now, huh?" she said.

"Yeah, it doesn't seem that long," I said, doing the math in my head. "A little more than two months, I guess."

"You *like* having them there, don't you?"

"I do."

I didn't tell my mom, but I decided right then that I needed to confess to my boss that the Wessons were living with me, especially if this was going to be a more permanent thing.

But before I had a chance to tell him, he asked me if I would be willing to change jobs. He needed me to work indefinitely as a reporter on the morning show in our South Valley bureau. My new office would be about forty-five miles from my home, and my new schedule would be 2:30 A.M. to 11:30 A.M., the exact opposite of my current 2:30 P.M. to 11:30 P.M. shift. Although that was difficult to swallow at first, I figured it would be better for everyone if I were so conveniently removed from the Wesson story, at least for now.

I decided not to say anything to my boss until or unless he told me I was back covering the case. I still felt no regret about my decision to help the Wessons, regardless of possible future consequences.

FOR THE FIRST few weeks of my new shift, I got only two or three hours of sleep each night, but that had its benefits. Getting home around noon meant I had a full day of sunlight to go swimming or lie by the pool.

I knew that the Wessons had lived periodically on boats, so I was shocked to learn that Marcus had never taught them how to swim. I wondered if they were ever afraid to make the journey to and from work in their little rowboat each day.

"Let's go to the pool and learn how to swim," I suggested one afternoon.

Rosie and Kiani giggled, as if they weren't sure I was serious. Elizabeth said nothing, so I figured she'd never take me up on the offer. I had been a swimming instructor when I was a teenager and assured the girls I had taught plenty of beginners. I saw no reason to tell them my students had all been under six years old.

"What will we wear?" Kiani asked worriedly.

They still wore modest shirts, skirts, and high heels every day. I knew there wasn't a chance I could get them into bathing suits, so I didn't even try.

"Whatever you want," I said. "I have some shorts and T-shirts you can put on."

I glanced back and saw that they were blushing. I couldn't believe Kiani and Rosie were more embarrassed by the thought of wearing shorts than they'd been by talking about sex with Marcus.

They followed me to my room, where I gathered my most conservative workout gear for them to try on. They disappeared into their bedroom for twenty minutes, during which time I could hear consistent laughter and playful screams.

Kiani stuck her head out for a minute, hiding her body behind the door.

"No one will be there, right?"

"Right," I said. "If anyone shows up, we'll leave."

My apartment complex had three pools. The two with showers, vending machines, and bathrooms were usually busy, so I planned to take the girls to the one without those amenities, which was always quiet.

Kiani disappeared into their room for another twenty minutes of screaming and laughter. Finally, she and Rosie tiptoed into the hallway and stopped near the front door.

I was determined not to comment on their outfits, but it wasn't easy. Kiani was wearing a long-sleeved T-shirt and sweatpants, while Rosie wore a T-shirt and her regular black skirt; both were still wearing high heels. I'd put on a bikini and flip-flops and had wrapped a towel around my waist.

"Let's go," I said, ushering the girls out the door. "Elizabeth, why don't you at least come watch us?"

"I'll be out there in a minute," she said, relieved to see that Kiani and Rosie were so excited. "Have fun!"

Our odd trio sauntered across the asphalt parking lot until we reached the tall iron gate surrounding the pool.

I unlocked the gate and swung open the door, holding it for the girls.

"Oh, good, no one is here," Kiani said with a nervous giggle.

I followed, relieved as well. The gate slammed shut, which caused Kiani to jump and let out a high-pitched scream. Her yelp startled Rosie, but the emotional chain reaction stopped with me.

"This is not off to a good start," I said, trying to calm the girls. "Are you okay?"

"We're fine," they said, laughing.

I threw our towels on a patio table and kicked off my flip-flops. The girls bent over and unstrapped their shoes, which they placed neatly under a chair. Almost in unison, we started skipping across the scorching pavement toward the pool, yelling "hot, hot, hot."

We hopped onto the first step in the shallow end, then Rosie continued down to the second step, which put the hem of her skirt an inch below the water line.

"I hope the chlorine won't bleach your skirt, Rosie," I

said, worried she would ruin her favorite article of clothing.

"It will be fine," she said.

I scooted past the girls, then plunged all the way under. "It's not that cold," I said. "Get in."

Kiani and Rosie waded down to the three-feet marker and waited for further instructions. I had them put both hands on the edge of the pool and extend their bodies while kicking their legs. Because they had never engaged in any sporting activity before, their bodies looked awkward, but they were good sports about it.

I reached under Kiani's torso and held her up with my forearms to give her some leverage. She began kicking harder and was nearly keeping herself afloat.

"You're doing it, Kiani, you're swimming," I said.

"I want to try," Rosie chimed in.

As I eased my hold on Kiani, she panicked and tried to grab my wrist as she started to sink. She sprang up, spitting out water, with a terrified look on her face.

"You okay?" I asked. "You just have to relax. You were doing so well."

"I want to try," Rosie repeated, just like one of the five-year-olds I used to coach.

I supported Rosie's upper body as I had Kiani's, and she began kicking ferociously, splashing water four feet into the air.

I could see Elizabeth peeking over the gate. Kiani gladly jumped out of the water to let her in.

"Oh, good job, Rosie," Elizabeth said, pulling a chair into the shade. "It's so hot out here."

Half an hour later, the girls were making good progress,

especially with treading water. Elizabeth fanned herself and clapped each time the girls looked over at her. It was the first time I'd seen them so carefree; I didn't want the moment to end.

We'd been so wrapped up in negativity lately, talking for hours each day about the darkest things imaginable: child abuse, murder, mind control. The Wessons needed an escape, not only from the guilt and pain of losing their children but also from the grim realization that they didn't fit into mainstream society. I needed a break from all the heavy emotions, too. I'd begun feeling like an outcast myself, and I yearned to feel normal again, even if it was just for an afternoon.

"Let's go to the movies," I suggested.

"Really, Alysia?" Kiani asked, excited. "We've never been to the theater before."

"I know. That's why I want to take you. Let's go change."

The girls jumped out of the pool, their clothes sagging with water. We grabbed our towels as Elizabeth held open the gate for us. On the way back to the apartment, I was pleased to notice that, for the first time, the eager girls were walking ahead of me.

The chill of the air conditioner hit us as soon as we walked in, and I warned the girls that movie theaters were even colder than my apartment.

"Maybe you should wear some of my pants," I said, teasing them.

"I'll wear pants sometime," Rosie said.

"Just not yet, huh?"

I didn't push it. I was too excited to take them to their first movie. I imagined this was what it felt like to introduce your children to new things.

It was a Wednesday afternoon, so there were only a few people in the theater and I didn't worry about anyone seeing us together. I had already told the girls about the concession stand, so that was the first place we headed.

"Wow, the ceiling is so high in here," Rosie said, her chin in the air.

Kiani, whom I'd playfully nicknamed Candy for her love of anything sweet, was preoccupied with the huge selection, ranging from M&M's to Sour Patch Kids and Goobers.

"Pick something out," I said.

I ordered an extra-large popcorn with extra butter for us to share. Kiani was in charge of ordering the candy, but she was taking forever to make a decision and the cashier was growing impatient.

"We'll take this and this and this," I said, pointing to items on the top shelf. "The movie's going to start soon."

We wanted to see *Spider-Man 2,* but the showtime was a few hours away, so we chose *The Bourne Supremacy* instead.

"Where should we sit?" Kiani asked.

"I'll follow you guys," I said, chuckling at their enthusiasm.

They chose a row in the middle of the dimly lit theater. I watched the three of them plop down into the overstuffed seats with blue velvet cushions. I couldn't help but smile as I thought about Marcus sitting alone on his cold, hard prison bed under the harsh fluorescent lights.

The lights went dark, and as the previews started rolling, I saw Kiani clapping next to me.

"Wow, this is loud," she yelled.

"What?" I asked.

"This is loud in here, I said."

"What?" I asked again, smiling.

"Alysia!" she said, swatting at my arm, never taking her eyes from the big screen.

This was the first time they'd ever heard surround sound, and they flinched at every sudden noise. The movie was one long series of car chases and explosions, so it probably wasn't the best choice. Luckily, there weren't any love scenes, which made the girls uncomfortable. I always thought it was weird that Elizabeth covered her eyes whenever two people even came close to kissing on TV. Kiani and Rosie always looked away but didn't go to such extremes.

I ended up not seeing much of the movie—I was too busy watching them. I marveled at how the dimple on Rosie's left cheek never left because she and the other two women never stopped grinning.

Eleven

From the moment Elizabeth married Marcus, her husband took her on a religious journey the likes of which most people have never seen. Her children got the same treatment and then some.

After giving birth to Sebhrenah in 1978, Elizabeth was baptized in the Seventh-day Adventist church, donning a white robe and being immersed in a heated pool behind the minister's pulpit. She gave up her jeans and makeup for long skirts and long-sleeved shirts, while Marcus, who had been baptized at fourteen, rededicated himself to God. Together, they changed their diet and gave up Elizabeth's favorite foods—hamburgers, spareribs, steaks, Kentucky Fried Chicken, and pizza—to become vegetarians as the church required.

The Wessons lived on peanut butter, rice and beans, oatmeal, whole wheat bread, vegetables, and fruit. There was no alcohol in the house, no candy and no caffeine. Elizabeth even used baby formula to make Cream of Wheat for the kids to comply with the restrictions against butter, milk, and sugar.

After years of watching her fellow churchgoers line up and salivate for vegetarian hot dogs and veggie burgers,

Elizabeth persuaded Marcus to allow the family to eat the real thing on special occasions and at family barbecues at her mother's house. Elizabeth saw no difference in God's eyes between craving meat and actually eating it.

Marcus, on a continuous quest to expand his religious knowledge, studied Mormonism, Jehovah's Witnesses, Eckankar, Hari Krishna, and Buddhism, adding facets of these belief systems to his Seventh-day Adventist base. He also collected literature about groups such as the Children of God, whose founder, David Berg, preached free love and polygamy. Marcus was fascinated by Berg, who encouraged his female followers to seduce men in bars, a calculated method of bringing nonbelievers into the fold that won them the nickname Hookers for Jesus.

Despite being a leader in his own home, Marcus was easily influenced by controversial religious leaders like Berg. Often, he would try to emulate these figures by donning robes, carrying a walking stick, or ordering his girls to wear head scarves and long skirts, the boys to dress only in brown. Over the years, he wove these influences into a strange spiritual tapestry, colored by his own interpretations to rationalize corporal punishment, polygamy, and incest—even vampirism.

In a letter to a friend, he wrote that he used discipline, spanking, and criticism on his children for their betterment, "to create the love they have today." That meant Marcus beat his children from the time they were infants. If they looked, spoke, or acted the wrong way, he would leave welts and bloody wounds on any of them who cried too much. He demanded perfect behavior during the morning and evening prayer sessions he held daily, testing his children's devotion and self-control by holding the second session late at night.

Elizabeth hated when he did this, so she sat near the youngest children in order to nudge them if they dozed off. She also made sure each of them had gone to the bathroom before Marcus began his sermon. They had to hold out as long as possible, because if any of them got up to go before Marcus was finished, he would beat them.

Marcus preached that Jesus was married—and not just to one woman but to many. Sometimes, he talked about God being a woman. God, he said, was very sexual.

In the late 1990s, while Elizabeth was reading the work of the gothic novelist Anne Rice, Marcus asked his children to be vampires for the Lord. He likened Jesus to a vampire because He had eternal life and his followers drank his blood. Marcus later gave three of his children vampire names at birth: Sedona Vadra, Marshey St. Christopher, and Jeva St. Vladensvspry, whose first name combined "Jesus" and "vampire."

"My children have never been to church . . . but we have built into many understandings," Marcus wrote in a letter. "All we know of my Father is from my head. The Bible simply conveys principles of the Father, like a map, depicted in the lives of various people. . . . I, the Christ, walk in this temple called Marcus."

Marcus's religious fervor escalated until he came to see himself as God, saying he would ultimately become thin and fit, wear his hair short and blond, and have blue eyes. Like most wives, Elizabeth learned to live with her husband's idiosyncrasies, although his were clearly more bizarre than most.

"Marcus, you're not crazy, but you're insane," she'd tell him. "You're way out there."

Marcus would just look at her and smile.

AS THE NOMADIC Wesson family moved from place to place, Elizabeth had three more children: Gypsy in 1983 in Fresno, and Serafino and Elizabeth, whom they called Lise, in 1985 and 1986, respectively, in Watsonville.

During this time, Marcus and Elizabeth would visit with her family on holidays for barbecues at Rose's house, where some of Elizabeth's brothers, sisters, and kids still lived. Her brothers never really accepted Marcus after he'd fathered a child with their mother, then run off and married their little sister. They also didn't like the way he isolated Elizabeth and her kids. The Wesson girls, knowing that Marcus didn't want them talking to outsiders, and men in particular, would sit near him at these gatherings to show their allegiance. They would be cordial to their uncles but usually limited their conversations to friendly hellos.

In the fall of 1986, the family began renting a second piece of land deep in the Santa Cruz Mountains for about $150 a month. The two-and-a-half-acre plot, which was about a mile away from their old house, was overgrown with trees and vegetation.

With winter quickly approaching, a dense, cold fog hung low over the rough terrain, nearly swallowing up their property. Knowing it would only get worse in the coming weeks, Marcus decided they needed to clear the land right away. By then he'd replaced his first used city bus with a powder blue Travelall, an oversize wagon-type vehicle made in the 1960s, with the hauling power of a modern SUV.

Needing all the free labor they could get, Elizabeth enlisted the help of three nieces, one nephew, and her little brother. Marcus loaded all sixteen of them into the Travelall, which was hitched to a small trailer full of hand-saws, sleeping bags, and a chain saw.

He played oldies on the radio during the long, bumpy ride, while the kids talked quietly among themselves, cramped in the back. Once they arrived at the property, Marcus lined up the children, handed out tools, and began issuing orders.

"The boys and I will be at the top, chopping down trees," he said. "The girls will cut the branches off all the trees, drag the brush to the bottom of the mountain, and get rid of it. The trunks need to go near the road, where they will stay for us to use as firewood."

The Wesson assembly line started up, while Elizabeth stayed at the base making sandwiches, nursing the children's cuts, and taking care of Lise and Serafino, who weren't old enough to walk.

When darkness descended, the family retired to their tents and sleeping bags, rising at dawn to start clearing brush once again. After two days of intense labor, it was time to head back to Fresno so Elizabeth's relatives could return to school. Marcus instructed his four oldest sons to stand on the trailer hitch so he could reattach it to the Travelall.

"Don't move," he yelled at the boys, aged four to twelve.

But the young boys weren't heavy enough to hold down the hitch, which slowly began to rise. They looked at one another in fear, frantically trying to anchor their small bodies so as to get the hitch to drop. But it was no use. "Dad!" they yelled. "Dad! Dad!"

Marcus walked out from behind the trailer, where he saw the boys riding several feet in the air. "What the hell is wrong with you?" he asked angrily. "You're idiots. You're all idiots."

Marcus shoved the hitch down. "Don't move this time!"

With that, he latched the trailer and drove the family home.

OVER THE NEXT few months, the Wessons frequently made the four-hour trip from Fresno, where they were staying with Rose and Rosemary, through the windy mountain roads of Santa Cruz to their property. Elizabeth's nieces and nephews came with them as often as possible. They enjoyed going to the harbor, where they would fish, collect cans, and barbecue hot dogs and hamburgers. By late summer, they had cleared nearly enough land for the house foundation.

Sofia, Ruby, Brandy, and Rosie especially loved spending time with their uncle Marcus. Once school started again for the three older girls that fall, they were sad they couldn't go back to the mountains with the rest of the Wesson clan.

"Please let us go with you," Sofia, the oldest, begged Elizabeth.

"I'm sorry, we can't take you," Elizabeth apologized. "You have to go to school, *mi hija.*"

At the time, Elizabeth had no idea Marcus had already staked his sexual claim on their daughters Kiani and Sebhrenah—let alone Ruby and Sofia—so she honestly felt bad that she couldn't bring her nieces with them.

Marcus called it "loving," telling each girl that the sessions were necessary to prepare her for her future husband. The progressive sessions began when the girls were about eight, just as they had with Elizabeth. At first, he touched them over their clothing, then after a year or so, he advanced to rubbing their bare breasts and private areas. When they were ten or eleven, he taught them how to touch his penis and, a year later, how to give him oral sex. Marcus didn't like it when the girls referred to him as Dad or Uncle Marcus, so they started calling him Baby, and it stuck.

Within a year, Elizabeth's nieces got their wish and joined the Wesson family full-time.

Rosemary had spent six months in jail on drug-related charges and was still fighting her habit, so she thought it best for Elizabeth and Marcus to raise her four daughters.

By this time, Marcus had moved on to wedding ceremonies, "marrying" eleven-year-old Ruby and her sisters and cousins when they turned thirteen or fourteen, using the same Bible ceremony as before. Although he made the girls swear not to tell anyone about these weddings, he gave each of them a symbolic ring to wear once they became his "wives" and the molestation had progressed to sexual intercourse. The rings made it clear who had joined the ranks, but the girls never spoke to one another about what was happening.

BECAUSE THE FAMILY always lived in such close quarters, contagious illnesses spread quickly among the children. When one of them acted sick or stayed in bed too long, coughing or blowing his nose, Marcus would let him have it.

"Get up," he'd yell, pulling the child upright. "You're not sick."

Elizabeth would run into the room and protest. "But Marcus, he *is* sick," she would say. "He needs to rest."

"It's all in his mind. He can't be making noise like that. He just wants attention."

Marcus would beat the child, then say to Elizabeth, "He'll never do that again. Next time, he'll control himself."

When a stomach bug was circulating through the Wesson home, Marcus would get angry just walking past the bathroom.

"Who was in here?" he'd yell.

One of the boys would come forward.

"That smells unhealthy. You've been sneaking food, haven't you? Get in the room!"

"The room" was where the kids went to get their punishment. Depending on where the family lived, it was a designated area of the house, woods, or boat. More often than not, the kids didn't know what they'd done wrong. Another child might have ratted them out, or Marcus would claim that God had told him.

They were usually punished in groups, told to file into the room and spread out with their backs against the wall like in a police lineup. Then, they'd wait.

Marcus would leave them there for a while to think about what they'd done before coming in with a beating implement. Sometimes, it was a spoon with holes, which pierced the skin, or a yellow broomstick; he reserved a metal pole for the boys.

During the beatings, Elizabeth would often stay outside the door and pace. In extreme cases, when Marcus seemed out of control, she would burst in. "Marcus, that's enough," she would plead. "Please, Marcus, just stop."

When the family lived in the mountains, Marcus would send the naughty children outside to fetch sturdy sticks to be beaten with. The children had to choose carefully, because if the sticks were too small, Marcus would swap them for ones twice the size and beat them twice as hard.

Marcus would often wave the stick around before giving a lengthy lecture, then, depending on their offense, he would hit the children on the hand or bottom. He'd have them lie facedown on the bed, drop their pants or lift their skirts, then he'd hit them anywhere from seven to twenty-one times—three times a day for the next two to four weeks.

Serafino, the youngest boy, got the worst of the beatings, so he was always relieved when Marcus left the house on an errand, knowing he would be spared the stick for a couple of hours.

But even then, Marcus would call the house and ask Rosie or one of the older girls who was misbehaving. As the girl whispered into the phone, the other kids prayed she wasn't tattling on them. But they found out soon enough. She would hang up, approach the guilty party, and say, "Dad wants you to wait in the room for him."

Often, it was Serafino she was addressing. While he lay bare-bottomed on the bed, his stomach would drop as he smelled the exhaust of Marcus's old car approaching. Even into adulthood, that smell still triggered fear in him.

Serafino got in trouble for many reasons. One of his worst beatings came after he committed the heinous crime of sneaking a spoonful of peanut butter from the cupboard. Marcus was so angry that he wrenched the thick TV cable from the wall and used it to whip his son for half an hour. Serafino knew better than to try to run away; if he had, the beating would have continued for days. He tolerated the pain by rotating slowly so that the cable struck him on different parts of his body. By the time Marcus had finished, Serafino was covered with welts and bruises.

Sometimes, Marcus would make the children *ask* for their thrice-daily beatings—before breakfast, before their afternoon nap, and before bedtime: "May I have my spank now, please?"

Serafino, who got smacked most every day, didn't always remind Marcus about his punishment—just to get a day's break from the pain, which mounted exponentially during a month's worth of beatings in the same spot. Bruises would develop on his bottom so severe that he could barely sit or walk, yet he'd have to keep asking for another spank. Sleep would help them heal a bit, but eventually he'd get to the point where he just couldn't take any more, regardless of the consequences.

When Marcus got so busy writing his book that he didn't notice Serafino had been hiding in the corner until the day's end without reminding him, he would add ten more days to the punishment, then another ten days two weeks later when Serafino failed to remind him once again.

AS A RESULT, the children tried not to anger their father at all, often keeping their illnesses to themselves.

Eight-year-old Gypsy was only halfway through her father's morning sermon when she felt the need to cough. Her throat had been sore for a few days, but she didn't dare complain. She'd already been holding in the cough for two hours, and the urge was growing increasingly difficult to control.

Her chest began to pulse, and she pursed her lips tightly to keep the cough from erupting. Her face turned red, and tears streamed down her sucked-in cheeks, until finally, the intense feeling passed. She took a long, deep breath. If only she could fight this off for two more hours, she knew she'd be safe.

Gypsy was strong, and she made it through. Sebhrenah wasn't as good at hiding her pain.

When she was sixteen, Sebhrenah felt a sharp throbbing in her side. Knowing she wasn't allowed to alter her routine, she tried to get through the day, but her body wouldn't let her. She was pale, sweaty, and doubled over in pain as she overheard her parents arguing in the next room.

"Marcus, there's something wrong with her. She needs to see a doctor."

"She's fine, Elizabeth. She'll get better."

"She is *not* fine."

"It's nothing serious. Stop worrying."

Elizabeth kept at him for two days. On the third day of excruciating pain, Sebhrenah was in even worse shape.

"Come look at her, Marcus," Elizabeth said. "She needs help."

Marcus reluctantly checked on her. "Fine. Go ahead and take her to the hospital."

Elizabeth gathered Sebhrenah's things and rushed her daughter to the emergency room. They arrived just in time. The doctor said Sebhrenah's appendix was moments away from rupturing; he wondered how she'd tolerated the pain for so long.

Elizabeth stayed by her daughter's side during the surgery. Marcus stayed home.

ALTHOUGH HE WAS absent when his children's health was in jeopardy, Marcus was a constant force in what he considered their character development—which any outsider would have described as character squashing.

Marcus didn't like it when his children expressed themselves, reprimanding them when they were loud or assertive. They soon learned that their only alternative was to be submissive.

Perhaps due in part to his autism, Dorian always felt a little different from his brothers and sisters, a characteristic Marcus never appreciated. Dorian was the most artistic of the children, and he also found it more difficult than his siblings to repress his emotions.

When he was eight, he decided to draw his father a picture. What could the harm be in that? Dorian sketched the Santa Cruz Mountains, added in some buildings, then enthusiastically showed it to Marcus.

"Here, Dad," he said.

In this case, Dorian made two mistakes—expressing himself creatively *and* drawing on a Saturday, the Wessons' holy day. No fun allowed.

"Take off your clothes," Marcus said crossly.

Dorian knew he was in trouble, so he stripped naked.

"Now go take a shower, and don't dry off," his father ordered.

The water only intensified the sting as Dorian stood there wet, naked, and humiliated while his father struck him twenty times with a switch, from his back to his ankles.

Dorian never let his father see him drawing on a Saturday again. And although his drawings were quite good, he lacked the self-confidence to develop his artistic talents any further.

Twelve

The thick fog that hugged Fresno each fall crept in every night like a vampire and vanished by sunrise. I hadn't noticed it the year before, but with my new hours, it became a nightly driving hazard during my forty-five-minute commute to Visalia.

I drove one of the station's marketing vehicles, a shiny white van that could hold fifteen passengers, was painted with our brightly colored logos, and put me at eye level with the truck drivers. The murky haze obstructed my view and, paired with the steady stream of air the heater blew into my face, almost lulled me to sleep. To get my adrenaline flowing, I had to pinch the top of my thigh periodically, creating an instant jolt and an ugly bruise that never got more than a weekend to heal. I made sure it was high enough to hide above the hem of my skirt, so it wasn't visible on TV each morning.

The grueling days of covering the Wesson case were a distant memory by now. I was enjoying the lighter stories that went along with the morning show, such as interviews with high school band members, the casts of touring musicals, and the senior citizen who won a multimillion-dollar lottery jackpot.

Another upside of the new shift was that it allowed me to spend more time with Elizabeth, Kiani, and Rosie. After I'd arrive home at noon, we'd go get lunch, then bring it back to my apartment, where we'd sit, eat, and talk. I tried but rarely made it to bed by 6:00 P.M., though I always got up at 11:30 to watch *Seinfeld* with the girls. Kiani would hand me my special Frank Sinatra mug full of coffee with milk and one sugar, and she would drink a cup or two with me. Around 12:30 A.M., I would get ready for work while the three of them got ready for bed.

One night in September, I walked into the bathroom, turned on the shower, and saw something shiny and metal on the counter.

"Did somebody leave their jewelry in here?" I yelled out, picking up the delicate gold necklace and dull gold band.

Kiani ran down the hallway and took them from me. "Oh, sorry, Alysia. Those are mine. I don't know what I'd do without them," she said, pulling them to her chest. She clasped the gold chain around her neck and slipped the band onto her ring finger.

Oh my God! That's her wedding ring from her father.

I wondered how Kiani could be so different from Gypsy.

Gypsy was coming over at least twice a week now, and when I was home, her visits were very refreshing for me, because I knew how much she hated Marcus and everything he stood for. She didn't verbalize her feelings in front of her relatives, but I'd learned about her opposing viewpoints during the preliminary hearing, when the prosecutor repeated some of the comments Gypsy had made to investigators.

We had an unspoken bond, going back to the first time she'd visited, when I'd caught her rolling her eyes at the girls' glowing remarks about Marcus. When they weren't looking, I made sure she saw me smile with approval.

It was the glimmer of hope I had needed to get me through the next months of listening to them talk about their "great" husband and father. I could tell Gypsy wanted to set the record straight about their warped perceptions, but she seemed to understand that they weren't ready to hear the truth. So, rather than confront the others about their delusions, we kept our frustration to ourselves.

One day, Elizabeth pulled me aside and told me Marcus would like me. I tried not to laugh out loud, but I couldn't help it. We both knew it wasn't true. I wondered what it would be like to meet him and what I would say.

After months of hearing about his good qualities and gentle nature, I still saw Marcus the same way I had that hot March night on TV: as a monster. As holy and powerful as he believed he was, I knew he was truly a selfish and lazy coward. I didn't think there was a chance in hell he had actually pulled the trigger that day. It wasn't in his character. He used religion to intimidate and manipulate everyone in his path, even to the point of murder. He lived out his illegal sexual fantasies, and may have ruined dozens of lives by doing so. There was nothing I could do to save the nine innocent victims who had died that day, but I was determined to do everything in my power to save the ones he'd left behind.

For whatever reason, silently ranting in my head made me feel better. It didn't make me hate Marcus any less, but it helped me deal with the girls who still loved him. Despite his hold on them, I felt good about the new world I was opening up for Elizabeth, Kiani, and Rosie, and although I hadn't anticipated it, they were teaching me things, too.

I had never been much for cooking, cleaning, or children. I loved watching the Food Network, but that's about as close as I came to a recipe. The girls were just the opposite: Rosie worked wonders in the kitchen, Kiani practically walked around with a duster in her hand, and Elizabeth went absolutely gaga over babies.

When I knew the girls' limited cash had run out, I began taking them to the grocery store to stock up on food they could eat when I wasn't around. Before they'd arrived, I had shopped at the high-end grocery store nearby, the one with the best cuts of meat and largest selection of vegetables. But now that I was shopping for four, I switched to the discount store where Marcus had taken the girls.

The first time we went, I engaged in my normal routine of rushing down the aisles, slowing just long enough to toss an item into my cart. The girls looked at me like I was crazy.

"What, you don't like chips?" I asked, throwing a family-size bag of Lay's into the squeaky metal cart.

"No, I love chips," Kiani said, laughing.

"Then what's wrong?" I asked, as I tossed in a bag of pretzels.

"Like that right there," she said, pointing to the pretzels. Looking at Rosie, who was also shaking her head, she said, "I just can't believe she's shopping like that."

"What do you mean?" I asked.

"Aren't you going to check the price? Look," she said, stopping my cart and grabbing two jars of salsa for comparison. "You have to look at the unit price down here, then see which one is a better deal."

Rosie chimed in. "We would spend all day at the store when we went grocery shopping."

"Yeah, but you were feeding an army!" I said. "Now, which one of those is a better deal?"

Kiani raised the jar in her right hand, so I snatched it from her and placed it in the cart. "Better?" I asked.

"Alysia, you're not going to eat *that,* are you?"

The girls made the best homemade salsa I'd ever eaten— a mixture of tomatoes, green and white onions, jalapeños, cheese, avocados, and an assortment of spices. Whenever they made some, I poured it on everything.

"I would never cheat on your salsa with this stuff," I said, returning the jar to the shelf. "Go get what you need to make a huge batch."

As the girls went off giggling toward the produce section, I mowed my way through the store, picking out household essentials and the ingredients to make a Greek dish called pastitsio, similar to lasagna, which I knew they'd never tried. I also grabbed a Rachael Ray cookbook from the magazine section and hid it on the side of the cart so I could give it to Rosie for her upcoming birthday. I couldn't wait for her to try out some of the recipes.

ROSIE'S BIRTHDAY WAS October 21, and I wanted to plan something with my roommates that they could all enjoy. Marcus didn't "believe" in birthdays, so Rosie had never really celebrated hers before. There was a Japanese teppanyaki restaurant nearby, where the chefs chopped and cooked tableside and calculatedly tossed food into the air. I knew it would impress the girls, so I decided to take them there for an early dinner. Gypsy, who was busy with school, didn't join us that night.

"You know this is the place where Scott Peterson took

Amber Frey on their first date," I said, feeling like a tour guide as we walked through the wooden doors, which must have been ten feet tall.

"Really? Wow," Elizabeth said, surprisingly impressed.

"Table for four," I said to the hostess, scanning the restaurant for familiar faces and hoping I wouldn't see any.

It wasn't very busy at 5:00 P.M. on a Thursday, so we had an entire table, set for twenty people, to ourselves. I sat down, unrolled my linen napkin, laid it on my lap, and opened the menu. The girls watched me nervously, then followed suit.

"You guys have been to a restaurant before, right?" I asked, confused by their copycat routine.

Kiani and Rosie looked at each other and laughed.

"You *haven't* been to a restaurant before?" I asked loudly.

Rosie shushed me. "We used to work banquets a lot, but we were always serving," she said quietly.

"Stop it!" I said, shocked. "I can*not* believe this."

A Japanese man the size of a sumo wrestler, wearing a tall white hat, pulled up a two-level metal cart, interrupting our conversation. He nodded, muttered something unintelligible in his thick accent, then went to work heating the rectangular table grill in front of us. When he poured hot oil on the surface, it made an intense sizzling sound and sent up a white puff of smoke that made the skittish girls jump in their seats.

"It's okay, it's just smoke," I said. "He's going to cook everything right here."

"Really, Alysia?" Kiani asked. "This is so neat."

The girls flinched as the chef pulled out two massive knives, one in each hand. He vigorously chopped the vegetables, then threw them down on the scalding hot grill. Halfway into his tableside show, he juggled the salt and pepper shakers and sent a lone shrimp spiraling off his spatula so it landed in the middle of Elizabeth's plate. She was too bashful to acknowledge the gesture, so I clapped for her.

By the end of the entrée, we were all stuffed, but we still managed to eat the vanilla ice cream that came with the meal. Rosie leaned back in her chair and looked past Kiani at me gratefully.

"Thank you, Alysia," she said.

"You're welcome," I said. "Happy birthday."

ALTHOUGH ROSIE HAD started out as the shy, silent one, she had turned into quite the practical joker. A few days after her birthday, the four of us watched *The Texas Chainsaw Massacre* together before I went to sleep. The girls had already seen it on video, so they spoke up right before the last scene, which was billed as authentic news footage of Leatherface attacking two police officers, then escaping.

"Alysia, you *have* to watch this part carefully," Rosie said insistently. "This really happened. They showed it on the news and everything. It's coming up right here, watch."

I stared at the TV in horror. My heart skipped a beat during the last frames of the movie, when it turned to static, à la *Poltergeist*.

"Tell me that wasn't real," I said, my voice growing louder. "Please tell me that wasn't real."

"It *is* real," Rosie said. "That was video from the police."

"That is the scariest thing I've ever seen. I can't believe you guys made me watch that before I have to go to sleep. That's so mean."

I loved watching horror movies, but I hated the nightmares they gave me. That night was no exception. I went to bed around 8:00 P.M., but I kept tossing and turning, thinking about Leatherface still being on the loose. I finally drifted off for a couple hours, but when I woke up, I immediately flashed on the masked man with the chain saw and wondered if he might be hiding in my walk-in closet.

If I could only get to the living room, where Kiani was brewing a fresh pot of coffee, I knew I'd be safe. I decided to jump out of bed and simultaneously reach for the light switch, so I reluctantly hopped onto the floor, and that's when it happened.

Someone—or something—latched on to both of my ankles.

I screamed louder than I'd ever screamed before. I couldn't move. It was pitch-black in my room, so I couldn't see a thing.

Leatherface is in my apartment and he's going to kill me!

Then, I heard laughter. *Hysterical laughter.* It was Rosie. She'd been hiding under my bed for an hour, waiting for me to wake up. It was the cruelest prank I could imagine, but frankly, I was a bit upset that I hadn't thought of it myself.

APPROPRIATELY, HALLOWEEN WAS coming up that weekend. A fellow TV reporter was having a party at her new house, and I needed a costume.

"Want to go to the Halloween shop?" I asked the Wessons, who jumped at the opportunity.

There were four Halloween stores within half a mile of my apartment. I pulled into the closest one, and we filed through the fake cobwebs that hung across the front door, which set off a wicked-witch cackle. Starting on the right side of the store, we worked our way through the hundreds of costumes, stopping near the section with the French-maid outfits.

"This would look good on Kiani," I said, holding one of them against her toned body. Marcus may have been out of shape and overweight, but he had kept the girls on a strict exercise regimen. Kiani had stuck faithfully to hers, doing hundreds of sit-ups and push-ups every day.

Kiani pointed at a revealing bunny getup and blushed. She picked it up and lunged at Rosie. "Here's you, Rosie," she said, chasing her cousin three steps with it.

I glanced ahead.

Uh-oh. Is that what I think it is? Fangs, fake blood, and black capes. Yep! It's the vampire aisle.

My father had always dressed up as Dracula to hand out candy to trick-or-treaters. "I'm coming to suck your blood, ha, ha, ha," he would bellow in a scary voice, flashing his plastic fangs at me and my sister, who were immune to the threat after the first year.

I won't be making any vampire jokes today.

Rosie and Elizabeth were still wearing predominately black but, for once, they didn't stand out, which was a nice break from the pointing and staring.

"What do you guys think about Wonder Woman?" I said, diverting their attention to the superhero aisle.

I'd been hooked on Wonder Woman ever since I first saw Lynda Carter in her shiny red, white, and blue outfit, deflecting bullets with her gold wristbands and taking on the bad guys in her invisible jet. Her combination of tough-ness and beauty made her my childhood hero, so I collected everything I could find with her image: comic books, clothing, and my favorite—a special-edition Wonder Woman Barbie. Even after my Maltese puppy chewed off the doll's hands and feet when I was six, I proudly carried my wounded doll wherever I went. The costume was the perfect choice, and the girls loved it.

A clerk wearing a striped prison costume, complete with a ball and chain, was working the store's only cash register.

Oh, God, this has to be a cosmic joke, but I bet it looks great on Marcus.

The girls got quiet. As I watched their faces fall, I could tell they were feeling guilty for having fun. Even behind bars, Marcus ruined everything.

I paid as quickly as possible and drove us home. I thought the Wessons could use a little inspiration from my favorite character, so I pulled one of my old comic books out of the patio storage unit and read some of her dialogue aloud.

"Listen to this one, you guys. You need to hear this," I said, hoping Wonder Woman could make the point that I couldn't. The girls gathered around as I read it slowly and deliberately.

"Some girls love to have a man stronger than they are to make them do things. Do I like it? I don't know, it's sort of thrilling. But isn't it more fun to make the man obey?"

"It says that, Alysia?" Elizabeth asked.

I handed her the comic so she could see for herself. "This is who you should be listening to," I said, satisfied.

GETTING ME READY Saturday night was a group project. Elizabeth sewed some extra padding into my starred headband, Rosie combed out the long black wig, which, coincidentally, looked exactly like her own hair, and Kiani painted my nails bright red to match my red and white pleather boots.

As usual, I was running late. Rosie straightened my red and blue satin cape as I dashed out the door like, well, Wonder Woman.

"Let us take a picture of you," Elizabeth called out.

I didn't have time to dig for the camera in my purse. "I'll take some at the party," I said, running down the stairs.

"Take lots of pictures."

"I bet she's going to have so much fun."

I heard their voices growing fainter with each step I took. I wished they could go with me. I had no idea that even *I* wouldn't make it to the party that night.

Thirteen

The Wessons often made the trip down the mountain to escape their everyday routine and spend the day in cooler climes, such as Twin Lakes State Beach in Santa Cruz. They also went to retrieve supplies from another used bus that Marcus had converted into a motor home, which they parked at a storage facility in a small town called Freedom, near Watsonville. Marcus, preparing for Armageddon, had stocked the vehicle with a year's worth of powdered and canned food.

But on this particular morning in the spring of 1990, Marcus, Elizabeth, and their nine children and four nieces had come to town so Marcus could go to court to face welfare fraud and perjury charges stemming from his purchase of a boat called the *Happy Bottom*. The county of Santa Cruz contended that the Wessons had been overpaid by more than twenty thousand dollars in welfare benefits and food stamps, claiming that any family able to buy a boat didn't need—or deserve—government assistance. What the county didn't know, however, was that the family never had enough money for food, clothing, or other necessities, specifically *because* Marcus had been using the welfare payments to buy the boat and used buses.

Fancying himself above the law, Marcus shrugged off the charges, telling Elizabeth he thought they were bogus. He said he'd return in a few hours to take them back to the big army tent in which they'd been living for the past few years.

"See you soon," he said nonchalantly just before he headed to the courthouse in Watsonville.

Elizabeth and the kids waited patiently in the motor home for Marcus to return and began to worry when he didn't show up as expected.

That afternoon, they heard a knock on the door. It was the man from the front office.

"Elizabeth?" he asked.

"Yes?" she responded nervously.

"Sorry to tell you this, but your husband just called from jail."

Her stomach dropped, and she couldn't catch her breath enough to respond.

"Yeah," the man went on, "he said they arrested him at the courthouse, and he'll be locked up for a few months."

Elizabeth collapsed, crying, which sent the kids into tears as well.

What were they going to do without Marcus?

At thirty, Elizabeth still didn't have her driver's license, so she was stuck with thirteen kids, ages four to fifteen, with no money and no way to get back up the mountain.

That night, Elizabeth called Linda, Illabelle's friend, and asked for a ride into town to pick up the Travelall. Marcus always parked it in the same spot near his lawyer's office, which was a couple of blocks from the courthouse; Elizabeth would often wait with the kids in it for hours.

Elizabeth felt lost and helpless without Marcus telling her

what to do, but she came up with the best plan she could for the family to survive on its own. During the day, they hung out in the motor home at the storage facility, leaving each evening in the Travelall so the manager would think they had somewhere else to go for the night. Elizabeth used her limited driving skills to find a place to park a few miles away, where they would stay long enough for the manager to leave. Then they would return to the storage facility, park outside, and creep back into the motor home.

In the dark and cramped bus, the large family whispered and kept their movements to a minimum so as not to alarm the two Doberman pinschers that roamed inside the locked gate at night.

Marcus didn't like them to use the portable toilet in the bus, so during the day, the kids held out until their aching bladders couldn't take it anymore; then they'd sneak outside and dig a hole in the rocky gravel to relieve themselves. At night, the dogs left them no choice but to use the toilet.

They had plenty of food on the bus, including macaroni and cheese, rice, beans, honey, evaporated milk, and oatmeal, but because Elizabeth had no way to cook, they quickly went through their supply of Spam and pound cake. And, as they had been doing for years, they ate the yogurt and cottage cheese that a nearby dairy store had tossed out after the expiration date.

Desperate for more help, Elizabeth called Linda again. Linda, who had always liked Marcus, agreed to take in what she'd assumed was his happy, healthy family. However, she couldn't let them come until her houseguests left in two weeks, so she suggested that the Wessons sleep in an abandoned video store in town in the interim.

A friend of Linda's had a key for the vacant store, and she snuck them in late one night so they could set up camp with their sleeping bags. Keeping a lookout for the landlord, the kids took turns peering out a small slit between the sheets of newspaper that covered the store windows. Whenever they saw people outside, they ducked behind the rows of empty shelves and kept silent.

As bad as things had gotten for Elizabeth, not all of her children felt the same. This was the first time that Gypsy had been happy. While the other girls sobbed on her shoulder about how scared they were and how much they missed Marcus, Gypsy searched for a way to help conjure up tears. She found one without too much trouble: she just had to think of the day her father would come home from jail.

THE COUNTY LOCKUP in Watsonville allowed family members to visit inmates once a week, but only on the weekends. So, leaving Sofia and Dorian in charge, Elizabeth went to visit Marcus that first Sunday. Hoping to avoid being pulled over, she drove the ten-minute route from the video store very slowly.

She'd never been away from Marcus for this long, so she wanted his guidance on how to provide the family with food and shelter. He, on the other hand, thought it was more important to talk about sex.

Marcus said he constantly had erections, so the female guards flocked to his cell every morning to watch him "pitch a tent." He also said he refused to eat any jail-prepared food because he was sure they'd dosed it with saltpeter—potassium nitrate—to quell the men's libidos. He said he would show them that he was wise to their scheme by not eating.

Elizabeth left more confused and frustrated than ever. Marcus was no help at all. He didn't even seem to care about what his family was going through, so she had to figure out what to do on her own. But, at this point, she had absolutely no clue.

MUCH HAPPIER TIMES came when Linda let them move into her cute little red house with white shutters, which was surrounded by mature redwood trees and a picturesque creek that flowed through the backyard. Elizabeth brought a couple of weeks' worth of food at a time from the motor home and used it to feed the kids four times a day—more often than ever before. She also let them roam outside, where the children climbed trees, played tag, and jumped into the creek. For the first time, the boys and girls could frolic together in nature with no rules and no fear. It felt like heaven.

They weren't completely carefree, though. As soon as Marcus got access to a pay phone, he started calling Linda's house every night to make sure the children weren't misbehaving, ultimately racking up five hundred dollars in collect calls that Elizabeth's mother and sister had to pay for.

As the kids passed the phone around, Gypsy nervously watched their expressions change from smiles to frowns within moments. Then it was her turn.

"Hi," she said with feigned enthusiasm.

"Do you miss me, Gypsy?" Marcus said with self-pity.

"Yes. I can't wait for you to come home," she lied.

Even though no one had told her why he was in jail, Gypsy prayed every day that whoever had put him there would hold him as long as possible.

Marcus Wesson with his niece Rosie (*left*)
and daughters Lise and Gypsy.

The Wesson family and their Solorio cousins
at Elizabeth's mother Rose's home in Fresno.

The Wesson boys (*left to right, back to front*), Adrian, Dorian, Almae, Marcus Jr., and Serafino in Watsonville. Six years after this photo was taken, Adrian and Dorian were abandoned in the Santa Cruz Mountains.

Brandy, Ruby, Sebhrenah, Gypsy, and Sofia (*left to right*), in the Wesson family bus, seem happy despite the stifling heat and cramped quarters.

Kiani, Sebhrenah, Rosie, Brandy, Ruby, and Sofia (*left to right*) in Rose's kitchen, wearing the modest clothing that Marcus required.

Rosie, Lise, and Gypsy. Lise and Gypsy were inseparable; their cousin Rosie was Marcus's "strong soldier."

Jonathan, Ethan, Illabelle, and Aviv belowdecks
on the family's houseboat the *Sudan*. All four children
were killed on March 12, 2004.

The *Sudan*. The girls, never allowed on deck in daylight during
the school year, sometimes went weeks without seeing the sun.

Ruby (*left*) and Sofia, pregnant with Marcus's children Aviv and Jonathan. When the women attempted eight years later to reclaim their children, most speculate that Marcus invoked the family suicide pact.

Sebhrenah holding her cousin Ethan with her nieces Illabelle (*left*) and Aviv (*right*). Sebhrenah was found, with gunpowder residue on her hands, on the top of the pile of those who died on March 12, 2004.

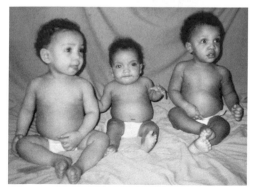

Sedona, Jeva, and Marshey. All three children were under two years old when they were murdered.

Author Alysia Sofios with Gypsy's daughter, the first Wesson child not to be fathered by Marcus. Gypsy named her baby Alysia, after the woman who risked so much to help them.

Kiani in Alysia's apartment. Kiani's sunny personality helped her acclimate to a life without Marcus.

Elizabeth (*left*) and Rosie's first roller-coaster ride

Little Alysia sitting at Alysia Sofios's desk. Gypsy's daughter brought new hope to the Wesson family.

Gypsy, Alysia, and Rosie on the Santa Cruz boardwalk

Marcus Wesson's booking photo. (*Fresno Police Department*)

Marcus Wesson, following his conviction on nine counts of first-degree murder and fourteen counts of sexual abuse. Once Wesson was found guilty, the officials at San Quentin were allowed to cut off his matted dreadlocks. (*California Department of Corrections*)

As the months of Marcus's sentence went on, the Wessons' lives continued to improve. Now that the kids were eating more, they had gained weight and were healthy, especially after being free from Marcus's beatings for so long.

Elizabeth was prospering, too. When an acquaintance offered to help her get a driver's license, Elizabeth cautiously accepted her offer. On Elizabeth's thirty-first birthday, she filled out the paperwork, took the tests, and proudly left the DMV with her license in hand.

Everything was moving in the right direction until September, when Marcus called Elizabeth. The jail was releasing him, so he told her to pick him up in three days, just after midnight. She had mixed emotions about the news. She was somewhat relieved that he would take over the decision making, but she dreaded the inevitable interrogations about the family's activities while he'd been away.

ELIZABETH PULLED INTO the jail parking lot as instructed, leaving the motor running while she listened to oldies on the radio. About ten other cars were parked in the spaces next to her, their headlights shining on the gate where the inmates would emerge from the tall metal fence.

Elizabeth had decided she was eager to see Marcus again. When the first man came out, she leaned into the windshield, hoping it was him, but she soon realized the man was too light-skinned. Three more men came out before Elizabeth finally turned off the engine.

Forty-five minutes later, a large man carrying a backpack walked briskly toward her, repeatedly looking over his shoulder, then broke into a run as soon as he was through the gate. Elizabeth recognized Marcus, and was pulling up to meet him when she heard him yelling as he ran to the car.

"Don't stop, keep driving," he said.

Elizabeth kept the vehicle rolling, watching his face for approval.

"Yes, just keep going," Marcus said, panting, as he caught up to the back door on the passenger side, which he opened, then dived onto the floor.

"What are you doing, Marcus?" Elizabeth said, frightened as she glanced back at her husband.

"Don't look back here. Just drive," he ordered, clearly in a high state of paranoia. "I don't want them knowing I'm in the car with you. They're going to follow us tonight, so we can't go back to the kids. I don't want them to know where we're staying."

Five minutes later, Elizabeth had reached downtown Watsonville, and Marcus sat up. "Go to a hotel," he said. "We'll need to stay there tonight, so they won't find us."

Elizabeth's sister had sent her some money to help with the kids, so she spent thirty dollars of it on a room.

The next morning, Marcus reunited with his children at Linda's house. After a round of hugs and kisses with the thirteen boys and girls, he backed away.

"I know you all have been breaking the rules while I was gone," he said. "I am going to have a talk with each of you to find out what's been going on."

As part of his probation, Marcus was ordered to search for a job and to pay off the outstanding harbor bills for the *Happy Bottom*. However, he complied with neither order, choosing rather to make up for lost time in disciplining his children.

Linda was gone for the day, so he used her bedroom to conduct his questioning. Beginning with the youngest kids, he grilled them about their thoughts and actions during his absence. He also demanded an accounting of every sibling's disobedience. He soon learned that the older girls had been talking to the boys, and that some name-calling had been going on.

Armed with this knowledge, he began to carry out weeks of systematic beatings on all the children. It was hard to believe, but his stint in jail had made him even more abusive—and perhaps even more resistant to government authority.

Gypsy didn't have to make herself cry anymore. The tears came far too easily.

MARCUS WAS MORE paranoid than ever. He reported seeing suspicious vehicles in the rearview mirror. He tried to lose the tails by taking roundabout routes to their destinations, never using his blinkers and taking sudden, sharp turns that made the tires squeal.

One afternoon, he was convinced he heard a helicopter overhead and panicked. As in a scene out of an action movie, Marcus believed that the government was searching for him from above. He drove erratically until he found a big tree at the side of the road and parked the Travelall underneath it. "They won't see us here," he told the family.

After hiding there for three hours, Marcus patted himself on the back for evading the government once again. But as soon as they got back to their property, he sent his children out to do a full security sweep.

"Look for bugs and wiretaps," he whispered, his hand cupped over his mouth. "I know they've planted them here."

"Why are you talking like that?" one of the children asked.

"Sssh. We are being watched," Marcus replied softly. "They are listening to us."

That night, he said he spotted shadowy figures lurking. When he went to confront them, however, they were gone. "They must have heard me coming," Marcus said. "But I found some cigarette butts out there where they were standing, spying on us."

Two days later, Marcus decided they needed to move in with Elizabeth's sister Rosemary in Fresno, so he packed up their supplies and drove everyone to the storage unit, where he loaded half the kids into the motor home and the other half into the Travelall. Three hours later, the Wesson clan arrived at Rosemary's duplex.

Each unit had one bedroom and one bathroom. Rosemary and the girls slept upstairs; the boys, Elizabeth, and Marcus slept downstairs, where he also conducted Bible studies, beatings, and weekly sit-downs with the girls.

Now that the county had cut off the family's welfare benefits, Marcus sent Dorian and Adrian out to work full-time jobs they found through one of Elizabeth's relatives— cleaning houses, apartments, and businesses.

Marcus had all eight girls working, too. He bought them strands of beads, bundles of string, and boxes of clasps, which the girls spent hours each day crafting into chokers, necklaces, bracelets, and anklets. Before long, each of them was churning out several pieces daily and selling them to friends and classmates of Elizabeth's brothers and nephews for two to ten dollars each.

* * *

OVER THE NEXT four years, the family lived at the duplex, occasionally driving to the Santa Cruz property for a week or two during the summer. Being in a more densely populated area like Fresno put the Wessons' illegal lifestyle in jeopardy, especially when the police started coming by the house.

The first time was during their morning Bible study. Three officers, looking for one of Elizabeth's brothers, knocked on the front door. When no one responded, they knocked again.

"Police," one of the officers yelled. "Open up."

Marcus had repeatedly said that the police and the government didn't understand the way they lived and would try to break up their family someday, so the kids sprang up and darted into the back room, piled into the closet, and closed the door. Dorian and Adrian held the door to the room shut while Marcus let the three policemen come inside.

"May I help you, Officers?" he asked.

The police asked whether Elizabeth's brother was around, and Marcus informed them that he was not.

"What was all that running going on when we were knocking on the door?"

"Nothing," Marcus answered.

"Can we take a look around?"

"Sure."

The officers went up to the barricaded back door and demanded entry. "Open up. This is the police."

Adrian and Dorian reluctantly twisted the doorknob. The uniformed men pushed their way through and walked to the closet, where they saw the children hiding inside.

"Come out here, it's okay," they said.

The frightened children filed out and stood before the officers.

"What is going on here?" one officer asked. "Why were you running from us?"

Gypsy wanted so much to tell them the truth. She wanted to scream and cry and grab on to one of them, begging them to rescue her from Marcus. But she couldn't bring herself to say a word. All the kids were silent, so the officers ushered them into the living room to join their parents.

"Why are these kids so afraid of us?" one of them asked Marcus.

"This is a bad neighborhood," Marcus explained. "We hear gunshots a lot, so we make them lie on the floor. They didn't know what was happening."

"But we're the police. We're here to protect people. Why don't they know that?"

"They were just confused, Officer."

"Well, why aren't they in school?"

"We're on vacation, visiting family," Marcus lied. "We live in Santa Cruz, and the kids are enrolled in school there."

"But it's not vacation time. I think we're going to need to investigate a little further."

The officers looked around. In the bedroom, they found Marcus's gun inside the familiar brown and tan leather bag. Everyone in the house knew Marcus kept a .22-caliber Ruger in that bag, because he'd take it out and polish it from time to time.

"Do you have a permit for this?" an officer asked.

Marcus said he did, but the officers were still suspicious

enough to call dispatch. "I think we're going to need CPS out here," one of them said. "We'll need two vans. There are a lot of children."

Gypsy was hoping she would be rescued after all, but Marcus confidently talked his way out of the situation. He promised to return his family to Santa Cruz that day, so the officers canceled the CPS request and walked out the door.

A FEW MONTHS later, the police came back, searching for another of Elizabeth's relatives. This time, Lise broke down, terrified. "Please don't take me away," she said between sobs. "I don't want to go away."

The officers were alarmed. "What made her think the police would want to take her from her family?" they asked Marcus.

Again, he told them that the kids were used to living in dangerous neighborhoods and that Lise was just confused. The officers didn't push any further, and left.

AFTER A HANDFUL of similar run-ins with the law, Marcus got nervous and, as a result, his rules grew more strict and his demands more outrageous.

For one, he instituted the "twenty-minute rule." In case the government came after the family, he said, the kids should be prepared to pack their belongings and leave within twenty minutes. That meant the children's clothing and personal possessions had to remain in bags; there wouldn't be time to retrieve their things from dressers.

Marcus began dropping hints during Bible study about what they should do if CPS stepped in. He warned that foster parents would separate and mistreat the family by feeding the kids greasy McDonald's food and sending them to public schools. Some of the kids thought that sounded pretty good, but they never dared say so. If this ever happened, Marcus decreed that their souls would be lost and their spirits contaminated by the outside world.

"Do not *ever,* under any circumstance, let the government separate you," he cautioned. "It will corrupt you. It is better to go to the Lord than to be apart from your family."

Over the years, he issued more specific—and brutal—instructions. Although it took on various forms, the suicide pact typically involved one of the older kids shooting the youngest children, then himself or herself. Initially, Marcus said he would shoot the children, then himself, but he later changed his mind. "I may not even be around when the authorities show up, so I'll need to train some soldiers to carry out the mission," he said. "Even if I am around, I will be too weak to do it, because it will hurt me too much. So, even if I tell my soldiers to back off, they need to be strong enough to follow through for me."

He didn't tell them exactly how to go about it at first; he simply described definitive ways to kill a person.

"Shooting someone in the chest or the head doesn't guarantee they will die," Marcus said. "But if you shoot them in the eye, it is a direct line to the brain and works every time."

To determine which children he would train as his soldiers, he held private meetings with a few of the girls, including Rosie.

If the police interrupted the plan before everyone had died, he said, all the children knew what to do: kill themselves at the first opportunity. Even if they were in a police cruiser, they should jump out of the moving vehicle. "If the door won't open, break a window. Just do whatever it takes to join the others as quickly as possible," Marcus instructed. "It is better to die than to be contaminated."

NOW THAT HE had established the suicide pact, Marcus decided he wanted to broaden his "new life" plan to make more children for the Lord. Only this time, it was directed at his daughters and nieces rather than Elizabeth.

One night in 1994, Marcus called a very important meeting with the girls. He always waited until Elizabeth was visiting her mother or sister to conduct these gatherings.

Marcus sat on the queen-size bed, his legs stretched out in front of him and his back against the wall; Ruby, Sofia, Brandy, Rosie, Kiani, and Sebhrenah sat in a semicircle around him. Gypsy and Lise were too young to be included, but he wanted them in the room, so they sat on the floor at the foot of the bed.

As was typical for his weekly rendezvous with the girls, Marcus turned off all the lights. The room was so dimly lit, the only thing the girls could see was the occasional flash of his white teeth.

"The world is getting bad," he said. "God is going to be here in a couple of years, and it's all going to end soon."

He told the girls that God wanted them to be fruitful and multiply, so they could bring as many children as possible to heaven when the world ended.

Gypsy and Lise knew they weren't really part of the discussion, so they whispered to each other, careful not to let their father catch them, while their older sisters nodded their understanding of Marcus's instructions.

"It is time for the oldest girls to have children for the

Lord," he continued. "Since no man in the outside world is worthy of you, the Lord will use me as the vessel to create the children. It will be like Lot and his daughters."

The girls knew the story of Lot well. According to the Bible, Lot's two virgin daughters incorrectly believed they were the only females to have survived the devastation that God had wreaked on their city and assumed it was their responsibility to perpetuate the human race. The girls developed a plan, which they carried out on two separate nights: they got their father drunk enough to have intercourse with them but too drunk to know what was happening. Each of them got pregnant.

Marcus said he wanted the girls to think like Lot's daughters and start having children as soon as they turned eighteen, but their plan had to remain secret from everyone else, including the rest of the family.

"The world is not going to understand," he said.

He told them to say they were going to a sperm bank to get artificially inseminated, then return a few hours later with literature as evidence of the trip.

"At the next family gathering, you will need to pull your uncles aside and tell them that you want to get pregnant, so they will not get suspicious," he said, referring to Elizabeth's brothers.

At the time, Sofia was the only one old enough; Kiani was seventeen, and Ruby was only sixteen. Ten-year-old Gypsy thanked God she had eight years to go. By then, she hoped, the world would already have ended. She and Lise didn't quite understand how their sisters and cousins were going to get pregnant; all they knew was they weren't supposed to talk about it.

In January 1995, Kiani got pregnant with her father's child, despite being under his stated age requirement. Four months into the pregnancy, Elizabeth's brother Jesse heard the artificial insemination story and threatened to call the police. He wasn't buying it.

Marcus got spooked. "It's getting dangerous for us here," he announced at the family's nightly prayer session. "We're going back to the mountains."

The kids knew the twenty-minute rule had been put into effect, so they rushed to pack their clothing and toiletries in backpacks and waited for instructions. But it was a week before the order came—at five o'clock in the morning.

"It's time," Marcus said.

The family obediently carried their things into the blue school bus Marcus had bought from a Baptist church a few months earlier with the older kids' paychecks. They drove away with him into the darkness, purposely neglecting to tell Elizabeth's relatives where they were going.

Fourteen

Trying not to sit on my freshly steamed cape, I carefully gathered the red satin around my torso and buckled my seat belt. My coworker's party in the trendy Tower District of Fresno was about fifteen minutes away, and I hoped my costume would hold up during the ride.

I have to remember to take pictures to show the girls.

It was almost eleven on an unusually fogless night, and I had promised the hostess that I would be there already. Because most of the guests would arrive around 11:30 or midnight—after the news—I was supposed to get there early to represent the morning show folks.

Maybe if I had an invisible jet . . .

We would switch back to standard time in a few hours, which meant I would have an extra hour to spend at the party. I made a left turn onto the main road and accelerated to the full forty-mile-per-hour speed limit. All of a sudden, a bright light blinded me. I could see nothing but white as the high-pitched squealing of tires overpowered Frank Sinatra on the radio. Before I knew it, a white van had jumped the curb and crashed head-on into my small SUV.

I watched the front of my vehicle crunch toward me like

an accordion and the dashboard plow into my kneecaps. My body shot up and forward, shattering the mirror on the visor. On the way back down, my cape settled on top of my rigid shoulders, and the long black waves from my wig came to rest on the steering wheel.

After a few seconds, I felt around with my tongue to make sure my teeth were intact. They were fine, but my mouth tasted like blood and I realized I had bitten the inside of my cheek. I struggled to regain my bearings.

I wonder how the other driver is. They must be drunk. I need help.

My vision was fuzzy as I looked through my cracked windshield and saw the driver of the van get out and start running toward my car, staring straight at me. In spite of the circumstances, I welcomed his help.

But the next thing I knew, he'd raced past the passenger door and kept on going.

Oh my God, he's running away!

I didn't have the energy to yell at him or ask why he wasn't stopping to check on me; I just opened my car door. Luckily, another driver who had seen the collision rushed to my aid. She and her passenger, a younger woman, stuck their heads into my car.

"We called 911, honey. The ambulance is on its way," the older woman said. "Oh my God. Are you okay?"

"I don't know," I said, feeling around for injuries in my stomach, which was hurting, and my thighs. A sharp pain was shooting through my right ankle, which had gotten scrunched during the impact, and my knees were aching where the dashboard had smacked into them.

"We need to call someone. Is your husband or family nearby?"

Much to my surprise, the first people who came to my mind were the Wessons.

"I'm not married, and my family lives in Michigan," I said weakly.

I thought of the Wessons again. In this time of crisis, it was so clear. *They* were my family now.

"Can you call my neighbors?" I asked, trying to keep our relationship a secret as long as I could.

I dictated Elizabeth's phone number to the woman as I tried to step out of my mangled car and onto the curb, a foot away. But I felt light-headed and immediately realized I wasn't going to make it.

"I think I need to sit down," I said, getting back into the car with their help.

I heard the woman calling Elizabeth. "Your neighbor Alysia has just been in an accident," she said, pausing. "No, she's going to be okay, but she'd like you to come out here. We're on Brawley Avenue . . ."

As the woman gave Elizabeth directions, I heard the unmistakable wail of police and ambulance sirens. Although I was disguised as a superhero, the several police officers who responded recognized my name and picture on my driver's license. They tried to help me relax with small talk while we waited for the paramedics to wheel over the gurney.

"So you're not on the air tonight, huh?" one of them joked.

"Not tonight," I said, trying to smile through the throbbing pain in my head.

The paramedics were loading me onto the gurney when I saw Elizabeth, Kiani, and Rosie running up to my car. I knew that the police would recognize them and that the scene could turn into quite a story at the precinct: "That news girl got hit head-on by a drunk driver. And she was dressed up like Wonder Woman, with the cape and everything. Then Marcus Wesson's family came to see her."

But I was too dizzy to care. The girls bent over me with tears in their eyes, their faces pale with worry. The image was strikingly similar to video I'd seen of them the night of the murders.

"Oh no, Alysia," Elizabeth said, gently stroking my arm. "Oh no."

"We'll see you at the hospital," Rosie said quietly.

"One of you can ride with us," a paramedic said to the girls.

Kiani stepped forward and jumped into the front seat of the ambulance. The other paramedic rode in the back with me, checking my vital signs along the way.

Herndon Avenue seemed bumpier than usual during the ten-minute ride, but it all became a blur until I was being wheeled down the hallway of Saint Agnes Medical Center— my faux dark hair flowing over the sides of the stretcher and my stiletto boots hanging over the end. One of the gurney's wheels was askew, so each time the paramedic loosened his grip on the metal handle, the lower end shifted to the left, nearly hitting the nurses running by.

"We've got a Wonder Woman here," a hospital worker yelled behind me.

"All right! Chalk another one up for me," another male voice responded.

Apparently, the emergency room staff had made bets on the costumes that would come through that night. I appreciated the humor more after a few painkillers. The nurse had to cut the back of my costume to get it off, then helped me into a faded blue cotton hospital gown that tied in the back. I still had on my wig, headband, and glittery red, white, and blue false eyelashes. I could tell the costume startled the doctor when he walked through the floor-length curtain.

Both knees and my right ankle had swelled to twice their normal size, and my head and neck were pulsing with pain. After hours of IVs and X-rays, the doctor told me the good news: I hadn't broken any bones. I did, however, have a concussion and a knot the size of a golf ball at the bottom left of my neck from whiplash.

The doctor sent me home with painkillers, muscle relaxants, and orders to follow up with an orthopedic specialist. Elizabeth, Kiani, and Rosie, who had gone home to get me something to replace my ripped leotard, were back. They still looked pale and worried.

"Where's my car?" I asked through my drugged haze.

"I think they towed it," Elizabeth replied. "Don't worry about that. I'll pull the car around and wait for you guys."

I slept on the way home, lying down in the backseat with my legs propped on Kiani's lap. Elizabeth pulled into the parking space; then Rosie and Kiani each took one of my arms and helped me upstairs and into bed.

"Do you need anything else?" Elizabeth asked. "Are you in pain?"

"Yes, but I'll be fine," I said, trying to find a more comfortable position. "Can you take me to the doctor in the morning?"

"Of course, Alysia. The doctor said we need to wake you up every couple hours because of your head, so we'll be in soon to check on you."

As they closed my door, I leaned my head against the pillow that Rosie had propped up for me and thought about the strange twist of events. I had never asked for help before, and it humbled me to know that, this time, I couldn't get by on my own. What would I have done without the Wessons? My immediate family was thousands of miles away. Taking the Wessons in had actually saved *me*.

I COULDN'T EVEN remember the last time I'd had a day off, so sitting at home resting was all new to me. I'd always been an overachiever. In high school, I was a diver, gymnast, runner, and jumper, and by my senior year was poised to earn twelve varsity letters. When I found out another girl in Michigan had already earned twelve letters, I joined my school's competition coed cheerleading squad so I could get thirteen and break the state record. I had always been under pressure and on deadline, so it was quite an adjustment to try to relax for three whole months.

But now I had no choice. For the first week I relied on the Wessons to get me around and to take care of the apartment. I couldn't move much, so they went grocery shopping, cooked meals, and served me food in bed. I was able to take care of paying the bills and managing our household finances while Elizabeth brought me my prescription pills and a glass of water every few hours. Elizabeth drove me to and from my doctors' appointments and also to physical therapy three times per week. After raising nine kids, four nieces, and their seven children, she was quite comfortable with this caregiving role. Only now she was free to follow her instincts, dispense medication, and express affection without Marcus getting in her way. She seemed to blossom in her new role, and I began to see the strength that had helped Elizabeth survive so much tragedy.

For their part, Rosie and Kiani rented videos and arranged a cushy spot for me on the couch so we could watch them together. Sometimes, Rosie would come into my physical therapy sessions, keeping me company while I was hooked up to the thermal ultrasound machine to try to ease my pain. The girls, who had never been able to reveal they were in pain any more than they could openly take care of each other, seemed to enjoy stretching their new caregiving muscles as well.

I tried to go back to work a couple of weeks later, but after a few CAT scans and trips to the orthopedist, I learned that my injuries weren't going to heal overnight. When I continued to have migraine headaches and my neck pain kept shooting down my back to new and unexplored places, the orthopedist decided I shouldn't be running around on deadline, so he ordered me to take three months off work for a stress-free recovery. I had no choice but to accept that I had to bring my life down several dozen notches. It helped that all the Wessons were growing more independent—rather than being my houseguests, they were truly my family now.

Once I was more mobile, I broke out my old Nintendo system and taught the girls how to play *Super Mario Bros.* and *Tetris*. We stayed up late playing video games and laughing. We also had a lot more time to talk and exchange stories. Theirs usually involved something positive about Marcus. It had been more than seven months since the murders, and I wanted to speak out against him more than ever, but I could tell they still needed someone to just listen.

The more I talked about my childhood experiences, the more I could see slight improvements in Rosie's and Kiani's grips on reality. They were beginning to question some of the things Marcus had taught them about the world—and recognize that school, boys, and friends weren't as bad as he'd told them.

With so much in limbo, I was reevaluating my own life, too. I spent a lot of time writing in my journal.

> I have no idea what the next year of my life has in store. Absolutely nothing is planned. It's the scariest, yet best feeling I've ever had. I wouldn't change anything right now. Even though I was just hit head-on by a drunk driver in a van, I live with the family of a mass murderer, and my entire career is in jeopardy. When I see it on paper, it doesn't look so good.

I was still in a lot of pain, but I knew it was important to stay positive in front of the girls, and they responded well to my motivating speeches. When I told them they could do anything if they set their minds to it, I didn't realize how naïve I was being.

Kiani and Rosie seemed to be getting more serious about going to school. Rosie fixated on the idea of working with animals someday; Kiani just wanted to get a college education. But realizing they would need tuition, they decided to find jobs first. They hadn't worked in more than two years, and their only work experience was in the food industry. So they picked up applications from several chain restaurants in Fresno, including Chili's, Chevys, and Macaroni Grill. I encouraged all of this, knowing that working would build their self-confidence and self-sufficiency, and also would help them meet new people.

"Alysia, what should we put here?" Kiani asked, pointing to the line on the application that said "education" and asked for the applicant's high school, then college, followed by any postgraduate studies.

After struggling for an answer, I said, "I guess just write 'home-schooled.' "

"But we don't have diplomas," Rosie said, concerned the managers wouldn't understand.

"Maybe you can explain it during the interviews," I offered.

It didn't get any easier after that. The applications also had lines asking for the reasons they had left their previous jobs. I hardly thought "abusive father" constituted an acceptable response.

"Should we put 'pregnant'?" Kiani asked.

I tried to think of a better alternative but couldn't.

"I guess so."

A few days after they turned in their applications, it dawned on me that no local establishment would hire them. Kiani Wesson and Rosa Solorio were household names around Fresno.

This community had been so generous to crime victims in the past, donating money, clothing, and scholarships. The police department had honored other victims, recognizing what they'd been through and asking them to speak about their experiences. Following the disappearance of pregnant Laci Peterson, the city of Modesto was covered with yellow and blue tribute ribbons, even after her body and that of her unborn son were discovered. But when it came to the

Wesson family, few people in Fresno had shown any compassion for the surviving members.

I was outraged. How dare people judge these poor people and treat them as if they had the plague? It wasn't as if these women were asking for a handout; they just wanted a job.

Needless to say, Kiani and Rosie didn't get any calls back. The whole situation left me nauseated.

HALFWAY THROUGH MY recuperation, my dad came to visit from Michigan. He was retired now, but he still taught graduate business courses at two colleges. The girls seemed excited to meet him, but when he and I got back from the airport, they were nowhere to be seen. Their car was out front, so I peeked into their room. Still no one. Then I heard noises from inside the long mirrored closet.

"Don't tell me you guys are in . . . ," I said, pulling open the sliding door to expose Elizabeth, Kiani, and Rosie, red-faced from laughing. "You're hiding in the closet? How long have you been in there? You know what? I don't even want to know. Get out of there and come meet my dad."

"We're scared," Rosie whispered.

"Why? He's only the nicest man on earth. Come on!" I said, pulling Rosie out of the closet and pushing her forward as she tried to walk backward.

"Okay, we'll go out there," Elizabeth said, finally giving in.

"Good. I'll lead the way," I said, praying they would follow me.

"Dad, I'd like you to meet Elizabeth, Kiani, and Rosie."

"Hi, I've heard so much about you," my father said with a smile, getting up to shake each of their hands.

He tried to strike up a conversation, but he could sense how nervous they were and left them alone. They waited a few seconds, then walked back toward their room. "Nice meeting you," Elizabeth said over her shoulder, too quietly for my dad to hear.

They hid in their room the rest of the day. My dad went out and got us dinner, then picked up our plates when we were done eating. I could see it made the girls uncomfortable, as if they felt they should be cleaning up. The following day, he brought some Chinese food for lunch. This time, the girls jumped up and tried to serve him.

"Go ahead and sit down," he said. "I can get it for you."

They looked at each other with shocked expressions. I glanced up at my dad and saw the antithesis of Marcus Wesson. Physically, he was tall, thin, and tanned, with neatly trimmed gray hair, a pointed Greek nose, and a large, bright smile that never left his face for more than a few seconds. Emotionally, he was optimistic, gentle, and caring. I knew his kindness was putting Marcus's paternal behavior in a whole new light for the girls.

"Your dad is so nice, I can't believe it," Kiani said.

Her father had never even let her speak to men outside the family. She had never seen another father-daughter interaction so closely before, and I sensed that watching my dad treat me so differently—and with so much respect—was difficult for her.

A few days later, Kiani decided to move into Adrian's apartment in Santa Cruz. Unbeknownst to me, things had been building up for a while. Gypsy had invited Kiani to go to Universal Studios with her and her boyfriend, but after Rosie said she'd report her to Marcus if she did, Kiani decided to stay home. Kiani also had developed a crush on one of her brothers' friends and knew she couldn't take that any further as long as Rosie and Elizabeth were watching her every move.

Kiani clearly felt she couldn't get on with her life without making a break from Elizabeth and Rosie, who were still pining away for Marcus and didn't want anyone in the family to go against his teachings. I was happy for Kiani but could see she was going to have a rough road ahead of her.

My FATHER WENT home, and we all celebrated our first Christmas together with a tree, stocking stuffers, and gifts.

Late on Christmas afternoon, my mom called, crying. "Alysia," she said. "Dad is in the hospital. It's his heart."

"Is he going to be okay? What happened?"

"We're not sure. The doctors say he'll need bypass surgery, and they may need to replace his aortic valve. It's very serious, babe, but please don't worry. I'll call you when we know more."

I froze. Marcus Wesson's vile image popped into my head, and I couldn't get it out.

"What's wrong, Alysia?" Elizabeth asked sympathetically.

At that moment, I didn't want to talk to her or Rosie. I knew I was being irrational, but it just seemed so unfair. How could my dad—the nicest man I'd ever met—be in the hospital, while Marcus was alive and well in his jail cell? My dad would never hurt anybody and he was the one with the heart condition? It made me sick.

Why can't they just trade places?

I wanted to offer Marcus up for the operating table

instead. If he didn't make it, everyone would be better off. No painstaking trial, no more public scrutiny.

If he was sentenced to death, it would be a joke. He would probably live another twenty years on death row before he was executed—if he didn't die of natural causes first.

AS MY CONTEMPT for Marcus grew in the coming days, Marcus's family finally got permission to visit him. While Elizabeth and Rosie touched up their makeup and put on perfume for their first weekend visit, I stewed in my room, wanting to stop them. I was afraid he would send them secret messages to kill themselves.

They seemed depressed when they got home, as if they felt bad leaving him in jail, and I could tell from their red eyes that they'd been crying. As mad as that made me, I told myself that they'd actually thought they were happy all those years. Which meant, I guess, they *were* happy. How do you tell someone she wasn't happy?

Marcus had convinced these women that he was a good man. An unemployed, overweight, middle-aged, abusive, controlling, delusional, insecure pedophile had convinced these smart, beautiful, intelligent women that he was a god. I understand why they fell for it as kids, but now that they had been exposed to mainstream society, enough was enough.

Elizabeth and Rosie had *four* children who were murdered. He'd left them out on their asses without the tools to succeed. Now he was locked up, they were stuck fending for themselves and, still, they felt sorry for him. I couldn't bite my tongue any longer.

"Do you think *he* feels sorry for *you* guys right now?" I blurted out.

The girls looked at me, stunned, and didn't answer. I felt so cruel for stating the obvious, but I realized that my home was the only place in the world where I was in the minority for hating Marcus Wesson.

AFTER A SUCCESSFUL quintuple bypass and with a new aortic valve, my dad joined me in recovery. And on February 1, my doctor cleared me to go back to work.

When I called my boss with the good news, he gave me some news of his own.

"How would you like to come back to work in Fresno, back on the night shift?" he asked.

"Really? Like a normal schedule again? No more foggy drives in the middle of the night, pinching my leg?"

"Nope. What do you say?"

"I say thank you, and I'll start tomorrow!"

"See you then."

I would be back in Fresno just in time. The Marcus Wesson trial was set to begin a month later. Now I *had* to tell my boss about my roommates.

Fifteen

*I*f there was ever a time when the Wesson family seemed normal, it was on Friday nights, when Marcus allowed his children to watch movies on the VCR. The kids enjoyed the weekly treat so much they would mark a 6 in the corner of their diary entries every Saturday, kicking off the countdown. It was the only thing that made life bearable.

Marcus would bring home large tubs of Neapolitan ice cream and bulk boxes of vanilla and fudge cookies, the only sugar the kids were allowed. The little ones were given small portions before being sent to their room, while the older children built wobbly houses of vanilla, strawberry, and chocolate ice cream, supported by cookie walls, which they carefully carried to their assigned seats in front of the television.

The family didn't have a TV until 1990, when one of Elizabeth's brothers sold them his old eighteen-inch set. Marcus began buying previously viewed videos from a liquidator, and within a few years, the Wessons had accumulated a movie library with dozens of titles in each category. Nonetheless, Marcus often replayed his favorites, including *Pretty Woman* and *Road House,* until the kids knew the lines by heart.

By the same token, the children learned when to cover their eyes or turn their heads while Marcus fast-forwarded through the scenes featuring sex or extreme violence. If he caught any of them peeking, he would wait for the movie to end, then beat them.

After the films, Marcus would put on dance tapes. The boys danced in one half of the room, the girls and Marcus in the other, romping around until the early hours of the morning.

Sometimes Marcus and the boys would perform Friday night skits for the girls. He'd have the boys put on hobo costumes, and he would don a long dress and red lipstick.

When Dorian was fifteen, Marcus took his son into a room to get dressed for that night's performance. He pulled out some cosmetic powder and eyeliner and began applying it to Dorian's face.

"What are you doing, Dad?" Dorian asked, surprised.

"This is what actors do," Marcus said, explaining that he used to take theater classes in Beverly Hills.

Dorian found all of this very strange, given that Marcus often quizzed the boys individually about their sexuality.

"Are you gay?" Marcus would ask.

"No, Dad."

"You know, homosexuality runs in our family. But I'm not raising any fags."

Although Marcus attempted to emasculate his son, Dorian still had the dreams of a typical teenage boy—going to high school and playing football—even though he knew his father would never allow it. But one day, Dorian's athletic urges got the best of him. "Dad, I was thinking that I'd maybe like to go to high school," he said.

Marcus turned to his son and squinted, his nostrils flaring like those of an angry bull. "I'd rather see you dead than see you in school," he said.

Dorian never brought it up again. That was why he was so confused a couple of years later when Marcus pulled him and Adrian aside.

"Do you want to go to school?" Marcus asked.

The boys looked at each other, knowing it sounded too good to be true.

"Yes, of course," Adrian said, waiting for the punch line.

"Are you serious, Dad?" Dorian asked.

"Yes. I have decided to allow you to go to a school for Japanese martial arts," Marcus said. "You will learn nonviolent ways of self-defense and discipline."

It wasn't football, but the teenagers gladly signed up for aikido classes at a studio in Fresno, which they subsidized by doing yard work for the neighbors. They didn't even care that they had to foot the bill themselves.

AS HIS OLDEST sons matured, Marcus beat them even more savagely. After having separated them from the girls for years, he decided he didn't even want them to interact with each other. The two oldest boys had become close friends, and Marcus seemed set on breaking that bond.

Marcus tested Adrian's allegiance by forcing him to watch Dorian get beaten with a metal pole. Adrian wanted to do something to stop his brother's pain, but he did nothing, knowing that any action against his father would only escalate the conflict.

Adrian had already seen where challenging Marcus would lead. One summer the family was crammed into the Travelall for a trip down the mountain to pick up supplies in Watsonville. It was a sweaty, grueling ride with no air-conditioning. Clouds of dust often engulfed the vehicle as they careened along the winding dirt roads, but Marcus usually rolled down the windows once they hit pavement.

This time, he didn't.

Adrian, who had been diagnosed with childhood asthma, had been inhaling dust all the way down and had been unable to take a deep breath for twenty minutes. When he couldn't take it anymore, he asked his mother to roll down the window.

"Don't do it," Marcus said to Elizabeth, who obeyed her husband.

"Mom, why don't you come back here and see how hot it is?" Adrian asked.

No one said a word, and the windows remained closed.

Ten minutes later, the family reached its destination— a used tire shop on the outskirts of the city. Everyone got out, gasping for fresh air, except Marcus.

"Adrian, don't go anywhere. Come back here," he said. "Now lie down on the front seat and lift your shirt."

Adrian complied, lying facedown on the seat. Marcus pulled out a thick tree branch, wet and heavy with sap, and beat his son with it.

Leaning in close to Adrian, he said, "Every time you scream or make a move, I'll start the count again."

Strike after strike, Adrian finally realized his father wasn't counting. His brothers and sisters waited outside, wandering around the stacks of old tires and rusty car parts, until Marcus finally stopped.

"Get up," he said as Adrian tried to pull his wounded

body into an upright position. "If you ever get smart with your mom again, I will bury you. I will kill you and put you in the ground."

"Okay, I'm sorry," Adrian said, regretting his misbehavior and leaning over to give his father a hug. "I love you, Dad."

Although the children loved their father, they were terrified by the prospect that he could murder one or more of them, and no outsider would ever be the wiser. They had already seen that he was capable of killing.

They were walking toward Rosemary's duplex in Fresno when they accidentally disturbed their uncle's dog, Charlie, who had been napping under a tree. Charlie, startled awake, snapped and lunged at Elizabeth, but because he was tied to a tree, the rope wouldn't let him get close enough to make contact. Without even flinching, Marcus reached down, whipped out his hunting knife, and stabbed Charlie seven times in the neck as the children looked on in horror. Marcus dug a hole at the foot of the tree, buried the dead dog, and went into the house without another word.

The children took note that the slaying seemed of little consequence to Marcus. One of them could be next.

IN EARLY 1996, sixteen-year-old Brandy ran away and moved back in with her mother, Rosemary. For two days after she disappeared, Elizabeth was frantic, sending the kids to search the hills for her missing niece. She begged Marcus to drive her down the mountain to call Rosemary, and when he finally did, she found out that Brandy was safe after all. When Elizabeth questioned Marcus about what had happened, he called a family meeting and announced that Brandy had run away because she was jealous. She'd wanted to be part of the plan to have babies for the Lord, and she'd grown angry when Marcus said it wasn't her time. Elizabeth, along with the Wesson girls and Elizabeth's other nieces, believed his story.

That fall, Marcus decided Dorian and Adrian should leave the family, too.

The boys, now in their early twenties, had been working for a couple of years at McDonald's in Santa Cruz. Without a car, they had to stay in town during the week, often having nowhere to sleep but the streets or the beach. On the weekends, they would walk or hitch a ride up the mountain, where eating meals with the family and sleeping on cots inside the tent made for a nice treat.

After a tough hike up the mountain one Saturday morning, Dorian and Adrian were shocked to find no one at their family's campsite. The tent was still up, but the supplies, food, and, most important, the people, were gone.

"I can't believe they left us," Adrian said.

For the first time, the oldest Wesson boys were completely on their own.

ABANDONING HIS SONS was just one of the adjustments to the family's living arrangements that Marcus decided to make now that there were some new additions.

Starting in September 1995, Marcus had had a daughter, Illabelle, with Kiani; a son, Jonathan, with Sofia; and a daughter, Aviv, with Ruby. After he left the boys behind, Marcus moved the family back to the duplex in Fresno for a few months until he was able to find them a new home: a boat called the *Sudan,* which was docked in Tomales Bay in Marin County.

Life on the boat ran relatively smoothly until 1998, when Ruby took off. She had run away before, but this time she was determined to stay gone. For the past few years, she had been Marcus's favorite, so he was noticeably agitated when she betrayed him. He followed her to Fresno, where he would stay for days, hoping she would have a change of heart.

While he was away, Marcus left Sofia in charge of her siblings and cousins. Sofia took her responsibilities seriously and kept watch for any potential problems. She knew to keep the kids quiet and hidden on the lower deck so outsiders didn't get suspicious and call police.

In early 1999, she saw a van marked "Progressive" repeatedly driving past the *Sudan*. Unaware that the van bore the name of an insurance company, Sofia had everyone worried that the driver was with the government or CPS and had come to break up the family. After weighing her options, Sofia decided it was time to put Marcus's suicide pact into motion and send herself and the children "to the Lord."

The only problem was, she wasn't familiar with Marcus's gun.

"I don't know how to load this," she said, searching through the manual. Following the instructions, Sofia fully loaded the clip with twelve bullets, one for each of them, then told the kids to write their half-page suicide notes.

"This is nobody's fault," fifteen-year-old Gypsy wrote. "We did this on our own. We do not want our spirits contaminated. This is want we wanted. No one is to blame."

Although Sofia thought Marcus would approve, she felt uneasy about carrying out the plan without checking with him. So she told Kiani and Rosie to row ashore and call

Marcus on a pay phone while she and the rest of the family prepared to meet the Lord. She and the girls washed and dressed the babies in clean outfits; then Gypsy and Lise changed into their nicest clothes, did the dishes, put away books, and wiped down the tables.

Twelve-year-old Lise took one last look at her favorite possession: a thick stack of celebrity photos she had cut out of magazines and kept hidden in her backpack. Marcus didn't allow the girls to read pop-culture publications, but the older girls had been sneaking old *TV Guides* out of the hotel conference center where they worked and giving them to Lise. She often dreamed of going to Hollywood someday to meet Tom Cruise, Brad Pitt, and her personal favorite, Chuck Norris.

"I can't leave them behind," Lise said to Gypsy. "I want to take them with me."

Gypsy watched Lise pick up a cutout, thinking she was going to look at it more closely. But to her surprise, Lise opened her mouth, shoved the paper in, and started chewing.

"Now they can be a part of me," Lise said, stuffing in a picture of Chuck Norris.

"Eat Nicolas Cage for me," Gypsy said, handing her one of her favorite stars.

Lise swallowed it down as well, and by the time she finished, she'd eaten a dozen of them.

The whole family gathered around the two small windows on the lower deck while they waited for Kiani and Rosie to return with a thumbs-up or a thumbs-down.

"I can see them," one of the children yelled.

Kiani and Rosie had their hands in the air, their thumbs

pointing down. Marcus had aborted the mission and sent word he would come talk to them that night.

He was beaming when he arrived around 9:00 P.M., and even happier when the oldest girls ushered him to a drawer to hand him the suicide notes.

"You are true followers of God," he said, smiling. "This was a true test for you."

Tears came to his eyes as he read them, one by one. They had never seen him so proud.

But the good feelings didn't last long. After Sofia reported that Lise had picked up the loaded gun, Marcus threatened to spank her.

"Don't you know that's dangerous?" he yelled.

Gypsy couldn't believe the irony. Earlier that day, they had been moments away from killing themselves with that same gun.

But Lise was more worried about her upset stomach than about getting a spanking. After having ingested all that glossy paper, she didn't feel very well.

"I can't believe I ate my favorite pictures," she whispered to Gypsy, frowning. "Now they're gone."

JUST TWO YEARS apart in age, Gypsy and Lise were practically inseparable. They sat together, did chores together, and even acted alike. Marcus had been too busy spending time with the girls he considered his wives to notice that Gypsy and Lise were avoiding him until one day he startled them in the hallway. He gave them a sour look, then brought up the incident that night in front of the others.

"Today I was walking by these two," he said, pointing at Gypsy and Lise, "and these idiots cowered. Gypsy never says hi to me anymore, and she's been hiding from me. Now Lise is following this idiot, and it's going to stop."

With that, he implemented a new rule for the pair, whom he often called the "black sheep" of the family. From that day forward, they had to give him an enthusiastic good-morning hug and kiss. If they didn't seem sincere, he would beat them. Marcus's two youngest daughters with Elizabeth went through the motions and feigned affection for the next couple of years, but he could clearly sense that he didn't have the same power over them as he did over the older girls. He was right. Gypsy, in particular, wished he'd just leave her alone. She wanted nothing to do with him.

Marcus gave up on her and Lise in 1999, when he decided to leave them on the *Sudan* with Serafino and three of the babies while he, Rosie, and her new infant, Ethan, moved with the rest of the family to Fresno to buy a house to fix up. Marcus visited his six children on the boat every so often, but for the most part, they lived by themselves for the next year.

AT FIRST, LIFE on the boat was tolerable for fifteen-year-old Gypsy. During the summer, the kids were allowed to be seen above deck. But when fall rolled around, they had to retreat below again so no outsider would report them for not being in school.

Sometimes Gypsy would sneak out in the dark, but it was so cold and damp that she felt like a prisoner. The sun hadn't hit her face in months, there was no television, and every day she endured the same routine: she cooked breakfast, bathed the kids and schooled them, washed dishes and cleaned, played with the kids, put them down for a nap, fed them dinner, washed dishes, and went to bed.

As sunlight shone through the two windows, Gypsy dreamed about being on land and going to a real school, in a real classroom. When dusk descended, she turned on their two small kerosene lamps so she could read. Elizabeth had bought dozens of books for the boat at the thrift store, including Nancy Drew and Hardy Boys mysteries, but Gypsy read her favorites, *Anne Frank: Diary of a Young Girl,* and *Little Women,* over and over.

During the rainy season, she was often awakened by water dripping on her head, her bedding soaked around her. She grew increasingly depressed, and although she often plotted schemes to sink the boat, she never followed through. She wanted to die, but she was too afraid of the pain to do anything about it. The only thing that kept her going was the knowledge that she was almost old enough to get a job somewhere.

At night, she would get on her knees and beg God to save her. "I will do whatever You want," she said, sobbing. "Please help me. I will never forget to pray to You."

When she turned seventeen, her prayers were answered. Marcus moved them all back to Fresno and sent Gypsy to join her sisters on the Radisson staff.

By this point, Marcus had kicked Sofia out of the house for having a relationship with a man she'd met at work. At least that was the story Marcus told the rest of them. In truth, he had stabbed her for wanting to leave the house, then kicked her out after she decided to stay.

After the Sofia incident, Marcus imposed even stricter

rules for the girls to follow at work: they were not to look at, talk to, or touch their male coworkers.

"What if someone asks us a question?"

"Don't answer and walk away," he instructed.

"May we say hello?"

"Absolutely not. Pretend like they are not there. You must ignore them at all times, or they may get the wrong impression and think you want a relationship with them."

Marcus charged his strong soldier Rosie, the loyal one who *never* disobeyed him, with enforcing the rules. Although he told all the girls to spy on one another, Rosie was the most regimented, watching her cousins' every move for the slightest hint of inappropriate behavior and reporting any violations to him each night.

"Is there anything I need to know about your sisters?" he asked one night.

"Well, Gypsy was carrying trays of food and one of the workers opened the door for her, and she walked through it," Rosie said.

Shaking his head in disapproval, Marcus said, "Thank you, Rosie."

He walked into the room with the girls, each one praying she hadn't done something wrong. Gypsy held her breath when he stopped in front of her.

"Gypsy, I need to see you in the room."

The door-holding incident flashed into her mind. Why had she walked through that door? She'd had a feeling Rosie was watching. It was just that she was carrying so many trays, and she couldn't put them down.

Marcus closed the door. "Is there anything you'd like to tell me?"

Please don't hit me.

She made her case, but he wasn't swayed.

"Next time, you walk to the other door and open it yourself," he said. "What's wrong with you?"

He struck her violently with the switch. Next time, she vowed to open her own door.

AS THE CHILDREN grew older, they confided secrets to one another and also to their diaries, a family habit the Wesson sisters and cousins practiced to record their personal thoughts. As the year approached 2000, their entries—especially Sebhrenah's—increasingly reflected Marcus's philosophies.

Sebhrenah used a white day planner as her diary, crossing out the "1996" date and writing in "2000." On the cover, she wrote in cursive "Sebhrenah April Wesson," then drew a dove.

> *The world tries to destroy God and all that he has made, but these are the last days, and things will get worse. They take away our children. . . . They take fathers out of their homes so he has no control. They give women power. They teach [women] not to be faithful and [not to be] loyal wives. This world is twisted. God needs to come very soon.*

> *The Lord says be fruitful and multiply. . . . The world does not like children, so they say teens cannot have babies. If they do, they're taken away and put in foster care, to be raised up without love and care. They take away the man, which is the head of the house, and put him away if he tries to control his family.*

Always keep to the Lord and stay with him always. He is the only way toward peace and redemption. . . . Trust in him in these last days, because there is no one else to turn to, only Jesus.

Although Sebhrenah mostly wrote of doomed times, she also penciled an occasional message of hope into the margin.

There is always light behind the clouds.

Now that Gypsy was working, she didn't spend as much time writing in her diary. When she did write, however, she never repeated Marcus's rhetoric. She may have agreed to follow his rules, but she still didn't agree with them.

Before she left for work each day, Gypsy pulled her long hair tightly into a bun, adhering to Marcus's rigid dress code.

"Get into the room," he demanded one morning, interrupting her.

"Why?"

"Do you wear your hair like that to work all the time?"

"Of course."

"Your cousin saw you and said you had your hair down."

"Well, sometimes I'll pull it down after work while I'm waiting to go home."

"Why would you do that?"

"Because it hurts. I get a headache."

Marcus yelled for his loyal niece, who came running.

"Rosie, does Gypsy ever look different at work?"

"Yes. I've seen her putting on makeup and fixing her hair."

Gypsy tried to protest.

"Shut up. You're lying. You're just showing off," Marcus said, raising his voice. "You want to show off? I'll shave off all your hair. Would you like that? I'll make you bald and see if you want to show off. Don't think I won't do it. Now get your ass over there and get the spoon."

Gypsy retrieved the dreaded metal utensil from its usual place.

"Hold out your hand."

Gypsy held out her right hand and rotated it to reveal her palm. She wasn't sure why, but the left hand always hurt more than the right.

He began to strike her, the sound of metal smacking against skin reverberating in her ears as she held her hand as steady as she could. If anyone moved during a beating, Marcus would start his count over.

By the thirty-sixth hit, Gypsy couldn't take it anymore and dropped her hand.

"Get out of here," he said, disgusted.

She was grateful that he'd stopped. Her right hand was numb and had already swelled to twice the size of her left. The holes in the spoon had pierced her skin, and the lacerations were bleeding.

She hurried to her catering job, where she had to lift heavy trays and serve hot plates. All through the night, the pain grew more intense until she could no longer hold back the tears.

"What's wrong, Gypsy?" a female coworker asked, concerned.

"Oh, nothing," Gypsy said, hiding her hand behind her back as she walked away. What would people think? She was eighteen years old and still being beaten by her father. It was horribly embarrassing.

The bruising set in the next day, and so did Gypsy's resolve to escape to a better life.

Sixteen

*B*etween my time on the morning show and at home in recovery, it had been more than six months since I'd worked the afternoon shift, which was just long enough to forget my old routine.

Now that it was February, the weather was getting warmer, so I opted for a brightly colored spring blazer and skirt to celebrate my return to work. My winter suits would remain untouched until the following year.

My hair had grown out a bit since my accident, and it hung just past my shoulders. I hoped Max wouldn't notice. Shortly after I'd moved to California, he'd sent me off to the salon to get a more "credible look." The stylist had turned my long, curly hair into a short, straight do, cropping off a chunk of my identity in the process. Now the length was somewhere in between—just like me.

Although I felt I was returning to my old self physically, every other part of me was evolving into a more understanding, more compassionate, and more sensitive person. As I walked through the doors of the bustling newsroom once again, I wondered how well my new outlook would last in the unforgiving world of journalism. More important, what would happen when everyone found out my secret?

It was one month shy of the Wesson trial, and newsrooms across the city were humming with anticipation. This was going to be one of those major stories that demanded a higher-than-usual level of coverage, which meant journalists' regular work schedules would be changed and vacation requests would be denied. On the upside, plenty of overtime would be approved.

Speculation was rampant among reporters and photographers about which of us would get to cover the big trial. A few weeks later, a dozen of us were waiting for Police Chief Jerry Dyer to take the podium at a news conference about gangs, when one of the TV photographers patted me on the shoulder.

"Good thing you're all healed up, Alysia," he said, tapping me a bit harder than necessary to prove his point. "I have a feeling this one's going to keep us on our toes."

I hadn't seen many of my media colleagues back in the field until now, so they were asking questions about my injuries and recovery. I still had the occasional postconcussive headache, but I was energized to be in the middle of the action again. It surprised me how much I'd missed the competition, the chase of the stories and the pressure of making deadline. The nightly adrenaline rush could be addictive, and I had forgotten how good it felt to work the evening news.

"I'm ready for it," I said, knocking on the wood podium in front of me.

"Thank God this one is in town," a male TV reporter said. "I'm sick of driving."

He and a few others in the room had spent months covering the recent Scott Peterson trial, three hours away in Redwood City, where the judge had moved it. The new venue was almost a hundred miles from Modesto, where Peterson had gotten so much negative publicity.

I hadn't covered any of the actual Peterson trial—or any other high-profile, out-of-town cases for that matter—but from what I'd heard, they were fun for the first few days, but they lost their appeal after weeks of living in hotel rooms, eating fast food, and commuting on weekends. Even though Marcus was being tried for twenty-one more charges than Peterson, legal experts expected the Wesson trial to be a similar six months in length.

Marcus faced a total of twenty-three charges: nine counts of first-degree murder and fourteen counts of raping and molesting his daughters and nieces. The DA's office had added a "multiple murders" special circumstance allegation to his charges, making him eligible for the death penalty if convicted of murder.

Three of the sex counts were for oral copulation and the continuous sexual abuse of Sofia; seven were for the rape and continuous sexual abuse of Kiani, Ruby, and Brandy; three were for the rape of Rosie and Sebhrenah, and one was for the continuous sexual abuse of Gypsy. Except for Brandy's, each rape charge corresponded to a child Marcus had fathered with each woman.

"Do you still keep in touch with the family, Alysia?" a male newspaper reporter asked.

"Just the girls," I said, not divulging how closely I'd stayed in touch with Elizabeth, Kiani, Rosie, and Gypsy.

"How do they feel about testifying against him?" another reporter asked.

"I'm not sure," I said honestly. "I know they're nervous."

Just then, the chief walked in. "Are we ready to get started?" he asked, watching us scatter to pick up our notebooks and turn on our cameras.

It was perfect timing. The chief had saved me from having to talk any more about my covert relationship with the Wessons.

THAT SAID, MY secret actually wasn't much of a secret anymore. As is typical in the news business, my trusted friends had had a hard time containing the juicy gossip, so word had already spread about my living situation. To my knowledge, though, my coworkers had at least kept it "in the family" at our station.

A couple of my coworkers alluded to it in casual conversation, and when I asked them what they meant, they said, "Everyone knows. It's no big deal."

Given the usual flow of information, I was fairly certain that "everyone" included my boss, although I figured he still didn't know the full story. I was nervous about his reaction, but I was also somewhat relieved that everything was finally out in the open.

I didn't think I'd lose my job over my actions. Worst case, I figured Max would simply take me off the story. I just wanted to get the conversation over with. I'd been thinking about it for months and had even played over possible exchanges in my mind. But with my changing jobs to the South Valley and then the car crash, it had just never seemed to be the right time. That said, I felt bad about letting ten months go by without saying anything.

Max was meeting with the reporters in line to cover the trial, and I was sitting at my desk, anxiously waiting for my turn. I was staring at a picture of Cosmo when my phone lit up. Max was calling me to his office.

I'd heard the plan: we were going to have a reporter in the courtroom from 8:00 A.M. to 5:00 P.M. to take notes on the proceedings and set up any necessary interviews; a second reporter would do a staggered afternoon shift to turn the information and video into a story for the evening news at 10:00 P.M.; and a third reporter would stay in the newsroom, ready to head to the courthouse or turn a new story that night by interviewing legal experts about issues raised in that day's testimony.

I nervously climbed the stairs to Max's office with no idea how, or even if, I would fit in to this plan.

"So, how are we going to handle this trial with *you*?" he said with veiled innuendo, as if he wanted me to know that he was already aware of my situation, a common power play in journalism.

I looked at him, but I still couldn't figure out what he was thinking, so I took a deep breath and started talking.

"As you may or may. not know, I have gotten close to the family over the last few months," I said matter-of-factly, trying to play down the significance of our relationship.

"Uh-huh."

"Very close, I guess you could say."

"Uh-huh."

So far, so good. He isn't jumping down my throat. At least not yet.

"And the Wesson girls have been in my apartment."

"Okay, let me suggest something," he said abruptly. In retrospect, I realized he'd wanted me to stop talking, but at the time, I felt this compulsion to explain myself, so I kept going.

"Well, I was going to talk to you about this earlier, but then I went to the South Valley and then my accident—" I said.

"What I was going to suggest," he said, interrupting in a fatherly tone, "is that you cover *only* the family aspect of the trial, and we have another reporter cover the hard-news angle. You know the family, they feel comfortable with you, and you think you can do a good job telling their side of things, right?"

"Absolutely," I said. "That sounds like a good solution."

By then I sensed that he didn't want to hear the whole story, and I was relieved that I didn't have to disclose anything more. It had been my decision alone to take in the family, after all, and I didn't want my boss or anyone else to get in trouble for my actions.

"Let me run this by a few people before we make a final decision," he said, referring, I assumed, to his superiors at the station.

"Understood," I said, nodding. He began nodding, too, as we looked at each other across the cluttered table. Max broke the silence with an uncharacteristic gesture to allay my tensions.

"Let me tell you a story," he said.

He proceeded to tell me about one of his former female reporters who kept getting tips about big stories long before anyone else in the market. She would also show up at crime scenes and get the exclusive scoop, giving the station an edge on the news each night.

I felt my heartbeat slowing and a wave of relief washing over me as Max said he thought she was a crackerjack reporter, so he wasn't surprised when she eventually went on to a bigger market. Years later, he found out why she was always first to the scene: her boyfriend was a cop and had been tipping her off. Max said it didn't change the fact that she was a good reporter because she never showed a bias, and it still gave the viewers great stories they couldn't find anywhere else.

"Now get back to work," he said, ushering me out the door. "And I'll get back to you about how we're going to handle this."

He didn't have to tell me twice. I darted out of the office with a new lightness in my step, confident everything was going to work out.

About a week later, Max told me to stay behind after a staff meeting in the upstairs conference room.

"Concerning what we talked about in regards to the Wesson trial, everything is all set," he said, looking at me over his glasses. "I spoke with the people I needed to speak with, and we're okay the way we planned to cover things."

"Great," I said, not knowing exactly what or who he was talking about. I also had no desire to find out. "So, I'll cover the family angle?"

"That's right," he said. "Now get back to work."

I laughed, jumped out of my seat once again, and dashed downstairs to my desk, ready for whatever came my way.

THE WESSON FAMILY, meanwhile, was not feeling very optimistic about the next few months. They knew the prosecutor planned to call them to testify but, never having attended a trial, they didn't know what that entailed. Elizabeth's only knowledge of the criminal court system came from watching reruns of *Perry Mason* and *Matlock*.

"It's nothing like it is on TV," I told her, explaining there would be no snappy dialogue, no witnesses bursting breathlessly through the courtroom doors at the last minute, and, unfortunately, no model-handsome lawyers.

"I know, Alysia," Elizabeth said. "It's just scary."

"What are they going to ask us?" Rosie asked.

"They'll ask you about your childhoods, and about the day it happened, and about Marcus . . . ," I said, pausing.

"What *about* Marcus?" Rosie asked.

"Mostly about the way he was. Like his religion and philosophy, the way he treated you guys, and, you know, *other stuff*." We all knew "other stuff" meant the uncomfortable details about their private sex lives with Marcus.

Rosie, who was sitting on the floor, dropped her head and picked at the carpet with her long nails. Elizabeth exhaled loudly, then twisted around in her chair to stare out the window. I could tell by their hopeless expressions that they were thinking about the "other stuff," and how difficult it would be to say these things out loud. It was one of the only subjects that we had never touched, and I certainly wasn't going to try to go there now.

"Do we have to answer every question?" Rosie asked, peeking up through her long black hair.

"I can't tell you what to do. I, personally, think it's best to tell the truth. You just have to get it over with and it will be done forever," I said, trying to minimize what I knew must seem to them like an insurmountable challenge.

In fact, I wasn't sure if they could get through the trial without breaking down, but I kept that fear to myself and tried to lighten the mood.

"Rosie, you look like the scary girl who crawls out of the TV in *The Ring* right now," I said.

She responded immediately by flipping her thick hair down over her face, then slowly clawing and slithering her way across the beige carpet toward me.

"Aaaahhhhh! Stop it!" I screamed, backing away from her reenactment, which was creepily spot-on. The three of us laughed heartily and managed to avoid thinking about the trial for the rest of the night.

THINGS TOOK A new twist in my apartment when the judge issued a gag order that prohibited every family member from talking about the case not only to the media but with one another as well. Up to this point, Marcus had dominated most of our conversations. Now we couldn't say a word about him. God only knew how long the trial would last.

My roommates and I sat down and carefully discussed our dilemma.

"Okay. So how are we going to do this?" I asked.

"I guess we'll walk around silent all day," Rosie said half-jokingly.

"So we can't say *anything* about my husband?" Elizabeth asked.

"Probably not. You want to be on the safe side. The last thing you guys need is to get arrested."

"You think your apartment is bugged?" Elizabeth asked, chuckling.

I knew she wasn't kidding. She was nothing if not a conspiracy theorist.

"Would you stop that? You got it from Marcus," I said. I covered my mouth. "Oops. I just talked about him. I hope the police who are listening didn't hear me."

"Wait, *you're* allowed to talk about the case, Alysia, just not us," pointed out Kiani, who was down visiting from Santa Cruz.

"That's true. I think I'm going to like this gag-order thing. I can say anything I want about Marcus and you guys can't say anything back. I can have some fun with this."

Rosie rolled her eyes at me. I jumped up to tickle her, and she ran into her bedroom to escape.

"Don't roll your eyes at me," I said, catching up to her and wrestling around. Nine times out of ten she overpowered me, so it was rare that I got the upper hand.

"Say mercy," I said, laughing. For obvious reasons, I never told her to say "uncle."

If the trial went the way I hoped, Rosie's uncle would never come near her—or anyone else for that matter—again.

"Mercy, mercy," she said, finally giving in.

Elizabeth wasn't in any mood to play. I walked out of the room to find her pacing up and down the hallway. I could have sworn she was searching for a bug, but I decided not to confront her about it. I considered the irony of all the time and energy Marcus had spent over the years looking for imaginary surveillance devices.

If only someone had *been watching Marcus, he would've been locked up years ago.*

GROWING UP, I could never sleep the night before the first day of school, and that's exactly what happened on the eve of the trial. I was a mix of nerves and excitement that I hadn't felt in years. Kiani got a ride down from Santa Cruz to Fresno because she, like several of her relatives, had been subpoenaed. Elizabeth had to be there, too, but Rosie was off the hook for a few days.

Kiani and Rosie went into the girls' room and sifted through their closet full of dark clothing. The few brightly colored shirts I had given them stood out, but the girls pushed those hangers aside on every pass.

"What are you going to wear, Kiani?" I asked from the floor near their closet, where I was sticking my finger inside Cosmo's cage to pet his sleeping head.

"I don't know," she said as she browsed through the hangers again.

Kiani took a shower, then sat Indian-style on the floor so Rosie could straighten her hair, with a brush in one hand and a flat iron in the other. When she clamped the iron down on Kiani's damp hair, a burst of steam rose to the ceiling.

"What is going on in there?" Elizabeth asked after seeing the steam drifting into the hallway, where she was doing laundry.

Kiani and Rosie were laughing too hard to respond. It may have been nervous laughter, but given the timing, I was happy to hear it. Kiani would be staying in my apartment off and on throughout the trial, and we were all glad to have her around again. I couldn't help but notice how much more they smiled these days. They spoke louder, and saw a future for themselves. I knew the next few months would be torture for them, but it would be nothing compared to what they'd been through already. I could only guess how hard it would be to sit on the witness stand across from Marcus and talk about the horrible things he'd done to them. I had no idea how I would handle watching them cry on the stand, trying to imagine how much pain and embarrassment they were feeling.

Even with all of the uncertainty concerning their future and mine, I knew I had done the right thing by taking them in. I had given up a lot over the past year, emotionally and financially, but I felt I was already stronger for it. I'd realized it was more important for me to act on my personal beliefs at times than to strictly adhere to the objective paradigms and guidelines of my profession.

Before I'd met the Wessons, I had interviewed Presidents Clinton and George W. Bush, taken college courses in England and Scotland, and partied with rock stars. With all that life experience, who would have thought that four women who had led such sheltered lives could teach me such important lessons?

Seventeen

Gypsy couldn't hold up her end of the solid mahogany coffin anymore. It was *so* heavy—too heavy for two teenage girls to carry—and she kept losing her grip on the slippery varnished wood.

"I need to put it down. I'm going to drop it," she said to Sebhrenah, lowering the casket onto the concrete steps that led to the basement of the big burned-out house they'd bought as a cheap fixer-upper on Cambridge Avenue in Fresno.

"No, don't stop!" yelled Sebhrenah, who was struggling to hold up the other side. But it was too late. The coffin was already so close to the ground that Gypsy couldn't pull it back up, so she put it down, trying not to send the casket and her sister tumbling down the narrow stairwell.

Sebhrenah was upset because Gypsy had already stopped ten times between the yellow school bus and the basement. Each time, Sebhrenah complained.

"What the hell is your problem?" she asked, losing her balance. "Pick it up and keep going. We're almost there."

"I don't even know why he's making us do this. Why does he want these stupid coffins anyway? We're never going to make them into something," Gypsy said. Marcus had said they would use the wood to build furniture for the boat, but she knew better.

She never would have had the guts to make such comments in front of her father, but he was over by the bus, issuing orders, so she felt safe mouthing off about him. Her insubordination, however, angered Sebhrenah even more.

The girls finally managed to get the coffin downstairs, where they stacked it on top of the one they'd already carried down. Gypsy headed back up with her to get a third, but Sebhrenah had other plans.

"There is no way I'm carrying another one with you," Sebhrenah said, panting from the exertion as she stomped up the stairs ahead of her little sister.

Before Gypsy knew it, Kiani was standing in front of the bus with a frustrated expression. "I guess *I'm* with *you* now. Let's go," she said, grabbing another coffin and waiting for Gypsy to lift the other end.

Kiani thought Gypsy and Lise had it easy—they'd been at home when the other girls had lugged all twelve coffins from the second floor of Dugovic's antique store into the elevator and out onto the bus earlier that day.

Marcus loved shopping at Dugovic's. He had seen the collection of hand-carved Indonesian caskets there about a year ago and just had to have them. But the caskets were too big to fit into Marcus's old van, so he asked the owner to deliver them to his house. She said no, they were too heavy; he'd have to find a way to transport them on his own. After a year had gone by, she told him she was tired of storing them and he needed to pick them up.

So Marcus came back in the school bus with his "muscle"—Kiani, Sebhrenah, Sofia, and Rosie. But once he led them upstairs, all he did was bark out orders, making them do the heavy lifting. The four girls couldn't fit all twelve caskets on the bus at once, so they had to make two trips.

This wasn't their first big purchase at Dugovic's. Over the years, the family had bought cannon replicas and a number of intricately carved dressers, armoires, and tables as well. From the time he was a teenager, Marcus had loved antiques. Although he mostly collected pieces that could have come from a junkyard, he also had an eye for nice things.

"Let's get these," Marcus would suggest to the girls, who always agreed and pulled out their checkbook to pay for the items.

The coffins, which averaged five hundred dollars apiece, were the Wessons' most extravagant acquisition yet. Still, they would lie dormant in the basement until the family moved from a shack behind the Cambridge Avenue house to the three-bedroom place they bought on Hammond Avenue in 2003.

The family was used to sleeping on the floor, but once they moved into the new Hammond Avenue house, Marcus had Ethan, Illabelle, Jonathan, and Aviv—four of the smallest children—sleep on top of the coffins. He arranged three of the caskets side by side like a makeshift bed frame, laid a blanket over them, then set a half-inch plank of plywood and some bedding on top of it. The other coffins were placed on their ends throughout the house, where the girls used them as dressers or for storage.

RELATIONS BETWEEN GYPSY and her father were growing increasingly strained—and with good reason. By 2002,

Gypsy was nearly nineteen, and she was the oldest daughter or cousin who had yet to marry or have a child with Marcus. Somehow, she had slipped through the cracks.

Until the family could find another place to live—which ultimately turned out to be the house on Hammond—Gypsy, Elizabeth, Serafino, and Marcus Jr. stayed with Janet, Almae's girlfriend. Marcus still carted Gypsy, Kiani, Sebhrenah, and Lise back and forth to stay on the *Sudan* when they had time off from work. Things went on that way for months.

"How old are you now, Gypsy?" Marcus asked.

"Nineteen," she said, sensing something ominous behind his question.

"I've been thinking. It's not fair to you that I've married the other girls and not you."

Gypsy cringed inside but forced herself to smile. Any other reaction would have made him suspicious.

"We'll have to do something about that," Marcus said.

Over the next few weeks, he dropped more hints, pressing up behind her and whispering, "I love you. I want to marry you."

She was sickened by his "loving" gestures, so she picked up every possible work shift she could, went in early and stayed late, trying to avoid—or at least delay—the impending "wedding." Unfortunately, Marcus didn't back down. Instead, he carved out some alone time on the boat with Gypsy.

"Gypsy, it's time," he said. "Go get the Bible."

Despite all her efforts, the dreaded moment had arrived. Gypsy walked into the bedroom and glared at the Bible with contempt.

How could something so good cause so much pain?

She grabbed the Bible, knowing Marcus would not consider their union "official" without it. Thinking quickly, she stuffed it underneath the sheets and blankets, then walked out, shrugging.

"The Bible is not in there. I think we took it to Fresno," she said.

Marcus shot her a skeptical glance, then smirked. "That's okay. There's another one right here," he said, reaching for a Bible he found nearby.

Gypsy wanted to scream out at God.

How could you do this to me? Why did you allow another Bible to surface?

Marcus performed the hand-on-the-Bible ceremony with a speech full of gibberish, but Gypsy didn't hear a word of it; her hateful thoughts were drowning out his rhetoric.

Even though God had failed her, she continued to ask Him not to let Marcus consummate their "marriage."

Marcus had already had sex with the other girls, including her younger sister Lise. Although he had been molesting Gypsy since she was a little girl, Gypsy had somehow managed to avoid intercourse. She knew she'd been lucky. She also knew that she couldn't emotionally survive sex with her father. Unlike her sisters and cousins, she was very much aware of how wrong it was. She just didn't know why. Maybe it was because she read more books and had gone to work earlier than her older sisters had. Or maybe it was because she had a more cynical and insightful personality than the others.

A few days after the ceremony, Marcus got Gypsy alone again. Not liking the look in his eyes, she instinctively pressed her thighs together. Her father leaned over and tried to pry her trembling knees open, explaining his intention to have sex with her.

This time, Gypsy couldn't hide her emotion as heavy tears rolled down her cheeks.

Marcus looked at her indignantly. "What's wrong with you?" he asked, continuing to pull at her legs. But then something in him gave way and he stopped fighting her. "Get out! Send Rosie in here."

Gypsy numbly scooted off the bed, still crying. "He wants you, Rosie," she said.

Rosie, who was in the living room with the other girls, walked slowly into the room and closed the door behind her.

The next day, Marcus had a talk with his defiant daughter.

"Gypsy, there are going to be some changes around here. You are quitting your job, and I'm taking you back to the *Sudan*. You are letting yourself be negatively influenced, and you need to get back to what's right."

He told her he would wait for her in the car while she packed her clothes in the apartment. But Gypsy was done following his orders. She knew if he got her back onto the boat, she would never get off it again. She couldn't take one more day of the insults, the molestation, and the beatings from the man who dictated her every move.

Brandy, Sofia, and Ruby had already broken free from his manipulative hold and started new lives elsewhere.

Now it was her turn.

Gypsy could hear the blood pulsing inside her head as Marcus honked his horn, clearly growing impatient with her. She paced around the room, psyching herself up to finally run away. She could do it. She had to do it.

He honked again—twice this time. She knew he was angry that she was making him wait. It was now or never.

Quietly, she opened the front door of the second-floor apartment and tiptoed as fast as she could down the concrete stairs. She was wearing her work uniform, which consisted of a black skirt and white tuxedo shirt with a black bow tie and vest, and she was carrying her nearly empty purse. Nothing else.

Escaping seemed like an impossible task, but it was one she was willing to die trying to achieve. Marcus was parked on the opposite side of the complex; however, she peeked around the corner anyway, just to make sure he couldn't see her. The coast was clear.

He was honking repeatedly now, her heartbeat speeding up with each blast. It wouldn't be long before Marcus realized she was no longer in the apartment. Where could she hide?

She immediately thought of the laundry room in the white and green apartment building next door, so she started walking as briskly as she could in that direction, trying not to draw any undue attention. She could hear that he was still in the car, yet somehow it felt like he was right behind her. She could practically feel him breathing down her neck, and she was terrified of what would happen if he caught her.

Reaching her destination, Gypsy hurried into the closet-size room. The door always stayed open, so she left it cracked to keep him from getting suspicious and squeezed into the narrow opening between the washer and dryer. She took a deep breath of temporary relief, inhaling the lingering aroma of detergent and dryer sheets.

The sound of Marcus's horn echoed in the small room, sending a vibration through the two metal machines hugging Gypsy's sides and the wall pressing against her back. Then the honking suddenly stopped.

It was completely silent. Too silent. The stream of thoughts blaring through her head now seemed so loud that Gypsy was certain Marcus could hear them. Marcus had always claimed that he had ESP and that God told him what everyone was thinking. Gypsy held her breath for long intervals, hoping to squelch her booming thoughts.

Over the years, she'd prayed for many things she didn't believe in, things for which Marcus had ordered her to pray. But that morning, she was on her own. She asked God not to lead Marcus to her cramped corner.

The next hour would be critical. She chewed on her nails until her fingers were almost bleeding, hoping to make the time pass more quickly. Although she didn't know Marcus was circling the apartment complex looking for her, she could feel his presence nearby.

If she could outwait her father, she hoped he would give up and go away. But it wasn't the waiting that was difficult— she would rather spend the rest of her life in that corner than live another day with him. It was the wondering.

If she could really escape him, what would become of the other children? What would she do without Lise? She wished Lise and all the little ones could come with her, but she knew that would never happen. Because Lise didn't work, she had no opportunity to escape. And the little ones? Well, they were too small to understand what was in store for them. Maybe someday, she could go back and set them free, too.

With each passing minute, Gypsy grew more confident that Marcus wasn't going to find her. For the first time she could remember, she felt safe.

Gypsy peered outside. Seeing no one, she let her eyes adjust to the bright sunlight for a minute, then ran back to Janet's and asked her to drive to the Radisson so Gypsy could pick up her paycheck. She lay down in Janet's backseat on the trip over, still worried Marcus would spot her.

She cashed her check, looked down at the few hundred dollars in her hand, and felt guilty. It was Friday, and the kids were at home waiting for their weekly ice cream and cookies. She was the family's only source of income, and without the money she was holding, Lise and the others wouldn't get any ice cream. She couldn't let that happen.

Gypsy pulled forty dollars out and put the rest in an envelope, which she placed under the washing machine that had sheltered her earlier that day. She asked Janet to call Elizabeth and tell her where to find the money. This was the first time Gypsy hadn't given her father every cent of her earnings.

She stayed in a thirty-five-dollar-per-night motel on the south side of town and cried the entire night. She knew he would come for her eventually. It was just a question of when.

AFTER THE MOTEL, Gypsy moved in rent-free with some female coworkers she had befriended. Two months later, she found a more permanent home back at Janet's apartment.

Marcus showed up at the Radisson the following month, just as she'd suspected, to reclaim what he felt belonged to him.

Gypsy knew she shouldn't get in a car with him or he might make her pay, stabbing her like he had Sofia. But when he came to collect Gypsy at work, he brought Rosie and Sebhrenah as backup, sending them inside to fetch her. It was so cruel. She missed the girls so much it hurt. Still, when she saw him sitting in his car in front of the hotel, gesturing for her to get into the front seat next to him, Gypsy was determined not to make the same mistake her cousin had.

"Get in," Marcus said. "We need to talk."

Until recently, she'd always done what he told her. Only this time, she felt it would be safer to climb in the backseat, where she sat in between the other two girls. Rosie's face didn't register much emotion, but Sebhrenah looked really sad. Gypsy could feel Sebhrenah's disappointment in her for leaving the family.

Marcus didn't talk much as he drove them to the Hammond house. After pulling into the driveway, he began to deliver a contrived speech, but Gypsy couldn't process the words. Over the years, she'd gotten good at drifting in and out while looking interested during his hours-long sermons.

". . . So God is telling me I need to get all my flock together," he was saying. "I'm going to go get Ruby and Sofia back. I am the shepherd, and I've got to find my sheep. We've got to get back to what's right, get back to the Lord. They will come back to us, just like the prodigal son, and you're going to come back, too. Satan is picking up the family, bit by bit, and I've got to do whatever it takes to get it back together. Are you ready to come home now?"

Gypsy wondered if he was actually delusional enough to

think that one lecture could erase nearly twenty years of abuse.

"Gypsy, don't you miss the babies?" he asked.

There he went, preying on her biggest weakness. He must have known Gypsy would feel guilty for leaving the others behind. Of course she wanted nothing more than to see the kids again, if only to say good-bye properly. So that was what she decided to do. She'd see them one last time, then leave the past behind.

"Yeah, I do miss them," she said. "I miss them a lot."

She was ready to head into the house when Marcus turned his huge frame around and, through his thick dread-locks, stared piercingly into her eyes.

"First, Gypsy, I need to know. Are you still willing to die for the Lord?"

She had answered that question thousands of times over the years, always with an emphatic yes. But today was different.

She knew he'd chased after Sofia and Ruby when they ran away, and had gotten a yes from them in answer to this same question. They may have been ready to die, but Gypsy wasn't. And she wasn't going to fold to his whims today. She just wasn't.

"No, I'm not," she declared. "I want to *live* for the Lord. Only God can decide when we die. We shouldn't decide for ourselves."

Marcus gasped. But Gypsy didn't break eye contact with him. In her peripheral vision, she could see Rosie and Sebhrenah shaking their heads, looking down at their laps.

The empowering feeling of standing up to her father was painfully short-lived.

"What did you say?" he screamed.

Gypsy blinked, realizing he had no intention of letting her see the kids. The yelling escalated into insults. She regretted ever getting into that car.

Her cell phone rang, but Marcus barely missed a beat of his tirade. When her phone rang a second time, he wasn't as forgiving.

"Who keeps calling you?" he asked testily. "Sebhrenah, take her phone and turn it off."

Sebhrenah snatched the phone away and, with it, Gypsy's chance to call a coworker—or anyone else—for help. Marcus was telling her that he was going to tie her to the bed until she came around, but she knew that wouldn't be the worst of it. In his mind, defiance was a cardinal sin, and she had just committed it. Gypsy wondered if she should jump out the window. How else could she get out of this alive?

She finally figured out what to do: She crossed her fingers behind her back and tried to cross her toes inside her work shoes.

"Dad?" she interrupted. "I want to move home. I realize I was wrong, and I want to come back."

Marcus seemed skeptical. "Why should I believe you?"

"Because you are right," she lied. "I lost my way and I miss my family."

As they talked some more, Gypsy could feel Marcus giving in.

"Can I go back to work to get my things first?"

"You don't need to go back there! You can't work there anymore. It's a bad influence."

She, too, could sense people's weaknesses, so she homed

in on the family's financial difficulties. "I need to get my purse," she said. "I left it there."

Marcus went silent for a moment, deep in thought. He looked first at Rosie, then at Sebhrenah.

"You know what? I'm going to let your sisters decide your fate. Girls, do you think Gypsy is being honest? Should we let her go back to work?"

Gypsy prayed they had fallen for her story.

"I think she's lying," Rosie said. "You shouldn't let her go."

It was harder for Sebhrenah to sell her sister out. "I don't think she's telling the truth," she said reluctantly.

"You know what I'm going to do," Marcus said to Gypsy. "I'm going to try something different. I'm going to take you back to work and trust you. I know you will do the right thing."

There must be a catch.

Gypsy tried not to let her renewed hope show in her face. "Okay," she said quietly. "I mean what I said."

Marcus turned on the engine and backed out of the driveway. Gypsy took one last look at the house and knew she'd never go inside. She was on pins and needles all the way back to work, wondering if Lise and the rest of her siblings had been aware that she'd been right outside.

"Finish your shift and I'll pick you up at midnight," Marcus said as he pulled up to the hotel. "Be here waiting and don't talk to anyone."

Gypsy didn't like the look on his face. She recognized that look.

"Oh, and Gypsy?"

"Yeah?"

"You need to come over here and give me a kiss. Just so I can *feel* that you're telling the truth."

Gypsy had promised herself that she would never touch him again, so it took everything she had to pull it off. But she knew it would be the last time. She was kissing her abuser good-bye.

Then she had to face her sisters. She hugged Rosie and tried not to look her in the eye. Next, she hugged Sebhrenah, who cried as she held Gypsy tight.

"Please come back," Sebhrenah pleaded.

"I will, Bhrenah," Gypsy said. "I promise. I love you."

Gypsy backed away and closed the car door behind her.

As Marcus drove off with his two somber passengers, Gypsy dropped her poker face. She burst through the glass doors, ran hysterically down the hotel hallway, checked in with her supervisor, and then took off, escaping from Marcus once again.

Against all odds, she'd made it out in one piece. Freedom tasted sweet.

Later, that moment would become searingly bittersweet. At the time, she'd had no idea that would be the last time she would see Sebhrenah alive.

Eighteen

I t was unusually hazy the morning of March 3, 2005, when fifty people were lined up waiting to get into the Fresno County courthouse on Van Ness Avenue. Wanting to avoid the line, I walked around the crowd and ducked in the side door. Technically, it was the attorneys' entrance, but the security guards let media in, too.

One of the guards, whom I'd met during Marcus's preliminary hearing, held out a cup for my keys and cell phone so I could walk through the X-ray machine.

"Good morning, Alysia. It's the big day today, huh?"

"It is," I said, sliding my shiny new laptop and notepad through the scanner. "Aren't you going to get sick of hanging out with us every day?"

"No way," another guard said, yelling from behind the X-ray machine. "This is the most excitement this place has seen in a long time."

The courthouse had two elevator cars that always seemed to take forever. I waited along with the twenty other impatient people gathered in the lobby, where we stared up at the lighted sign indicating where the elevators had stopped. Only half of us were going to fit at a time, and when the first car came, I made sure to cram my way in.

"Five, please," I said, after realizing I couldn't reach the numbers. The mix of freshly applied musky colognes and floral perfumes made my eyes water, and when the double doors opened, I couldn't push my way out fast enough.

Scooting around the corner into the main hallway, I was stalled again by a large group gathered in front of the courtroom. Other than the verdict, the opening statements drew the most media during a trial. I saw at least a dozen video and still cameras, with at least twice as many reporters and photographers. I assumed some were from out of town because I didn't recognize them.

As soon as a tall, skinny bailiff pushed through the crowd and unlocked the courtroom, I headed straight for the defense table and sat as close as I could—on the wooden pew behind it. I opened my crisp new notebook and wrote "WESSON TRIAL: Day One."

The rectangular courtroom was split by a dark wooden divider a couple of feet high, with a swinging door that squeaked each time someone walked through it. The judge, attorneys, clerk, court reporter, and defendant sat on one side, while the spectators and media sat on the other, known as the gallery. On that day, the gallery was filled mostly with media and a few people who looked like Elizabeth's relatives.

Elizabeth and Kiani were escorted into the room, both of them hiding their faces, but they were told to come back the day the prosecution was ready to call them to testify. As witnesses, they weren't allowed to watch the proceedings.

Two bailiffs opened the door behind the judge's seat, peeking both ways before escorting a shackled Marcus Wesson toward us. Wearing glasses, black pants, and a black, button-up shirt with short sleeves, he had lost some weight since I'd last seen him. He kept coming and coming until he was closer to me than he'd ever been.

As always, he searched the crowd before turning around, then sat in the wooden chair right in front of me so that I was looking at the back of his massive head. If I'd stood up and leaned over the divider, I could have touched him. I couldn't take my eyes off his dreadlocks, which were the most disgusting thing I'd ever seen. After a year in jail, they were a huge, matted mess that draped down past his waist and nearly rested on the carpet. He could have hidden an arsenal in those things, or hanged himself with them.

Why hasn't the jail shaved them off?

I couldn't imagine touching them, all caked with dirt and who knew what else. The girls told me they'd always been his personal groomers, trying to make sure his hair was neat and in order, but they could do only so much. He'd just say the word, and they would swarm around him to scratch his scalp or armpits, or to shampoo his dreadlocks. No matter what, their fingernails would be black with grime. In the last few years, Rosie had taken over the task of tidying his hair each day. She would meticulously separate the clumps, then secure them into a low-hanging ponytail, just as she had done the day of the murders.

Elizabeth told me that during the 1960s, when most boys were growing their hair long, Marcus's father regularly shaved his young son's head, which caused him to stand out at school. In 1984, a decade into Elizabeth's marriage to Marcus, he told her he'd gotten a message from above about his hair. "The Lord has told me to grow dreadlocks," he said.

He started growing his hair out that day, and by the looks of it, he hadn't cut it since.

I noticed that one of his thickest dreads had almost split into two partway down, with only a skinny clump of gray knots holding it together. The urge to grab it and yank almost overpowered me, and I couldn't stop staring at the giant rat tail. The guard who'd let us into the courtroom saw me and chuckled.

"Why can't they cut off that hair in jail?" I whispered to him.

"It's a civil rights thing, I guess," he whispered back. "He wants to keep his hair long, so if we cut it and then they find him innocent, he could sue us."

We both rolled our eyes.

Like anyone would find him innocent. Wait! Could someone really find him innocent?

Although a trial verdict was never a foregone conclusion, this case seemed different. I knew the gist of the testimony the jurors were about to hear, and I couldn't imagine them letting Marcus loose afterward. I definitely felt he was guilty, but I would never reveal that opinion or let it color my stories.

"All rise," the bailiff called out.

Judge R. L. Putnam walked in, and when he sat down, so did the rest of us. Everyone was in position. The jury, culled from a pool of 540 potential panelists, was sitting nervously in its box; the attorneys were ready for battle at their tables; and we reporters and photographers had our pens and cameras on point. I checked the droopy dreadlock. It, too, was standing at attention.

* * *

JUDGE PUTNAM HAD taken over the case and would preside over both phases of the trial. He reminded me of Alan Alda. He was tall and lanky, with fine gray hair. But unlike the characters Alda typically played, Putnam was soft-spoken and reserved, speaking only when necessary. He seemed nonplussed during most of the trial, and retired a couple of years later.

Prosecutor Lisa Gamoian, chief of the district attorney's homicide division, was quite the opposite. She was tightly wound and always seemed to be in motion. She looked to be in her forties, wore shoulder-length dark hair, glasses, and conservative skirts or pant suits, with dark lipstick that faded as the day went on.

She had a strong case, but for a prosecutor, she seemed to be more on the defensive much of the time. Many of her witnesses were not very cooperative or expressing the answers she wanted, so she paced the courtroom, seemingly agitated, and appeared increasingly tired as the trial progressed.

Proactively taking the wind out of the defense's argument, Gamoian told the jury that Marcus probably wasn't the one who actually pulled the trigger that day. But, citing the suicide pact he'd made with his children, she said he was responsible for the murders nonetheless. To convict him under the theory of aiding and abetting, she had to prove only that Marcus had "instigated, promoted, or encouraged" the killings.

This wasn't news to me, because I knew that investigators had found no fingerprints on the gun, and no gunshot residue on Marcus or any of the victims but Sebhrenah. Marcus was the only person who knew for sure what had happened, and he wasn't talking. But it was widely believed that Sebhrenah had pulled the trigger, because they'd also found her DNA on the gun. If it *was* Sebhrenah, she must have lined up her brothers, sisters, and her own son, Marshey, then shot them one by one.

What must that have been like for her, killing the child she wanted so much? Could she really have done it?

Even after covering the case for a year, I was still confused by the Wesson family tree. Gamoian apparently guessed it would be difficult for jurors to follow as well, because she produced a diagram with photos to show the family ties. For the seven youngest victims, she used generic cutout figures—blue for the three boys and pink for the four girls.

For the older girls, she used stern, straight-faced photos from their DMV identification cards, but they looked nothing like the smiling faces I had seen in my apartment and in family photos. I felt bad that these emotionless photos were the images the jury would have of them, but the defense team's comments about Sebhrenah being fascinated by guns made her look even worse.

Marcus's two attorneys from the public defender's office seemed to work well as a team, often consulting each other before speaking. Ralph Torres was fortyish, a sharp dresser with neatly groomed, thick black hair who always wore sunglasses outside the courtroom and strode through the hallways with confidence. His much taller cocounsel, Pete Jones, was more conservative, and the more experienced of the two. He didn't say much during the guilt phase but sat at the defense table every day, conferring with Torres and making objections. Marcus sat between the two men, who always wore suits and ties.

The defense had already lost its pretrial motion arguing for a change of venue. Stuck with a local jury that had been exposed to all kinds of negative publicity about his client, Torres went all out to lay blame for the murders solely on Sebhrenah.

He said the physical evidence showed that she had killed her eight siblings in the back bedroom, then turned the gun on herself. He said the evidence also proved that Marcus was not in the room when the first seven children were killed, referring to the coroner's estimate of time of death and an audiotape recorded by one of the relatives trying to rescue Jonathan and Aviv.

Torres said the tape showed Marcus had been calmly trying to quell the custody dispute and even *wanted* police intervention, saying, "This is a kidnapping. The police should be here already. . . . Police [are supposed] to protect us from being like idiots."

After the murders, Torres said, seven of Marcus's adult children denied the existence of an official suicide plan and dismissed any such thing as being part of their father's typical ramblings. Torres did not dispute the sex charges, however, conceding that Marcus was a polygamist who practiced incest.

"He was a flawed man who expressed it with deviant behavior," he said. "But he is a deeply religious man, a zealot, who believes in the Lord, Jesus Christ."

Later, Torres acknowledged that Marcus "had his own way of raising his children."

That's one way to put it.

One day down, who knew how many more to go.

* * *

ON THE DRIVE home that night, I didn't blast my car radio as I normally did. Instead, I mentally explored the possibility of Marcus getting off. I knew the girls secretly believed he would get out someday, but I felt quite sure he would be behind bars for at least a century on the sex charges alone, given that the DNA evidence proved he'd had children with his daughters and nieces. I relaxed a little.

The girls were waiting up when I got home. We all said hello, but nothing else. I was uncomfortable. They seemed uncomfortable and sad. Even Cosmo was hiding. I tried to use him to break the tension where the elephant was dancing and trumpeting about.

"How was your day?" Elizabeth asked.

"Fine. Yours?"

They all just nodded at me, so I kept talking.

"The weather was a little strange today. We're allowed to talk about the weather, you know," I said, trying to make them laugh.

How are they going to make it through their testimony?

I could tell by the prosecutor's opening statement that she wasn't going to take it easy on them. She didn't seem to tolerate any pity toward Marcus, and the girls were still relentlessly defending him. I couldn't imagine how terrified they were to take the stand. In all the criminal trials I had covered, this was the first time I'd witnessed the emotional toll the legal process could take on a family.

IT SEEMED LIKE bad timing all around, but the one-year anniversary of the murders was only a few days away. Coincidentally, however, a much happier day was also on the horizon: Gypsy's due date.

Of all the Wesson women, Gypsy was having the most stressful month. Not only was she dealing with the first stages of the trial and the last stages of pregnancy but she was also taking final exams to finish her high school diploma.

Gypsy had signed up for classes right after she'd run away from home. The counselor had told her she could get a GED in less than a year, but once she'd enrolled, another student told her she could get a diploma instead. Gypsy had been dreaming about earning a diploma since she was a little girl. To her, it seemed like the Holy Grail. So she went back to her counselor.

"I'd like to try for my diploma," she said with determination.

"Gypsy, I don't recommend that," he replied, adding that it could take up to four years if she went part-time. "I'd advise you to get your GED."

But she didn't plan to go part-time. She planned to throw herself into school and finish as soon as possible. "No, I've thought a lot about it. I really want a diploma."

"Are you sure you're willing to make that kind of commitment?"

"Yes, I'm sure. Please sign me up."

All those dreams she'd had about the day she would be in a real school, with real teachers and real lessons, had finally come true.

On her first day, she took an empty seat in the back of the classroom and sat upright with anticipation. Gypsy looked at the desk next to hers and imagined Lise sitting there, thinking how much fun the two of them would have had together. She set her mind on graduating for Lise and

Sebhrenah and the Wesson kids who would never have a chance. It was the only way she could see to get revenge against her father.

Taking pride in every assignment, she took diligent notes and studied hard for each test. Her teachers were impressed with her eagerness to learn and wondered why such a bright, motivated young woman didn't have a diploma. When the news about the murders broke, they learned the reason.

Gypsy missed two weeks of class, but other than a few absences necessitated by her court appearances, she stuck to her schedule. After just eighteen months, Gypsy had earned enough credits to get her diploma. She was scheduled to graduate that June.

As HER DUE date approached, Gypsy was worried that her delivery would fall on the same date as the murders. "I'm not having my baby on March twelfth," she said emphatically.

"Maybe it's a sign or something," I said, preparing her for the possibility. "Like something we can positively associate with the day."

"There will never be anything good about that day, Alycia "

"Let's not worry about it right now. Have you thought of her name yet?"

"I'm still not sure," she said. "I guess it will just come to me."

ON THE NIGHT before the one-year anniversary, Elizabeth, Kiani, and Rosie were crying. Elizabeth was in her usual spot on the couch, and the girls were in their bedroom. I had the next two days off, but I almost wished I had to work so they could have some privacy to grieve. Then again, I didn't want them to be alone.

Trying to get their minds off their dead children, I got them all into the living room, where I showed movie after movie and told lighthearted stories. They stopped crying for a little while, but after we retired to our bedrooms, around 2:00 A.M., I could hear them sobbing again.

The next morning, we sat silently in the living room. The TV, which Elizabeth always kept on, was black and cold. The only noise in the room was the crackling and popping of the bowls of cereal no one was eating.

"Why don't I go get some flowers today and we can place them at the house and have a little memorial service?" I asked.

They all nodded. We decided to wait until after dark, when we figured the reporters would have left.

JUST BEFORE SUNDOWN, I packed my car full of Wessons and drove them over to the house on Hammond Avenue. Reporters and photographers were still hanging around out front, so I pulled into the burger place behind the house. I stayed in the car while the Wessons snuck into the backyard, where they hoped none of the reporters would see them.

I watched in my rearview mirror as they solemnly placed nine long-stemmed red roses at the side of the house under a pine tree, where another family member had lit nine tall prayer candles. The girls hugged and cried while I bowed my head and said a silent prayer. It reminded me of the funerals, only this time the mourners were coming home with me.

After struggling for the right words to say, I decided it was best to say nothing. Everyone cried all the way home. We needed a diversion in a major way. I hoped that Gypsy's new baby would provide that for us.

Gypsy went into labor five days later, on St. Patrick's Day. The Wessons rushed to the hospital, but I was in Modesto, covering a news conference right after the Peterson trial, so Kiani called me every half hour or so to update me on Gypsy's status. I waited with bated breath for news of the birth—how big the baby was and what she looked like. I knew she would be a blessing for the family. A brand-new beginning.

Kiani called with the news that Gypsy had finally delivered a cute and healthy baby girl. I had never really wanted children, but that day, I was overcome with joy and happiness. I couldn't wait to meet her.

I had the next day off, and my boyfriend, Juan, had sent me green roses for St. Patrick's Day, so I grabbed a handful, drove to the hospital, and followed the signs to the maternity ward. Elizabeth, Rosie, and Kiani greeted me in the hallway, smiling and looking happier than I'd seen them in weeks.

I knew this would help them.

The three women led me into the room like proud parents. I realized this was the first nonincestuous baby from a Wesson daughter, and the thought made me hug Gypsy even tighter.

Thank God he will never be near this child.

"Congratulations," I said with a grin. "Aaaw, is that her?"

I walked toward the window, where the baby was lying in a bassinet, wrapped in a soft pink blanket. She had dark, wavy hair, bright pink, heart-shaped lips, and long black eyelashes. She was perfect. I picked her up and nestled her against my shoulder. She smelled sweet as I laid her warm head in the crook of my neck.

"I love her," I said.

I counted her fingers and toes, then examined her hospital bracelet. I couldn't believe what I was reading. I felt the pinch in my nose as tears came to my eyes.

"Her name is . . . really?" I asked.

"We named her after you," Rosie said. "Welcome Baby Alysia into the world."

The gesture touched me in a way I had never felt before. I saw hope in the new life before me; I felt honored and proud to be a part of it.

"Hi, Alysia," I said, cooing. "We are going to make sure you have such a great life, baby."

Nineteen

One by one, the prosecution's witnesses climbed the steps into the witness stand, starting with two of the Fresno police officers who had responded the day of the murders.

At first, Judge Putnam hesitantly allowed us to bring laptops into the courtroom to take notes, but that didn't last long. The sound of me and the other reporters pounding on our keyboards sent the elderly judge into a frenzy, so he snapped at us to ditch the computers. From Sofia's testimony onward, I stuck to a pen and paper, scribbling as fast as I could.

Sofia, who was on the stand for five days, smiled while answering some of the questions posed by Ralph Torres, Marcus's attorney. When asked about her cousin Sebhrenah's obsession with guns, Sofia said Sebhrenah was her best friend and liked to collect toy guns. She also said that the two of them used to play hunting games when the family lived in the Santa Cruz Mountains, and that Marcus liked to show the family "army movies."

But Sofia's voice cracked and her mouth seemed dry as she recalled the twisted details of her childhood and teenage years with Marcus, her brown skin growing flushed with emotion at times, pale at others. One of her stories made my temperature rise, too, and it felt like hives were forming down the back of my neck.

The day she told Marcus she wanted to leave the family, Sofia said, he offered to drive her back to Fresno. On the way there, he pulled over to the side of the road and asked if she was still ready to go to the Lord. She said yes; then, as Marcus leaned in to hug her, she was surprised to feel a sudden and sharp pain in her chest. When she pulled back, she realized that he had stabbed her with the hunting knife he always wore on his ankle.

Hearing this, one of the jurors let out a surprised yelp. I almost did the same thing when Sofia pulled down her shirt to expose the inch-long scar that his knife had left. Two of the jurors began to cry as Sofia described how Marcus beat one-month-old Jonathan until his legs bled. I searched the side of Marcus's face for expression and saw none.

How can this not faze him?

THAT WAS NOT the case once Ruby took the stand a week later, when Marcus repeatedly wiped away tears as she answered questions about their "marriage" and the first time they had intercourse. Elizabeth and Gypsy had always told me that he'd been partial to Ruby, and so far, her testimony seemed to be affecting him the most. When Ruby outlined the severe beatings he gave her after she ran away the first time, Marcus cried again and shook his head.

Ruby testified that Marcus had the family watch television news reports about the protracted battle between federal agents and the Branch Davidian leader David Koresh, a polygamist who died with nearly eighty of his followers during the fifty-one-day siege in Waco, Texas, in 1993.

Marcus, she testified, told them that he related to Koresh. "This is how the world is attacking God's people. This man is just like me," she quoted him as saying. "He is making children for the Lord. That's what we should be doing, making children for the Lord."

After that, Ruby explained, she and her sisters and cousins all agreed to have one baby each with Marcus. Later, after she and Sofia left the house and got married, they came back to get their children because they no longer wanted Marcus to raise them. They were also worried that the kids were not getting enough to eat or a proper education.

After hearing about Sofia's and Ruby's experiences, I applauded them for being so honest and brave on the stand. I hoped that, when all of this was over, they could reunite with the other side of the family. It seemed obvious how much they still cared.

WAKING UP ON March 23, I could hear the shower running as Rosie got ready for her first day in court. I stayed in bed, listening to her turn on the blow dryer, then fumble through her makeup bag. I contemplated going out to see how she was doing, but I got as far as my bedroom door before deciding against it and crawling back under the covers.

As I got ready for work a couple of hours later, I thought about what Rosie must be going through that very minute just a few miles away. I wouldn't get to see for myself because I had to work on another story.

I hope she's okay.

It was a good thing I wasn't in court for Rosie's testimony, because I was fairly sure I wouldn't have been able to handle it. There are some people who need a shoulder to lean on, and there are people like Rosie. She had issues like everyone else, but she didn't feel the need to share them and she certainly didn't want anyone's sympathy. Of all the Wessons I'd met, I could relate to Rosie the most.

In a way, I respected her toughness. I had once fiercely defended a Russian gymnastics coach of mine much as she stuck up for Marcus. My coach trained four or five of us, ranging in age from eight to fourteen, putting us through a seven-hour daily regime that would intimidate adult bodybuilders. He didn't tolerate us having fun or laughing; he didn't want us to show fear or pain. The gym owner eventually stepped in and fired him. Even though I knew he was too hard on us, I felt the need to protect and defend him to my parents. Similarly, Rosie had never changed her position about Marcus, and I didn't expect her to anytime soon.

At noon, I flipped on another TV station's news and listened to its reporter nonchalantly summarize Rosie's morning testimony. Rosie had testified that she loved Marcus and considered herself his wife. But what really got to me was that she said she was still willing to die for him.

I sat alone on my living room floor, shaking my head, my tears falling onto the carpet. *How could she still think that way? Would she ever break free from Marcus?* When the reporter said Gamoian had questioned Rosie about where she lived, I sat up and listened more closely. Rosie said she'd moved around quite a bit since the murders and was staying with friends.

I turned to Cosmo, who was sprawled out on the floor

next to me. "That's us, buddy," I said, getting up to shut off the TV. I didn't want to hear any more.

When I got to work that afternoon, I found notes about Rosie's later testimony on my desk. Apparently, things had gotten worse when Gamoian asked Rosie about her sex life with Marcus.

"I don't like to talk about my private life," Rosie said, explaining that she didn't want to state the names of male or female genitalia. Gamoian persisted, however, and Marcus cried from his chair as he watched his loyal niece struggle with the words. Rosie went on to defend Marcus's "loving," saying all the girls went along with it willingly, because Marcus told them he was preparing them to please their future husbands.

"We would be better women and we would have experience," she said, quoting his rationalization. She admitted she was still wearing the wedding ring that Marcus had given her when she was a teenager and said she would always remain faithful to him.

When I came home from work that night, Rosie was in her room with the door closed. She never stayed in there by herself at night.

"Is she okay?" I asked Elizabeth quietly. "How long has she been in there?"

"She's okay, Alysia. I think she wants to be alone."

ON THURSDAY, MARCH 31, Elizabeth was called to the witness stand. In exchange for her testimony, Gamoian had granted her immunity, an order that was upheld and signed by Judge Putnam. The immunity deal meant that nothing Elizabeth said could be used to prosecute her, but she could still face perjury and contempt charges if she lied on the stand. Elizabeth was the only Wesson to accept such a deal.

Gamoian started off by asking Elizabeth to state her age and date of birth. Elizabeth said her birthday was July 31, 1959, but then mistakenly said she was forty-four. She was actually forty-five, but I knew her world had shut down after the murders and her concept of time was off.

Gamoian was not so understanding. Her irritation with Elizabeth was immediately apparent, and it would grow increasingly so in the coming days, to the point where I heard her sputtering with exasperation. Elizabeth, in turn, appeared just as annoyed with Gamoian. The prosecutor's lack of compassion and sympathy for Elizabeth and the other female family members seemed quite obvious, at least to me.

Oftentimes, Elizabeth gave the prosecutor convoluted answers when it was clear that Gamoian wanted simple ones. For example, when she asked Elizabeth to identify Jonathan's mother, Elizabeth answered, "Sofia gave Jonathan to me, so I am his mother."

Forty minutes in, the judge called it quits for the day, so Elizabeth had three days off before she had to continue her testimony.

THE APARTMENT WAS very quiet that weekend. Kiani was back in Santa Cruz. Elizabeth sat on the couch the whole time, staring at the TV or writing down thoughts on a yellow notepad. Rosie kept mostly to herself, drawing animals in her sketchbook or playing with Cosmo. I ran errands and went out with friends, but I was just going through the motions. It was hard to have fun knowing that mental anguish was raging in my apartment.

When Elizabeth returned to the stand on Monday, she went over the past three decades of her life with Marcus. Her answers were always brief, and she and Gamoian often sounded agitated. The tension between the two was building, and I knew things could erupt at any time. It didn't help that Elizabeth often looked over at Marcus before answering a question.

The prosecutor confronted Elizabeth about why, if she was cooperating with police, her first interview with detectives was so scant on details.

"I just lost my children," Elizabeth said, adding that she had buried her children right before the detectives asked for a second interview.

"I just couldn't do it. Could you?" she asked Gamoian. The prosecutor said she could if that was what it took to bring justice to the nine murder victims.

"Well, I'm not you," Elizabeth said. She added that she and her family had been threatened and ridiculed by the general public, which only made life harder.

I was away from court covering other stories for part of the time, so I wasn't there to watch the fireworks on Tuesday afternoon, but I found out at the station what had happened. The conflict started when Gamoian tried to trigger more of a memory from her hostile witness and began grilling Elizabeth about what she saw in the back bedroom the day of the murders.

Elizabeth kept saying she didn't remember anything except Lise's eyes and a pile of blankets. "I just see her eyes," she said.

Gamoian continued to press her, but all that did was make Elizabeth cry and clam up. The prosecutor came closer and closer to the stand as she asked her questions.

"Why did you run away? It's a mother's duty to protect her children," Gamoian said.

Elizabeth, who was sobbing by this point, didn't respond.

"Is it because you didn't want to be killed?" Gamoian asked loudly.

"Objection, Your Honor," Marcus yelled, capturing everyone's attention. "The prosecutor is angry."

Judge Putnam scolded Marcus, telling him he could speak only through his lawyers.

"I didn't mean any disrespect," Marcus said.

Elizabeth grew increasingly overwhelmed with emotion. "I should have stayed," she kept saying as she struggled to calm down and catch her breath. When she couldn't, she turned to the judge and said, "I don't feel good. I feel dizzy. I can't breathe."

Elizabeth kept crying, turning to the bailiffs and begging them to "make it stop."

"I can't think no more," she said.

Putnam called a recess and told her that paramedics were coming to check on her. After the medics arrived, they tested Elizabeth's blood pressure, pulse, and blood sugar and said she was okay to continue.

On Wednesday, Elizabeth pounded the witness stand under Gamoian's questioning. "He didn't kill my children," she declared.

Elizabeth said she blamed Sofia and Ruby for setting off the shooting, but she told jurors that it was Sebhrenah who killed the children.

"I can't believe she did it," Elizabeth said.

"Sebhrenah?"

"Yes."

The judge ruled that her statements should be stricken from the record, but it was too late. The jury had heard her speak. Elizabeth and the prosecutor continued to battle, as Elizabeth told Gamoian she was tired of being mistreated.

The conflict ran into Thursday, when the prosecutor asked Elizabeth why she didn't sell their collection of videos if the family had no money.

"You're giving me stupid questions to answer," Elizabeth replied. "They are not even worth answering."

Gamoian stood so close to Elizabeth's chair that she was touching the witness stand. Elizabeth leaned farther and farther to her right to get away from the prosecutor until the judge finally stepped in and told Gamoian to give her witness some space. Gamoian backed up for a few questions but was soon in Elizabeth's face once again.

Putnam finally ordered the attorney to ask her questions from the prosecution table.

"Excuse me, Your Honor," she said, retreating behind the table.

From there, Gamoian continued to question Elizabeth about why she wasn't aware of everything that Marcus was doing to their children.

"I guess I was just plain stupid," Elizabeth said.

Next, Gamoian confronted Elizabeth for describing Marcus as a sensitive man, asking, "Is it sensitive to molest your daughters?"

When Elizabeth didn't answer, Gamoian threw another question at her. "As you sit here today, do you believe he fathered Kiani's child?"

Elizabeth said no, so Gamoian asked her to explain.

"I don't want to believe it," Elizabeth said. "It's not true."

After five days of feeling embarrassed and humiliated on the stand, Elizabeth finally couldn't take it anymore and called Gamoian a bitch.

Marcus, who had been crying while the prosecutor hammered at his wife, apparently had reached his limit as well and erupted with another outburst.

"Objection, Your Honor!" he said, accusing Gamoian of showing disrespect for the court and criticizing his attorneys for failing to stop her. Given that Marcus had made two such eruptions that day, his comments prompted the judge to excuse the jury while he, Marcus, and the attorneys discussed the issue.

BECAUSE ELIZABETH'S AND Rosie's testimony contradicted some of what they had told police the night of the murders, Gamoian played their taped interviews in court, sometimes for days at a time. Whenever there was downtime, I would stare at the big, ugly dreadlock and fight my recurrent urge to grab it.

We reporters usually left the courtroom during the breaks, wandering into the hallway to use our phones and stretch our legs. But I decided to stay for the break one day to observe Marcus's behavior for a story I was working on.

The courtroom had emptied except for me, a bailiff, and Marcus. I really wanted to talk to him but knew that I wasn't allowed. When Marcus began moving his fingers across the table, I startled to attention. He was playing an imaginary keyboard, swaying his head to an imaginary beat, and mouthing imaginary lyrics. Another reporter had seen him do this before, but I didn't realize how absurd it looked until I'd seen it for myself. It was almost as if he did everything he could to act sane in front of the judge and jury, showing his true self only during breaks. Completely counterintuitive for a man trying to beat a murder rap.

His lawyers weren't arguing insanity, as many of us had predicted. I later figured Marcus didn't want anyone to think he was crazy. Still, as I stared at the make-believe musician that morning, insanity was all I could see.

I picked up my pen and jotted down some notes: "10:30: During break, Wesson plays pretend piano on defense table." I talked about his odd behavior on the news that night.

When I got home, Elizabeth was staring at me. I knew she had something on her mind.

"I saw your story tonight," she said finally.

"Oh yeah? The fake piano?" I asked with a smile.

"My husband writes songs in his head. He's been doing that for years. He does this conducting thing . . ."

"Really?"

"We never thought it was strange. I guess we're used to it. That's all I wanted to say."

"What kind of songs does he write?" I asked.

"I have some of them in the room. Do you want to read them?"

"Sure, I guess."

I knew if his songs were anything like his book, I wasn't going to like them.

The next day, Elizabeth came out of the room bearing a stack of handwritten lyrics and makeshift sheet music. "Enjoy," she said.

"Ah, perfect poolside reading," I joked, taking the papers down to the pool.

I expected some eccentric, crazy lyrics out of the man,

but to my surprise, the songs were pretty benign. They were mainly about boats and girls.

> Some say a ship is a woman,
> Some say the sea is her soul.
> She's the guardian of the waters,
> The keeper of the winds.

I kept flipping through the pages and stopped at a song called "Haul Yard Girls."

> Some ask why do us girls haul yard.
> You're young, you have life, much to live.
> We spy each other, not to smile.
> Our smiles fade silent with the air.
> Our past holds secrets as our night.
> We leave while yet still standing there.

I wasn't moved. I kept flipping. I saw something labeled "The Seeds of Vampyr" and thought that sounded more like Marcus Wesson.

> My life is fulfilled with love's shattered expectations
> Only to find sadness in love's anticipation
> My hope when I see her she'll remember our past time
> Yet I fear when I lose her it won't be the last time.

I realized I was softly singing the lyrics to try to make sense of them. A guy lying near me at the pool gave me an odd look. If he only knew what I was singing.

* * *

AFTER BEING BOMBARDED with testimony defending Marcus, I was actually looking forward to Gypsy's testimony, which started on April 12. She was the only Wesson child who seemed to have told police and prosecutors the whole story. I couldn't wait for Marcus to hear one of his daughters tell the truth about how much he'd hurt her. I wanted someone finally to stand up to him, even if it wasn't one-on-one. But once she took the stand and was face-to-face with Marcus again, Gypsy didn't say what everyone, including me, was expecting her to.

I was in court for only one day while she was testifying, so I didn't have to hear her claim that Marcus had never raped or molested her. When Gamoian confronted her with her own statements to police that he had started touching her when she was seven years old, Gypsy contended that she had exaggerated her statements to police because she believed he'd killed all the children. However, she said, she had since learned that "the evidence" proved he didn't do it.

Gypsy also claimed that the kids didn't really take the suicide pact seriously, nor did they have clear instructions on what to do, further downplaying the severity of the situation. Because Gypsy had not delivered the anticipated inflammatory testimony and because some of it conflicted with her statements to police, Gamoian felt it necessary to play those interview tapes for the jury as well.

I was dying to know why Gypsy had changed her story. It was eating me up inside. She was the brave one, the only one who truly "got it." How could she have lied? I knew she hated Marcus and wanted to see him pay for what he had done. I had envisioned the moment as so triumphant. She was supposed to stare right at him and list the horrible things he'd done to her and her siblings, then turn to the jurors and tell them he should be locked up forever. Why had she caved? Unfortunately, the gag order was still in effect, so I couldn't ask her. Not yet, anyway.

I was angry with her for blowing her big chance. But deep down, I knew she didn't want to talk about such private things in front of strangers. She probably thought the jury had ten times the amount of evidence they needed to convict him. Still, it bothered me to see him look over at his youngest living daughter and smirk, as if he'd scored a victory of some kind. If even *she* couldn't confront him, what hope was there for the rest of the family?

NEARLY SEVEN GRUELING weeks into the trial, it was time for Kiani to take the stand.

"Will you be there, Alysia?" asked Kiani, who was staying in the apartment with us the night before her first day of testimony.

"I'll be there."

Neither of us knew she'd be on the stand for six days.

I'd already found out—from interviews with the police and the preliminary hearing—much of what Marcus had done to the girls sexually. Even so, I wasn't prepared for the intensity of their testimony.

With Kiani, the prosecutor went straight for the details about the sexual abuse.

"When did your father start touching you?" Gamoian asked. "How did he touch you?"

As the questions got increasingly invasive, I watched Kiani struggle to answer them, clearly feeling embarrassed and helpless. It was obvious she didn't comprehend the seriousness of what Marcus had done to her. When Gamoian asked Kiani to demonstrate how she touched her father's penis, I was so furious I almost jumped out of my seat. I wanted to throttle the prosecutor.

Give me a break! This is too much.

There was already concrete DNA evidence proving Marcus had fathered Kiani's two children. I watched Kiani cup her hand and make the up-and-down stroking motion and felt absolutely mortified for her, especially with Marcus sitting right there, watching.

Just as Rosie had testified, Kiani told the jury that she and her sisters were never forced to do anything sexual with Marcus; they did it willingly. All the girls were allowed to leave the house and get married if they wanted to, as long as they left their children behind with Marcus. When Gamoian asked how marriage was possible if he never allowed them to talk to men, Kiani said she didn't know.

"Did you want Illabelle to have 'loving' with her father?" Gamoian asked, referring to Kiani's eight-year-old daughter, one of the murder victims.

"No," Kiani said, sounding offended. "I wanted her to grow up different." She added that she wanted Illabelle and her younger daughter, Jeva, to attend public school and get married.

"Then is loving a *bad* thing?" Gamoian asked.

"I can't say it's a good thing," Kiani said sadly. "When I was young I didn't mind it. I just wanted something different for [Illabelle]."

Kiani began crying as Gamoian questioned her about her relationship with Lise and Sebhrenah, but she sobbed even harder when the prosecutor threw the facts in her face:

Illabelle's life had been no better than or different from Kiani's. Marcus had them both trapped in the house, with no way out.

Gamoian spent a couple of days going over Kiani's diary entries from 2000 to 2004, often asking her to read them out loud. I couldn't imagine reading my most intimate thoughts in front of a roomful of strangers who were taking notes to broadcast my words to the world.

Yet there was Kiani, spewing out loving anecdotes about her father, reading the entries that expressed sentiments such as "Dads are special in a girl's heart," "I love my Daddy very much," and "Daddy was very sweet today." When Gamoian asked her if the last statement was code for the times she had sex with her father, Kiani denied it.

Some entries had a more serious tone, such as the ones that discussed the Second Coming of Christ. In February 2001, for example, Kiani wrote, "It's truly the end of time. Dad truly wants to make sure we all get there. Reading some serious Bible text."

Other entries reflected Kiani's worries that her children had only rice to eat. "I hope we make it today," she wrote. "I can't take it any longer." She explained how they sometimes had to dig through the garbage at grocery stores, McDonald's, and other fast-food restaurants to find something edible.

Beginning in the fall of 2003, her diary entries reflected sadness and depression, saying her life "felt like a big, black pit." At that time, the family was living on the *Sudan* with no propane or money and little food. After that, Kiani said, the family moved into the Hammond Avenue house and life improved.

In the weeks that followed, the prosecutor called Adrian and Dorian to the stand and played their police interview tapes. By that point, I was busy covering other stories, including *American Idol* in Los Angeles, but I noted that Marcus's sons stuck up for him, too. I was amazed that, after all these kids had been through, they still showed their allegiance to such a monster.

Twenty

*I*n the weeks after giving their testimony, Elizabeth, Kiani, Rosie, and Gypsy were all very quiet. Elizabeth often looked as if she was about to burst into tears. When I asked Kiani how *she* was, she just looked at me with a blank stare and nodded, as if to say she was okay. But I knew she wasn't.

Rosie didn't play tricks on me anymore, or even laugh much when I tickled her. It was as if they'd gone back to being emotionally and physically numb. The trial had sucked the new life right out of them. Gypsy, who had been visiting quite frequently, brought little Alysia over for only a few minutes every other day, confiding that it was too depressing to be around her relatives any more than that. Having had to sit in front of Marcus and give explicit testimony about their sexual abuse had been debilitating for them. On top of that, the gag order prevented them from talking to one another about their pain, forcing them to keep it bottled up inside.

The Wessons weren't the only ones having difficulty following the gag order. It was affecting me, too. I was feeling empathy in a way I never had before, only I had no way to process it. I couldn't share my feelings with the subjects of those emotions, and I didn't want to worry my mom with them either. This was all foreign to me.

But I soon started to realize what was happening: these women had become so important to me that their feelings were now *my* feelings. We were connected. They were even more a part of my family and vice versa. Their tragedy was different from anything I'd ever experienced in my own family, yet somehow I still internalized what they'd gone through. I felt used; I resented sex.

That weekend I was at the gas station filling up my car and contemplating the situation. Four guys in a big white truck pulled up next to me and made catcalls about how hot I was. Normally, I'm not the type to get offended by such remarks. But on that day, I was disgusted. When I looked at that truck, all I could see was Marcus's face. I grew increasingly uncomfortable until the goons finally drove away. I climbed back into my car, where I sank into my seat and cried.

Those children were so damn young and innocent.

I thought of Marcus's huge belly and his long, dirty dreadlocks, lunging over their tiny bodies while he violated them for his own pleasure. Although I hadn't even met them at the time, I felt guilty that I hadn't been there to protect them.

FROM THE GAS station, I drove to the hotel where Juan was staying. I had warned him not to visit that weekend because I was still feeling uncharacteristically somber and standoffish, but he insisted he could cheer me up. He had moved from Michigan to San Diego a few months back so we could be closer, but I didn't feel particularly close to him or anyone else these days. It had been quite a while since I'd felt like my usual self.

Juan used to stay at my apartment, but I told him it was best if he stayed elsewhere because the girls were so uncomfortable in his presence that they often hid in their bedroom while he was visiting. I knew they didn't need another ounce of stress during the trial.

I sat in my car in the Piccadilly Inn parking lot, composing my thoughts and touching up the makeup mess my crying spell had caused. Five minutes later, I walked into the hotel, forced a smile for the desk clerk, then walked down the long hallway of floral carpet toward Juan's room. He greeted me with his usual enthusiastic hug, embracing me in his muscular arms. Sensing I needed the comfort, he held on even longer than he normally did. But when he leaned in to kiss me, I pulled back.

"What's wrong, babe?" he asked sympathetically, his smile fading.

"I don't know. Just don't do that, I can't breathe," I said, walking toward the bed and sitting down. He followed, sat next to me, and gently rubbed my back.

"Don't," I said, standing up to get some distance. "Don't touch me right now."

"Is it me?" he asked, sounding worried and confused. He was working with troubled kids as a school counselor now and always wanted to talk to me about my feelings. Usually, I put up with it, but I wasn't in the mood that day.

"No, it's me," I said.

"Tell me what's wrong. Please just talk to me. Is it about the girls?"

"Yes, I just *hate* him for what he did to them. And the

things he made them do," I said, shaking my head. "It makes me sick, and I just don't want anyone touching me right now."

"It's just me," he said, grasping my hand and stepping up to hug me again.

"I can't do this," I said, pulling my hand back. "I need some space right now."

"What are you saying?"

"I'm saying I want to be alone."

"For how long?"

"I don't know. A while. I just need space."

"Are you ending this, *just like that?*"

"I can't do it, Juan. I'm sorry. I don't know how else to deal with all of this."

We sat side by side on the bed as I tried to justify my irrational thoughts and behavior. Ten minutes later, I gave up and left the hotel, ending my two-year relationship with the man who had wanted to marry me.

As I drove off, I watched the hotel shrink in my rear-view mirror, wondering if I'd done the right thing. I almost turned around, realizing I was letting Marcus ruin *my* life, too. I felt unjustified having these emotions, knowing I hadn't experienced a fraction of the family's trauma. But, like the girls, I found myself shutting down emotionally. I felt drained and overwhelmed, and knew it would take something major to pull me out of it. Fortunately, my job provided me with that opportunity. By that time I was regularly covering *American Idol,* so I was able to escape once again into the alternate universe the show had become for me.

* * *

ON THE THREE-AND-A-HALF-HOUR drive to the CBS Studios in Beverly Hills, I pushed all the serious and sad thoughts to the back of my mind and tried to summon some happier ones. As soon as the security guard cleared me and my photographer to drive through the gate, I felt my old vigor and excitement trickling back. I couldn't help but smile when I saw Bob Barker's billboard-size grin next to the *Price Is Right* logo that covered the side of the building. When we walked into the media entrance near the back parking lot, we were smack in the middle of the action, surrounded by fans screaming and holding signs, and *Idol* contestants running around.

By the time the Wednesday night elimination show started, I had done an arm-in-arm interview with the Season 2 winner, Ruben Studdard, and a dancing-and-singing interview with the Season 3 winner, Fantasia Barrino. The reporters and photographers lingered backstage, hoping for a chance to interview the judges after the show. Most of the media were from L.A. or one of the national entertainment programs, so I was the tiniest fish in the pond. Initially, I didn't think anyone noticed that I was from a small market, but based on the inquiries from the other stations, I soon realized that I was wrong.

"So, where are *you* from?" an *Entertainment Tonight* photographer asked, looking perplexed at the logo on my microphone.

"The Fox affiliate in Fresno," I said, staring wide-eyed at the sticker on his camera.

"Fresno, Fresno, right. That's where that guy took out his whole family, huh? Wasn't that in Fresno? The big guy with the dreadlocks—"

"Marcus Wesson," I said, cutting him off. "Yep, that's us."

Before I knew it, the whole group was gathered around asking questions about the crime and the ongoing trial.

Just what I need.

The conversation fizzled as the judges started to stroll backstage after the show. The reporters couldn't wait to get their cameras focused on Simon Cowell, and I understood why. He was the closest I'd ever come to meeting *my* idol, Frank Sinatra; Simon had the kind of exaggerated swagger, charm, and ego you'd find in the leading men of yesteryear. Wearing his signature V-neck gray sweater and bright white smile, Simon made his way over to my camera.

"Hi, Simon," I said, taking a good look at his perfectly cropped haircut and guessing it cost more than I had in my savings account. "We're from Fox in Fresno."

"Ah yes, I remember. Fresno," he said in his thick English accent.

Please don't talk about the Wesson case. Please don't talk about the Wesson case.

"Where is Fresno again?" he joked, putting his arm around me and setting me at ease. "I'm just kidding. I love Fresno."

And so the interview began. I wished I could have stayed longer backstage, flirting with Simon, but I knew I needed to get my video on the air, and drive back to Fresno so I could be at the trial the next morning. As we drove out the gated lot, I turned around to look at Bob Barker's giant face and sighed.

Back to reality.

The next morning, I'd be staring down the dreadlock once again.

* * *

I WENT BACK to L.A. nearly every week for the rest of the season. The girls and I may not have been allowed to talk about Marcus, but we could talk about Simon all we wanted.

"Is he *really* mean like he is on TV?" Rosie asked.

"Not at all," I said, explaining that he was actually nicer to reporters than the other two judges were.

"I think he likes you," Elizabeth said, giggling, referring to the flirtatious comments he made during our interview.

"I think he likes *all* the female reporters," I said, laughing.

The girls paid close attention to the show each week and picked their favorites to win. It was refreshing to discuss something carefree and fun for a change. I was happy to hear the girls giggling again and not crying as much. It also helped that Gypsy had been coming by more often with little Alysia, which definitely lightened the mood.

Meanwhile, the cruel case of incest and murder continued to unfold in the courtroom, where I recognized a familiar look of desperation on the jurors' faces. It seemed like they, too, wanted to forget about the dark testimony and resume their normal routines, but it wouldn't be long now. The prosecutor had finally wrapped up her case, and the defense team was poised to take center stage.

I knew Marcus's attorneys had an uphill battle; their own client wasn't even cooperating with them. Before the trial began, Pete Jones told Elizabeth that Marcus had refused to submit to psychological testing, which could have been used to quantify his mental instability. To make up for his lack of cooperation, Elizabeth, Kiani, and Rosie met with the defense team at least a dozen times, trying to help in any way they could. When they visited Marcus in jail during the trial, he told them he was unhappy with the way Jones and Ralph Torres were portraying him in court. He thought they were doing a bad job all around.

Focusing on the evidence that pointed to Sebhrenah as the killer, Torres called the forensic pathologist Venu Gopal to the stand and questioned him about a bruise under her eye near her gunshot wound. Gopal said the mark could have been caused by the sight on the Ruger pistol if the weapon had been fired while upside down, all of which was consistent with a suicidal shooting.

Gopal also testified that Sebhrenah and Lise had died an hour or two after the younger victims, which supported the defense's theory that Marcus was not in the room when the other seven victims were killed.

As the last defense witness, Torres called the firearms expert and crime scene specialist Allen Boudreau, who said the black mark found on Sebhrenah's bloodstained right hand could have been caused by her firing the Ruger.

To help the jury visualize how the victims were stacked in the corner of the bedroom, Torres played a graphic slide show of their bodies, including close-ups of Sebhrenah's wounds. Marcus kept his head down the entire time.

THE DEFENSE WAS wrapping up its case just as the finale of *American Idol,* Season 4, was about to begin. I was ready to get out of town; I didn't want to see, hear, or think anything more about Marcus Wesson. I made a deal with myself to think only about the *Idol* finalists Carrie Underwood and Bo Bice for the next few days.

At the Kodak Theatre, I had one of the best seats in the

house, in an opera box on the left side of the stage. From my red-cushioned chair, I had an amazing panoramic view of the theater and the thirty-five hundred people packed inside, cheering for the finale to begin.

I looked down onto the stage where the Academy Awards had been held for the past five times, and thought about all of Lise's favorite Hollywood stars who had stood there. Every few seconds, a series of brightly colored spotlights flashed over my face. As I sat in a trance, listening to the loud music and the roar of the crowd, I felt Lise's spirit was there with me.

When Carrie and Bo waltzed onto the stage, the enormous room of fans erupted into applause, drowning out my thoughts. I finally let the stresses of the trial go and soaked up the positive energy.

I had to duck out of the finale early to get my stories edited in time for my live reports that night. Thousands of *Idol* fans gathered in the outdoor courtyard of the five-story Hollywood and Highland shopping center, gazing down at us working in a roped-off circle, surrounded by security, while more than a hundred reporters and photographers jockeyed for the best positions. When the show ended, the contestants and judges joined us, eliciting screams of excitement from the men, women, and children in the audience.

By midnight, the fans had gone and we West Coast reporters had filed our final reports. Exhausted from the long day but still basking in the afterglow of the glamorous evening, I gathered my belongings and pulled out my cell phone to listen to my messages. I had two from a crying Elizabeth, who said she was afraid to face the upcoming verdict, and just like that, my other life came flooding back to me. Even though I was three and a half hours away, I couldn't seem to escape the reach of Marcus Wesson.

THE JURY BEGAN deliberating on June 2. I half-expected the panel to tell the judge, "We don't need time to deliberate. He's guilty!" But, of course, that didn't happen.

With each hour the jurors were out, I grew more agitated; with each day, more anxious. I knew the sex charges were in the bag, but were they going to let him off on the murder charges?

One day. Two days. Three days.

I had a vision of Elizabeth and Rosie waiting for him—each with the intensity of a proud wife longing for her brave soldier husband to return from the war.

Four days. Five days. Six days.

I showed up at court each morning, hours before my shift was supposed to start, so I wouldn't miss the big moment. I was confident the jury would come back any minute. Each time I saw a bailiff saunter down the hallway, I'd search his expression for the slightest hint that the jurors were close to reaching a verdict. A few dozen blank expressions and courtesy smiles later, I stopped looking up.

Marcus Wesson's fate consumed every second of my day. I spent my time at work listening to people at bus stops and malls wonder aloud why the jurors were taking so long to find him guilty; then I came home to find Marcus's surviving victims praying on my couch for the jury to find him innocent.

Seven days. Eight days. Nine days.

The girls sat on the couch looking more distraught each

night and wondering the same thing I was. What was taking the jury so long?

The night before the tenth day of deliberations, I made myself stop thinking about the verdict. I was burned out, and I hadn't had more than a couple of hours' sleep a night in weeks. I didn't set my alarm clock and decided to arrive in court whenever I got there. I wasn't going to let Marcus control *my* life anymore.

The next morning, I stubbornly stayed in bed for an extra hour before I got up, and casually sipped my coffee while watching TV. I took a long shower, letting the hot water soothe my tired and tense neck muscles. When I got out, my phone was ringing and I ran into the bedroom to answer it.

It was Rosie. Her voice was shaky, so I thought she was laughing.

"What's so funny?" I asked, laughing myself.

"Nothing's funny," she said. "Alysia, the verdict is in. The jury is back."

Remembering I'd told her about my plan to sleep in and not worry about the verdict coming in, I still thought she was kidding. "Ha ha, Rosie," I said.

"No, the jury is back. Come here now. I have to go," she said abruptly, hanging up.

She must be kidding. It couldn't be in now . . . could it?

My phone rang again. It was my assignment editor.

"They're reading the verdict in thirty minutes. Get there!" she said, her voice edgy with deadline pressure.

The adrenaline rush was overwhelming and paralyzing. I stood naked, clutching my cell phone, wondering how I was going to get ready in just a few minutes when I normally needed an hour and a half to do my hair and makeup. The courthouse was at least twenty minutes away, and my station expected me to look like I was ready to go on the air at any moment.

That gives me five minutes.

I blow-dried my hair with one hand, using the other to pack a bag with makeup, my earpiece, and high heels.

Should I wear my red suit? The skirt could get in the way when I'm running. Why couldn't they have waited one more hour? God, please let me make it on time.

I pulled on the red suit and sped to the courthouse, where I sprinted from the parking garage, cut through the side door to save time with the security check, and pushed my way onto the elevator. Feeling like Superman, I used the ride to the fifth floor to finish getting dressed. Luckily, the elevator stopped on every floor, giving me a few extra moments to pull myself together. As I fished behind my back for the left armhole of my jacket, someone guided it around to me.

"Thanks," I said with a backward glance at the tall, athletic-looking man behind me.

Oh my God; it's the police chief!

I'd interviewed the chief more than a dozen times, so he wasn't a complete stranger. Luckily, he was also a nice guy, with a reputation for being charming. Chief Dyer bent down and handed me my other high heel, which had fallen out of my bag.

"I think this belongs to you."

I didn't have time to be embarrassed. "Hold this for a second?" I asked, thrusting my compact-size mirror at him.

He smiled and obliged. With his help, I brushed on two

coats of mascara in the overstuffed, smelly elevator, just in time for the alert bell. The doors opened onto a menagerie of flashing cameras, bustling reporters, and curious community members who had heard that the verdict was in and wanted to be there to hear it being announced. I turned to thank the chief, but he'd vanished in the crowd.

Around the corner, the hallway was just as packed. Security guards were setting up a checkpoint outside the courtroom, where all observers, including media, would have their pockets, purses, and bags searched. One of the guards told me they were trying to ensure that no one brought in a weapon to harm Marcus.

I spotted Rosie behind a group of people on the other side of the hallway. She was standing with some relatives near a bench outside the courtroom. I could tell the family was nervous because they kept fidgeting and looking around.

I elbowed my way to where she was standing and raised my hand to cover my mouth in true mafia fashion. "Where's Elizabeth?" I asked.

Without making eye contact, Rosie walked down the hall, through the reporters and photographers, and into the stairwell.

Aaah, the stairs.

I counted to five and discreetly followed. Elizabeth had chosen a great hiding spot. The Wessons always took the stairs to avoid the media, and soon the cold, stark stairwell was filled with about half a dozen of them and their significant others, all looking at me with forlorn eyes.

I told them how proud I was of them for testifying and that we would all get through this together, that everything would be all right.

"You guys can do this," I said, like a coach giving a pep talk to a losing team. "The hard part is already over. I'll see you in there, okay? Call me when you leave court. It's going to be okay."

It had become second nature to me by now to keep my relationship with the Wessons a secret from the rest of the media, so I casually walked back into the hallway and joined my colleagues on the benches.

"Hmmm, I wonder where the family is," one of the reporters said, looking around for them.

"I don't know," I replied with a shrug.

JUDGE PUTNAM HAD originally said he didn't want the family in the courtroom when the verdict was read, but he reversed his decision with no explanation before the jury came back. He ruled that family members could come inside if there was enough room, and if they could "control themselves," but he warned that he didn't want any emotional outbursts that could influence the jury's decision should the trial advance to a penalty phase.

The bailiffs made sure to save enough seats for the Wessons, but even *I* wasn't sure if they would be able to control themselves. Elizabeth and Rosie walked in with their heads bowed, followed by Rosemary, some of the boys, and their girlfriends. They sat in the back rows on the left side, where they cried quietly. Scanning their faces, I saw hurt, anger, and a helplessness I could never truly understand.

The past year and a half flashed before my eyes. I saw a bloody Marcus Wesson walking out of the house and surrendering to police. I saw the detectives carrying out the bodies of the dead babies, draped in white sheets. I saw myself running after the family with a microphone in my hand. I saw the girls crying on my couch, with Elizabeth repeating, "My babies are gone. My babies are gone." I saw Kiani and Rosie laughing as they bobbed up and down in the pool during their first swimming lesson. I saw Elizabeth's face glowing after Kiani, Rosie, Gypsy, and I decorated my apartment with streamers and balloons to surprise her with a birthday party. I saw little Alysia looking up at me from her hospital bassinet with her tiny hand wrapped around my finger.

It had all come down to this.

Twenty-one

My cell phone vibrated, sending it surging sideways on the wooden pew until it hit the reporter next to me.

"Sorry," I whispered, grabbing my phone and reading the text message that had just come in from Debbie,* one of my coworkers: "I FOUND OUT THE VERDICT ALREADY."

I gasped and hit the arrow button to scroll down the screen: "HE'S GUILTY ON ALL COUNTS!"

I read it a few more times, not knowing what to think. Neither the judge nor the jury had come in yet, so I knew I still had a few minutes. I hurried into the hallway, where hordes of people were lined up to get inside, and dialed the station. I didn't bother greeting Debbie when she answered.

"How do you know the verdict?" I demanded.

She explained that her friend worked at Wal-Mart with a juror's husband. Apparently, the juror had told her husband about the verdict and he told everyone at work about it.

"But she can't do that!" I said, exasperated.

"Well, she did."

"This is crazy. Okay, I have to get back in there."

I opened the doors with an uneasy feeling.

Should I report what happened? But what if she's wrong?

Because juror misconduct was such a serious offense, I decided to wait to see if the text message matched up with the verdict. I didn't want to create a commotion for nothing.

Why do I always get so entangled in this case?

I WAS STILL wrestling with this latest ethical dilemma when the bailiffs brought in Marcus, who was wearing the same short-sleeved black shirt and black pants he'd worn throughout the trial. With his hair messier and beard bushier every day, he certainly didn't look polished for his most important court appearance so far.

Most of the jurors went out of their way to ignore the disheveled defendant as they filed into the courtroom. I thought that could mean they'd found him guilty, but I still wasn't convinced. I studied each of the seven women on the jury, trying to figure out which one had blabbed to her husband.

What if the family has to go through this all over again because she couldn't keep her big mouth shut?

The courtroom was silent except for the sniffling and sobbing coming from the Wessons in the back row. Judge Putnam asked his clerk, Barbara Graves, to read the verdict. I held my breath and looked down at my notebook.

I've never heard anyone read so slowly. I wanted to yell, "Spit it out already, lady!"

Finally, she read the jury's decision on the first murder count: "We the jury, in the matter of People versus Marcus Delon Wesson, find the defendant guilty of murder in the first degree."

Guilty.

She repeated the same sentence eight more times for the rest of the murder counts.

Guilty.

Then she moved on to the fourteen sex charges. It took her twenty-three minutes to finish reading them all.

Guilty on all counts.

The dethroned patriarch of the Wesson family would never rule again. I didn't want to turn around to look at the back rows. I could already hear Elizabeth's weak sobs behind me, and I knew all too well what that looked like. As a friend, I wanted to respect their privacy, but as a reporter, I knew it was my job to look.

I raised my eyes to the ceiling, paused, then slowly turned toward the family. When I saw them, it was worse than I had expected. Tears were streaming down Elizabeth's face, and her mouth was open with an expression of near panic. Rosie was crying hard, too. Harder than I'd ever seen her cry before. They looked as if they'd lost their family all over again. I wanted to run back and hug them.

I turned toward Marcus to gauge his reaction. I could see only the right half of his face, and as usual, he was in his own world, staring straight ahead, apparently unaffected.

You're finally going to get what's coming to you.

The bailiffs walked over to Marcus and escorted him out. Then the reporters in the courtroom rushed outside to meet up with our crews, who were positioned on the side of the building. We had been allowed to text-message the verdicts to our stations while they were being read, so word of Marcus's fate had already spread. A large crowd had gathered nearby, and a few people cheered upon hearing the news. Amid the chaos and noise, I thought about erasing my first text message from Debbie and never saying another word about it.

After all, things turned out the way they were supposed to.

But I didn't erase it. I showed it to Max when I got back to the station. He said we needed to report it to Judge Putnam and let *him* decide what, if anything, to do about it.

The following week, before testimony began in the penalty phase of the trial, the judge held a closed hearing regarding my text message. I gave my cell phone to my boss in case he needed to show anyone the message, and prayed there would be no new trial.

Judge Putnam asked Max to name the source of the leak, but my boss invoked the shield law, which protects journalists from naming their sources. After two days, Putnam decided the information had not affected the outcome of the trial, and he kept the jury intact. The penalty phase was ready to move forward.

I had never really given the death penalty too much thought. In my eleventh-grade debate class, I was assigned to argue *against* capital punishment. I went to the library, checked out all the books on the subject, and read them cover to cover. When I closed the cover of the final book, I wished I was arguing *for* the death penalty. In class, it became the first and last debate I would ever lose.

The way I saw it, the world would be a much better place without people like Marcus Wesson. No punishment would be harsh enough for what he had done to his family. With him gone, though, maybe they could—and would— finally move on.

* * *

MARCUS REMAINED HIS usual unemotional self during the penalty phase of the trial. Scribbling away once again, he penned a note wishing good luck to his attorney Pete Jones, who would deliver the defense's opening statement. Marcus was taking an existential approach to his fate, saying his "father," meaning God, had told him to "let it go, let it flow."

> *You will win opening argument. . . . No matter what you present, the verdict will reflect the plan at hand. If God himself were on [the] stand, the verdict would be the same. . . . I am happy with the verdict—it reflects my father's will—as Jesus himself was convicted—I am no better, but the same. . . . You did your best within the parameters. . . . I will be freed either way—trust me. . . . I am here to loose [sic] weight only.*

THIS TIME DURING opening statements, Prosecutor Gamoian was brief, giving only a one-minute presentation. She introduced one new piece of evidence the judge had not allowed her to bring up before—a legal document from Santa Cruz County showing Marcus's welfare fraud conviction in 1990, proving that he had a criminal history.

Jones didn't have many character witnesses to bolster his case. Marcus's father, Ben Wesson, had died of cancer a year ago, and his mother, Carrie, said she was too ill to travel from Seattle. Jones had to settle for Marcus's sister Cheryl, who portrayed her mother as overly religious and her father as an alcoholic who had homosexual affairs and periodically left the family. While Cheryl was on the stand, Marcus kept his head down and eyes closed.

"Open your eyes, Marc," she said, trying to get him to respond. "I love you."

Greg Bledsoe, a childhood friend of Marcus's, also testified. I didn't think there were any more surprises left in store, but I was sorely mistaken. According to Bledsoe, Ben Wesson used to pay his son's friends to give him oral sex. Greg also thought it likely that Ben had sexually abused his children, including Marcus. That made sense to me, given that sexual abuse is so often repeated for generations. Greg also mentioned Ben's sexual affair with his nephew in L.A., noting that Ben moved back home with his wife and kids after Marcus and Elizabeth got married.

During the testimony, I looked around at the other reporters. None of their faces reflected any emotion.

Am I the only one who thinks this is the most bizarre case in the history of the American justice system?

For a brief second, I felt compassion for Marcus. He *must* have been abused. But my sympathy dissipated as quickly as it came. Millions of people were abused every day and *they* didn't act like him. Could this be happening to another family out there somewhere?

Gamoian, in her closing argument, asked the jury not to "give him the gift of life. He doesn't deserve it."

She projected images of the nine bloody children stacked in the back bedroom and the deadly gunshot wounds under their eyes. Some of the jurors cried as she talked about the children's last moments of life and how their father had played a role in their murders.

"He controlled their bodies, their hope and dreams," she said. "He controlled their deaths. He controlled the timing of it. He controlled the manner of it. Imagine the terror in that bedroom."

It was such a powerful message that even Marcus wiped away tears.

In Jones's closing, he argued that jurors should spare his client's life because he did not fire the murder weapon, contending that Marcus's acts stemmed from an obvious mental illness. Both of these points were mitigating factors. The jury's job was to decide whether such factors outweighed the aggravating factors. If so, the jury could recommend a sentence of life without the possibility of parole. If not, death.

Jones ended by telling jurors, "You've heard a lot of bad. But there's some good there." If sentencing Marcus to die by lethal injection could "undo the harm done, your job would be simple," he said.

This time, it took the jury only nine hours of deliberating over three days, and it took Clerk Barbara Graves only six minutes to read the panel's recommended punishment. The verdict was a finding for the penalty of death for the murders of Sebhrenah, Elizabeth, Jeva, Sedona, Marshey, Ethan, Illabelle, Aviv, and Jonathan.

The man who had ordered the end to his children's lives would be put to death himself. I felt very relieved—and that feeling alarmed me.

I'm relieved that another human being is going to die.

Marcus had his arms crossed, his hands grabbing his shoulders. He stared straight ahead and never turned around to look at the back row, where Elizabeth, Rosie, and four of his children were crying once again.

After it was over, the other reporters and I chased down the attorneys outside the courtroom. Although Lisa

Gamoian said she couldn't say anything yet, Pete Jones stopped to talk.

"Obviously, I'm extremely disappointed," he said, his face wilted with defeat. "I'm second-guessing myself of what more I could have done or should have done."

I wasn't sure what to expect when I walked into my apartment that night. I had stayed late at work to archive some of the video and my notes from the trial, so I didn't get home until after 1:00 A.M. Elizabeth and Rosie were still up, watching TV.

"How are you guys doing?" I asked.

Elizabeth looked more angry than upset; Rosie simply looked empty.

"He didn't have a chance," Elizabeth said after a few moments of silence. "They were going to give him the death penalty from the beginning."

Although I was sure this was a debate I could win, I knew it wasn't the time to engage them on the subject.

"I'm really tired. I'm going to bed," I said, removing myself from the conversation before I said something I'd regret. "Good night."

THE FORMAL SENTENCING hearing was a little more than three weeks away. The judge had told the family members that they had the right to address Marcus before he made his recommendation. Elizabeth thought she would be too emotional to stand in front of the court; Gypsy didn't want to either. So, instead, they decided to write letters to the judge, explaining their positions.

"Can I borrow your computer to type a letter to the judge?" Gypsy asked me.

"Sure. What are you going to say? Do you think your dad should get the death penalty?"

"No. I think it will make everything worse," she said sadly. "I don't agree with it."

She sat down and began composing her letter.

Your Honorable Judge R. L. Putnam,

I hope you take the time to consider my plea to save my father's life. I beg that you not adhere to the recommendation of death that the jury put forth to you.

I ask that you consider us, the family members. We have gone through so much sorrow since March 12th. Putting our father to death will only add to our grief.

I know many people believe the punishment fits the crime. But we ask that you take into consideration all the hardships we have been through and grant us this favor and not put our father to death.

There have been enough deaths in our family and I don't think that we can handle one more.

I hope that you take those into consideration. Thank you for your time.

Sincerely yours,
Gypsy Wesson

* * *

WHEN HE BEGAN the sentencing hearing, Judge Putnam acknowledged that he had read the family's letters, then asked if anyone wanted to address the court at the podium. About ten people accepted his offer, including Ruby, Sofia, Kiani, and several of her brothers, but some of them directed their comments at Marcus.

"Those were not children who belonged to you," Sofia said, with a sense of empowerment. "It was not your decision to take them away from this world."

Kiani stood up to defend her father and her family's lifestyle. "I am proud of all my family, of the way we were raised," she said, crying.

She and her brothers tearfully talked about the "good times" with their father and told Marcus how much they would always love him. It reminded me of a funeral. Family members talking about what they would remember most about their beloved. Except this time, the subject of their kind words wasn't dead.

Not yet, anyway.

Marcus nodded a few times, and at one point, I saw tears dripping down his long, dark face. I sat there, taking notes, secretly wishing I could get up and give Marcus a piece of my mind.

The judge sat stoically throughout the hearing; then he spoke directly to Marcus.

"Marcus Delon Wesson, it is the judgment and sentence of this court that you shall suffer the death penalty," he said. Putnam also sentenced Marcus to 102 years in prison for the sex charges.

Based on California's capital punishment history, Marcus's execution was decades away, so he would be safe and sound in isolation at San Quentin for the foreseeable future. It didn't seem fair.

I wondered if there was any possibility that he might "accidentally" end up in the general prison population, where other inmates could carry out their own form of justice. That often happened with child molesters. The serial killer Jeffrey Dahmer, who mutilated and ate seventeen young men and boys, died at the hands of a fellow prisoner.

Either way, his family would finally be safe.

THE JURORS MET in a room off the courthouse lobby to do interviews with the media. They talked about how much the case had affected them, and how they felt they had upheld justice.

If they only knew how much of the story didn't get into court and how much the case had affected the family members, especially after all they've been through.

A number of radio stations called—some national and some regional stations from other parts of the country— asking me to go on live or do a taped interview with a thirty-second summary of the case and sentence. I prepared a script and read it to each audience, and, occasionally, the host would ask me follow-up questions.

"What was Wesson's demeanor in the courtroom?"

"When will he be transferred to death row?"

I could answer those questions in my sleep. During the last interview, however, one question made me pause.

"We have about ten seconds left, Alysia. Can you tell us why the family members still support their father?" I wanted to laugh. *I've been trying to answer that question for almost a year and a half, and I'm still at a loss for words.*

I said the only thing that came to mind.

"Well, I think the family is still struggling with their tremendous loss and, up until his arrest, Marcus Wesson is all they knew. I'm sure they'll have a chance to go through the grieving process now that the trial is over."

That's when the reality set in: the trial was over. Marcus had lost his battle against the law.

Now what is everyone going to do?

In a weird way, the constant demands of the trial had helped the Wessons avoid coping with the tragedy. Now that the distractions were gone, they would finally have to drop their defense mechanisms. I wondered how they would handle their new reality.

Marcus's family members could do nothing else to help him at this point. All they could do was help themselves.

"What happens now?" Elizabeth asked when I got home that night.

"They'll transfer him to San Quentin and go through the whole check-in process, then put him in isolation. They don't think it's safe to put him with the other prisoners."

I almost told her what inmates did to child molesters, but I caught myself. "It's for *his* protection, not theirs," I said.

THE FAMILY WAS also dealing with another defeat. The victims' advocates had written a letter to the judge advising against family visitation, using the same arguments they did when Marcus first went to jail: they worried he could still influence and control some of his family members. By now, I knew they were right. The judge agreed and prohibited any family visits at San Quentin.

"The good news is, we can talk about the case again," I said sarcastically.

My joke didn't go over well. Elizabeth and Rosie rolled their eyes. Now that we had the green light to talk about him, we didn't have anything substantive to say.

"You know, they're going to cut his hair," I said. "And if you ask me, it's long overdue."

I would have done anything to chop off the malformed dreadlock myself. I felt like I'd earned it.

"He told us he was getting ready to cut it off anyway," Rosie said.

"He's only saying that because he knew they were going to cut it," I said. "God, he still has to act like everything is his decision."

"What are they going to do with it?" Rosie asked.

"Hopefully burn—" I started. "Oh, sorry. It's just so gross and unsanitary. Why? Do you guys want it or something?"

They shrugged.

"Oh my God! You want it?"

The thought of those dreadlocks lying inside my apartment made me cringe. "No way are those things coming here."

"He told us the prison would send us his belongings and his hair," Rosie said.

I had a vision of the dreadlocks escaping from their plastic bag and wrapping themselves around my body, tying down my arms and legs, and choking me while I slept.

The huge shredded one I'd been fixated on in court would definitely come and get me.

The girls cracked up at my reaction.

"You guys better tell me that you're not going to bring those things into the apartment."

They kept laughing.

"I'm not kidding. Especially you, Rosie."

I still needed to get her back for the Leatherface incident.

A FEW DAYS later, San Quentin e-mailed a new picture of Marcus sans dreads to all the media outlets, including our station. He looked almost normal. I prayed that the remnants of his haircut weren't on their way to my apartment.

I flipped on one of our competitors' news stations just as they were airing the hair story, so I turned it up loud. A reporter was saying that the hair would be donated to Locks of Love—a nonprofit group that makes wigs for children who have alopecia or who are undergoing chemotherapy. I couldn't imagine how they'd ever let a bunch of little kids run around with a mass murderer's hair on their heads. Still, I was relieved those demon locks would never come near me again.

Twenty-two

I felt like I needed a long vacation. We *all* needed a long vacation. Unfortunately, I didn't have the money or the time off. It was a nice daydream, though. *Someday,* I thought.

To escape from reality, the Wessons and I often spoke about *someday*. The day we would hop on a plane—a first for them—and jet off to the Greek islands. Fantasizing about what we would see and do and who we would meet somehow made the depressing times a bit more tolerable.

That said, sometimes no amount of daydreaming seemed to help. The children's birthdays were the worst. Elizabeth had a certain look on those days. I always knew by her face, but sometimes she would tell me anyway.

"It's Sebhrenah's birthday today," she'd say, or "Today's Jeva's birthday."

There was nothing I could say on those days. I just listened to her stories about that child, and in between the tears, she would smile. And in between my tears, I would smile. I wished her critics could have seen her during those moments. Maybe then they would understand that she never would have done anything to purposely hurt those children. The truth was, Elizabeth wasn't doing well. She was simply surviving.

* * *

"You won't believe this," she said to me one day as she handed me a printed envelope that said "Jury Summons." Her husband had just been whisked away to death row and the county wanted her to be a juror?

"I can see it now," I said playfully. "The defendant walks in and you're like, 'Your Honor, he's *not guilty!*' And the other jurors are like, 'But he confessed five times and there was the victim's blood and the murder weapon in his car.' And you're like, 'It was probably a setup. *Not guilty!*' "

"Alysia, I'm not that bad," Elizabeth said.

I shot her the Oh, really? look, and she laughed. I wouldn't have been surprised if Marcus himself got the next jury duty notice.

Elizabeth reported to the courthouse on the specified date and actually made it through the first few stages of questioning, but luckily, she was excused.

To be fair, Elizabeth was slowly beginning to acknowledge Marcus's mistakes. Still, every once in a while, she would say things that made me question her progress. Such was the case when we watched a true-crime program that focused on a serial rapist. The suspect would crawl through women's windows at night and sneak into their bedrooms to attack them.

Elizabeth shook her head, turned to me, and said, "I guess you're not even safe in your own home anymore, huh?"

I waited for her to see the irony in her statement, but it didn't happen. Didn't she realize that she and the kids would have been safer anywhere in the world *except* their home?

Even though the obvious often went right over Elizabeth's head, I could tell she was reexamining her life.

"You know, by the time I was your age, I had given birth *eleven* times," she said.

"You are crazy. I can't even imagine having *one* yet," I said, shaking my head in disbelief. "I'm surprised Marcus let you stop."

I knew it was nearly impossible for Elizabeth to talk about sex. If actors were even *kissing* on TV, she'd turn red and cover her eyes.

"I remember the first time I went to Planned Parenthood," she said, blushing. "I can only talk to you about this stuff, Alysia."

"I know, Elizabeth. I feel honored."

"Well, I went in there because I was pregnant. I was fourteen, and my mom had never told me about sex. I didn't even know where babies came out. I thought they came out of your belly button. I don't know why. But Marcus had to tell me about birth back then. Anyway, the lady asked me how much I was, you know. How much we were . . ."

She paused.

"Having sex?" I said, leaning toward her.

"Yes, well, having, you know, how much I was sleeping with my husband. So I didn't know what to say. So I lied and told her two times a day."

"Two times a day? Every day? When you were pregnant? What do you mean you lied?"

"You don't know Marcus. We would, well, he would want it five times a day."

"*Five* times? How many times did you do it?"

"Five times a day."

"Oh my God, Elizabeth!"

"So, I was embarrassed to say five. So I told her two, but I didn't know that was still a lot. So she looked at me with bug eyes and couldn't believe it."

"What did she do?"

"She handed me a huge bag full of condoms and another huge bag filled with that foam stuff for after I had my baby. I was so embarrassed because when I got out to the lobby, I saw all the other girls had these little dainty paper bags only half full, and I had two *huge* bags. Then I had to ride the bus home carrying them."

"Clearly you didn't use them. What did you do with them?"

"I gave them to my sister," Elizabeth said, laughing so hard that tears poured down her face. "Alysia, I didn't know any better. He was the only man I'd ever been with. The only man I have *ever* been with. And I was so young. And sometimes he wanted me to do things I wasn't comfortable with. So, I didn't satisfy him enough."

"How do you know?"

"He would tell me, you know? And I could just tell."

"He would *tell* you?"

"He would leave a lot and go to movies."

"Movies?"

"Yeah. He was frustrated and he would tell me he was going to *those* kinds of movies."

"Porn movies?"

"Yeah. He'd be gone most of the night, and then come back whenever."

"And leave you home with the kids?"

"I didn't mind. I knew I didn't satisfy him. I was always pregnant."

"Because he wanted so many damn kids!"

"Every year, I would go into the free clinic and the workers would get more and more upset," Elizabeth said, more serious now. "With my last three, they begged me to get my tubes tied. When I came back pregnant with Lise, they wouldn't let it go. They decided to pay for it themselves if I would have the procedure. So I finally did it. The day after I had Lise, I had my tubes tied."

I hoped she couldn't tell from my expression that I was grateful for those clinic workers.

AT HOME, I had turned into a life coach. It had taken Marcus years and years of manipulation to shape the girls into what they were. I knew I had no easy task talking them out of it, so I claimed a small victory every time they acknowledged he was wrong about something.

Rosie was the most stubborn, so no one in the family thought she would change her mind about Marcus. Maybe it was wishful thinking, but I was convinced she was coming around a little bit. She was young, smart, and beautiful, and she had missed out on so much. It sickened me to think she might be fantasizing that Marcus would get out of prison and the two of them would ride off into the sunset.

I could tell she felt guilty for even talking about the prospect of moving on. She told me that, although she loved children, she would never have any more.

"But when *you* have kids, I'll help you raise them, Alysia," Rosie said, smiling.

"I just may take you up on that someday."

"Aaaw, your kids would be cute, with big blue eyes and curly hair."

"Okay, it's a deal. How many should I have?" I asked.

"What about a boy and a girl?"

"That sounds good. Let's see, I would name my girl Athena, after my favorite relative, and my boy, um, I don't know what I'd name a boy."

"How about Simon?" she asked, pointing to the *American Idol* media badges that hung on my doorknob.

"I don't think so," I said, shaking my head. "Keep trying."

As she listed off possible names for my future son, I thought about *her* boy and girl who had been murdered. The only time Rosie ever cried was when we talked about Ethan and Sedona. By then, I was mostly desensitized to Elizabeth's daily crying. But when Rosie cried, it was different. I always thought releasing emotion was a good thing for victims, but that didn't seem to be the case for Rosie. She wasn't like most people, and I hadn't quite figured out how to get through to her about Marcus.

Rosie always came and sat on my bed to talk while I was getting ready to go to work or out with friends. Since the trial ended, I had used those casual conversations to nudge her in a more positive direction.

"I know you don't want to hear it, Rosie, but someday, you will get in a new relationship and be happier than you ever thought possible."

"Alysia!"

"You don't have to say anything, but I'm telling you, it's going to happen."

"No it won't. Don't say that."

"I know. You're convinced that I'm completely wrong. That's fine. But someday, you're going to be like, 'Man, Alysia was right.' And you won't admit it to me, but we'll both know the truth."

Rosie laughed. "You are so wrong it's not even funny."

"Then why are you laughing?"

AT FIRST, I could tell Rosie was uncomfortable even being in the room when I was speaking out against Marcus, but after a dozen such conversations, she not only listened to what I had to say but began contributing as well.

Rosie and I had gone down to the pool to get a little sun and do some swimming. Fortunately, she had graduated to wearing a tank top and knee-length shorts, a vast improvement over the skirt. We were both standing halfway between the shallow and deep ends, with our elbows resting on the concrete rim that bordered on a horseshoe-shaped pond. There, we watched a family of ducks float through the pond's artificially colored teal water.

"You want to know something?" Rosie asked.

"What?" I said, sensing I was about to hear a confession.

"You aren't going to believe me."

"Probably not."

She paused for about ten seconds, looked at me, then back at the ducks.

"I liked a boy once."

Coming from the mouth of any other twenty-four-year-old, it would have sounded crazy.

"Shut up," I said.

"I did," she said, looking me in the eye. "He worked with us at the Radisson."

"You liked someone? Did you ever talk to him?"

"No way! But he used to say hi to me all the time."

"Did you ever say hi back?"

"No way."

"Tell me more."

What began as a lighthearted story became increasingly serious.

"I thought about saying hi to him, and then . . . ," she said, pausing.

"And then what?"

"I found out I was pregnant."

There's the rub.

"I was afraid something would happen to the baby if I didn't confess."

"*Confess?* Confess what?"

"That I was beginning to like someone else."

"Please don't tell me you—"

"Yes, I told Marcus," Rosie said, finishing my sentence.

"What?"

"Yeah, I went to him and said I had feelings about a boy, but I'd never talked to him and I never would."

"Wow. I bet he lost it," I said.

"Well, he told me God would take my baby if I didn't straighten out."

"That mother fu—" I started.

"Alysia!" Rosie interrupted. "He told me to report the guy to Human Resources if he ever got near me."

"What ever happened with the guy?"

"Nothing. He ended up getting fired."

I wonder how Marcus managed that one.

* * *

EVERY SO OFTEN, Elizabeth's and Rosie's demeanor would visibly change. They seemed sadder, and they clammed up when I tried to talk to them. I came to learn that these changes occurred after they'd received a letter from Marcus, who was trying to "snap them into shape" just when they were making progress on their path to independence. I felt helpless, knowing he continued to dictate commands through the mail. I wished so much that I could intercept the envelopes at the post office. I wondered what he could possibly be saying to them.

I asked Elizabeth about his prison letters, and she reluctantly showed them to me, pulling out a stack of handwritten notes with curlicues and drawings all over the margins.

"What are those pictures?" I asked, looking more closely at one of the pages. "Is that a bumblebee?"

"Yeah, Marcus draws a bee in the parts where I'm supposed to read and a rose in the parts that are for Rosie," Elizabeth explained. "He's been doing that all along."

"Wow! So what were all those things he was drawing in court? Do you know?"

Marcus had spent hours doodling on lined paper during his trial. All the reporters tried to figure out what he was sketching, but we couldn't tell.

"I have some of them, Alysia. Do you want to see them?" Elizabeth asked.

"You have them here? Please, show me!" I said, realizing the answer to the mystery had been under my nose for months. Some investigative reporter I was! She returned with a stack of white and yellow pages, which included notes and questions Marcus had drafted to help his attorneys. I flipped through them with excitement.

Even his handwriting is creepy. I reached two conclusions after reviewing the documents. First, Marcus was severely disturbed, and second, he loved to write about himself and his bizarre worldviews. It got me thinking. If he liked to talk so much, maybe he'd be up for an interview with a reporter who had a zillion questions for him.

"Do you think Marcus would talk to me?" I asked Elizabeth.

"What do you mean?"

"Would he do an interview with me if I started writing to him?"

"Probably, Alysia. Marcus loves to talk and talk and talk," Elizabeth said.

I walked into my room, sat at my computer, stared at the blank screen, and began to type:

```
Dear Marcus,
```

Then I deleted "Dear." There was nothing endearing about the man, and I couldn't make myself be nice. Still, I needed to know more about him. Why were these women I cared so much about still devoted to him?

```
  Before I introduce myself, I want
to be completely honest. I'm not sure
how I feel about you. From the day of
the tragedy until now, I have regarded
you in a million different ways. I've
laughed while listening to funny sto-
ries from your family; I've cried out
of both anger and sympathy listening to
```

stories from the prosecutor; and most of
all, I've constantly wondered how our
paths got so intertwined.

I told him where I was from and that I was a reporter
who had covered his case. I didn't go into much detail but
left the door open in case he wanted to "tell his side of the
story." That phrase usually worked.

Frankly, I had forgotten about the letter until I was
flipping through the mail a couple of weeks later and saw
an envelope from San Quentin, penned by the monster
himself.

I almost didn't want to read it. I carefully tore open the
envelope, hoping he hadn't licked it closed, and pulled out
the two pages of scribbles.

Alysia,
    This letter is written in apprecia-
tion, gratitude and thanks. Thank you.
How are you today? I hope fine. I found
your letter most intriguing: You have
my granddaughter's name; correctly put,
she has yours!

I didn't even want him thinking about the baby. I read on.

    I can only ascertain; My Elizabeth
lives in your life and you in hers,
possible to the extent of co-habita-
tion? Never the less; I am sure: She is
in trusting hands wherever she is.

"My Elizabeth"? Not anymore, I thought. Next, he told me he didn't want to set the record straight, because doing so would endanger his family; he claimed society lacked "perspicuous views." I could tell he had a dictionary in his cell.

The only job I could help him with, he said, would be to protect his family from the prosecutors who had sought his "wrongful conviction."

The man actually believed *he* was the victim, and the government was to blame? He *was* delusional.

```
Do not get me started, I see now; you
are also a tactician: A woman-reporter,
saying key words and phrases to attract
the need to tell the truth—built up
within a man of whom has not talked for
two years almost, You!
```

That nonsensical statement was followed by a whole page of ranting about the "entire house of prosecution" that "conjured up stories" and harassed him and his family, as well as tried to "dissimulate all previous known values instilled by the defendant to his family."

Apparently, he also had a thesaurus. He thought the crazy beliefs that he'd instilled in his family were "values"? He was wrong about the prosecution "dissimulating" what he taught his family. In actuality, it was because the family was being exposed to society—mainly me.

```
I am afraid to meet you—you might
have me talking, while at the same time
```

swearing that I will not. The length of
this letter is indicative of my need to
talk. Well, Alysia: I did enjoy talking
to you Ç. I hope the experience was mutual. . . . This letter is written with
love and appreciation.

He was the last person in the world I could imagine
drawing smiley faces. He hoped the experience was mutual?
Somehow, everything he said sounded perverse. He was
afraid to meet me? How was that for a twist of fate? On
second thought, I realized, he *should* be afraid to meet me.

The intimate tone of his letter creeped me out, and I
didn't feel good about corresponding with him. On the
other hand, I didn't want him to get the last word, so I felt
I had to respond. I retracted my proposal to "tell his story"
and told him that a local attorney I had talked to must have
been mistaken when he said Marcus wanted to set some
things straight.

As for my letter, I did not intention-
ally choose my words carefully. I was
very honest about everything and I vow
to continue that honesty. I'm certain
you will grant me the same courtesy.

I appreciate your confidence in my
intentions in regards to your family.
I am honored your granddaughter shares
my name. She is a bright and beautiful
child. As you know, she brought hope to
everyone at a time when it wasn't easy

to come by. Your wife and children are amazing people. Anyone would be lucky to know them.

As for your case, I realize the appeals process can be long, convoluted and frustrating. I get plenty of letters from inmates describing the injustices. It's true, having an unlimited supply of money can only help one's prospects when faced with the legal system.

I can not pretend to know what it's like, because I've never been incarcerated. I can only relay information I've learned from others. . . . With that, Marcus, I will wrap up this letter. I am a bit stubborn, so I feel the need to defend my previous statements. Thank you again for your time.

Best, Alysia

I sealed the envelope, then copied down his inmate number and San Quentin's address.

"Elizabeth, do you have any stamps?" I asked, carrying the letter into the living room.

"Sure, how many do you need?"

"I don't know. How many stamps does it take to make it to death row?"

"Alysia!"

"I'm sorry. I'm serious, though. I'm sending this to your husband."

"What does it say?"

I wanted to respond with something sarcastic, but I restrained myself. "I just told him that I thought he wanted to talk, but I guess he doesn't after all."

"No, Alysia, he *does* want to talk."

"Well, he'll do it only on his own terms, I'm sure. Just like everything else in his life."

Twenty-three

I might have joked around about my new death row pen pal, but it wasn't so funny when his frightening image made its way into my dreams. Even though I didn't think I was afraid of him, I felt vulnerable and unsafe now that Marcus knew my name and address. The fear led to consistent nightmares about him. For a week straight, he became my personal Freddy Krueger, sadistically sneaking into my mind after I'd drift off to sleep. I stayed up late, turned on both lights in my bedroom, and kept my door open.

When I mentioned it to the others, they confessed they, too, were suffering from violent nightmares. In our own separate ways, we were all working through the damage that Marcus had caused. Talking about the dreams helped us process our complicated emotions.

My nightmares were similar to Gypsy's, in that they always involved Marcus coming after me somehow, whether in a room or on a deserted road. In Dorian's, Marcus was chasing him in the heavy black combat boots that he used to wear. Dorian was so afraid, he never broke his pace; he just ran and ran, his fear escalating. Adrian described his nightmares as savage. Marcus tore after him with a large machete, mowing down everything in his path as he closed in on his son.

GYPSY HAD BEEN talking more often and more freely about Sebhrenah and Lise, so I figured she must be hurting less these days. One day she told me a story that changed my image of her older sister for good.

Shortly before Gypsy had run away, Sebhrenah had been going through a rough time with her health. Sebhrenah had a history of stomach problems, but during that period, she was in severe pain. She would hide in the girls' room, curled up in the fetal position. Then, clumps of her hair began falling out. Some of her siblings knew about the ailments, but none of them risked telling Marcus about them.

"There's something very wrong with me," she told Gypsy.

"*What's* wrong with you?"

"I'm not going to say. But it's really bad. You'll be able to really tell in about eight months."

"Sebhrenah, what are you talking about?"

The murders came eerily close to that eight-month mark. I wondered what had been wrong with her. The coroner mentioned no sign of disease in her autopsy.

Even though the defense had painted Sebhrenah as a tough, gun-obsessed soldier, Gypsy was telling me about the softer side of her sister, a young woman who had dreamed of going to school, sharing an apartment with Kiani, and getting married someday. She had even summoned up the courage to tell Marcus of her plans, for which she was scolded and beaten for weeks. Gypsy said Sebhrenah finally told him she'd changed her mind and wanted to stay.

I kept trying to picture Sebhrenah pulling the trigger, but the image I had of her now was inconsistent with a killer. I still wasn't satisfied that she did it. On the other hand, Marcus fit the mold to a T.

I'D HEARD PLENTY of bad things about Marcus so far, and I hated him a little bit more with each new story. I could barely contain my anger at the man, but it was about to get even stronger.

Rosie had been acting strangely anxious and depressed for the past week, and I couldn't understand the sudden shift in her mood. She'd been making such strides, talking optimistically about going to school so she could work with animals someday. Something must have happened to bring her down; I immediately suspected Marcus.

I walked into her room and noticed that some of her clothes were neatly folded on the floor.

"What's going on?" I asked, pointing to the pile of clothing. "Where are you going?"

"San Francisco."

She didn't know a single person in that city. "Why San Francis—" I started.

Then it dawned on me. *Marcus* was in prison near San Francisco. She wanted to be closer to him. I was enraged. I wanted to scream. I wanted to give up. Rosie looked up at me apologetically with deep brown, lost eyes. Both of us were on the verge of tears.

"You're not going because of *him,* are you?" I asked, needing to hear the answer from Rosie.

"Alysia, I just need to go there."

"What do you mean *need*? Did *he* tell you to move there?"

She looked down but said nothing.

"Where will you live?"

"I don't know yet."

"Rosie, you don't have to listen to him anymore. He's never getting out," I said, feeling my anger take over. "You never have to see him again."

She turned her back to me and stared at Cosmo in his cage. I could tell she didn't want to face the reality of what I was saying.

"You have to do what's best for *you* now," I said to the back of her head. "He doesn't have a say in your life anymore!"

Grasping the thin, black metal bars of the cage, she looked over her shoulder at me with a trapped expression, almost as if she felt caged herself.

"I just have to do this, Alysia. I have to."

A WEEK LATER, she was gone. I called Elizabeth, who had driven Rosie to San Francisco, to find out the real reason behind the move. She promised to explain everything to me when she came home in a few days.

There was something different about Elizabeth when she returned to Fresno. She was distracted, jumpy, and wouldn't answer my questions about Rosie directly.

"I need to know, Elizabeth," I said. "He had something to do with this, didn't he?"

"I tried to get her to stay, but she doesn't want to listen," Elizabeth said, crying.

"What did he say to her? I won't get mad. Just tell me."

Elizabeth broke down and told me the truth. Rosie had asked her not to, but my constant badgering made it impossible for Elizabeth to keep her word. I was worried about Rosie, and I wasn't about to let Marcus take her away from me.

As I suspected, he was behind it all. Elizabeth said Marcus had sent Rosie a letter saying that the Lord told him she was on the wrong path and needed to be by herself, away from the negative influences. I was fairly certain *I* was the negative influence to which he was referring. Marcus had been sentenced to a lifetime of isolation, and now he wanted Rosie to live in solitary confinement as well.

Maybe it was a mistake to write him after all.

Marcus told Rosie to pack some clothes in a backpack, then ask Elizabeth to drive her to San Francisco and drop her at a random spot at the side of the road. From there, Rosie was supposed to find a boat to live on, enroll in sailing lessons, and wait for further instructions. He told Rosie to use the money from the sale of the Hammond house, money the family had planned to use to buy a new house, for her living expenses.

At first, Elizabeth told Rosie she wouldn't go along with the new plan, but Rosie said she would do it with or without her aunt's help. She would hitchhike if she had to. Whatever it took to follow Marcus's orders.

"I'm not going to drop you off in the middle of nowhere in a strange city," Elizabeth replied.

The two fought privately for days while I was at work until they reached a compromise. Elizabeth would take Rosie to San Francisco, but she would not leave her there alone. They would find a boat together, and as soon as Rosie was settled, Elizabeth would leave her there. So that's what they did.

Elizabeth couldn't keep up her entire end of the bargain, though, because she was too worried about Rosie being on her own for the first time. So she would stay with me a few days, then return to San Francisco for a few days. This went on for months.

Unfortunately, Marcus wasn't finished handing out orders to his faithful wives. He put Elizabeth in charge of bringing the family back together. He told her she needed to get another "trailer," which was his code word for "boat." He wrote that he'd had visions of the "trailer," saying it was "what the Lord wanted for the family." Once she bought the new boat, he said, the "children would flock back to her." He told her to find a fifty-foot trailer space—big enough for the whole family—but to hold on to the old car.

```
    It is perfect, it loves you. It will
run forever for you. Please keep faith
in our expectations. God reminds me
everyday. . . . Once you accomplish
the trailer spot, then the trailer
will come automatically. God promised
that you already have it and do not
even know it. . . . Once you accom-
plish everything, then I have a letter
for you already written. Give it to
Adrian. I feel that he wants to pur-
chase another car for himself and give
his old one to his brothers. God said
mail it to you. Be ready!
```

It was even worse than I thought.

When would this stop? Why is he allowed to continue his abuse from behind bars?

I didn't feel like justice was being served. Apparently, the First Amendment rights of a mass murderer or child rapist outweighed the health and well-being of his surviving family members.

Elizabeth left the letter on the table, knowing I would read it.

"What is all this?" I said, waving the letter at her. "Why are you letting him do this?"

"What do you mean?"

"Are you going to do whatever he wants, whenever he wants?"

"No, Alysia. I just ignore this stuff."

"But Rosie doesn't. Do you tell him you're not following his orders?"

"He knows," she said unconvincingly.

"Apparently he doesn't."

IT HAD BEEN months since Rosie moved onto an old houseboat that didn't run. She also had enrolled in sailing classes, just as she was told.

Why did he want her in sailing classes anyway?

I called my mom to vent and told her about Rosie's latest living arrangement.

"Do you think he wants Rosie to sail to San Quentin and pick him up or something?" Mom asked.

My stomach dropped. I knew instantly that she was right. Marcus had the deluded idea that he would get out of prison soon—and he wanted Rosie to come rescue him.

* * *

AFTER A FEW months, Rosie came to visit. She had been avoiding me, knowing I didn't approve of what she was doing. I tried to keep my opinions to myself and just enjoy her company, but she seemed distant, as if she was under his influence again. I couldn't stay silent, so I confronted her about it.

"Rosie, why are you taking sailing lessons?"

"What do you mean?" she asked, surprised that I knew about the classes.

"Why do you want to learn how to sail all of a sudden? I've never even heard you mention sailing before."

"I just want to, Alysia."

Her face was pale and gaunt. She'd lost at least ten pounds since I'd last seen her. I couldn't let Marcus do this to her any longer.

"But you said you wanted to go to school," I said, hoping I could appeal to her sense of logic. "And instead you're spending all your money on sailing lessons? Listen, you don't think you're going to rescue Marcus from the bay, do you?"

"Alysia!"

"Be honest. Because I promise, he's never getting out of there. Does he think he's going to escape, and you'll be there waiting?"

"No. I don't want to talk about it," she said firmly.

The last thing I wanted to do was push her away, so I quickly softened my tone.

"Fine," I said, smiling. "Would you please just start doing what *you want* to do, though? Forget all the crap he tells you to do. Do what *you* want."

"Okay, Alysia."

Rosie rolled her eyes at me. I may have sounded like a broken record, but I wanted her to hear it over and over until it sank in. I would never stop fighting my battle of wills against Marcus Wesson.

IT WAS THE worst possible time for this, but I was the next person in the household to get a jury summons. When I walked through security that morning, the guards at the courthouse got a good laugh out of it.

Actually, at that point I could have used a day off from work and the drama at home. Sugary snacks and a slew of movies in the jury room sounded pretty good. It was just my luck that the court's DVD player broke the day I showed up. I knew I was in trouble when a court worker wheeled out a dusty old VHS deck. As I sat for hours with the other potential jurors, I tuned out the 1980s movies with their constant lines of static and mentally prepared a list of reasons I'd be a horrible juror.

I'm a news reporter. I correspond with a death row inmate. I live with the family of the biggest mass murderer in this city's history.

The defendant agreed to a deal before I ever made it into the courtroom, so I never had to try them out.

I HAD BEGGED Elizabeth to change her ring tone for months. I didn't know what annoying song it was or what ungodly decibel she had it set to. All I knew was, it was blasting into my eardrum at 4:00 in the morning.

It was a familiar wake-up call by now.

"What's wrong, *mi hijo?*" Elizabeth asked frantically.

My feet were hanging off the end of the couch, both of them painfully asleep. I was way too tall for the thing, and it wasn't even comfortable. Even so, I slept on it sometimes when Elizabeth and I would have late-night talks. One of my coworkers had given me the couch once she learned of my living situation. It was an odd shade of blue, not my style, and matched absolutely nothing else in the room, but none of that mattered anymore. Function had replaced fashion in my world. Plain and simple, we needed more places to sit. Besides, I never had company over anymore. My left foot tingled awake, and I heard Elizabeth turn on the shower.

From her conversation, I could tell one of the boys in Santa Cruz was going through a crisis. I heard her tell him she'd make the two-and-a-half-hour drive there to help talk him through it.

The water stopped running, and Elizabeth walked into the kitchen. She jumped, startled to see me on the couch with my eyes open.

"You scared me, Alysia. Did I wake you? I'm sorry."

I was sitting up, so the answer was obvious. We both chuckled.

It didn't make sense. This woman was about to drive for hours in the middle of the night to help her son without thinking twice. So how could she have stood by while Marcus physically, mentally, and sexually abused the children?

"I'll see you later," she whispered. "Go back to sleep. Sorry."

I listened to the click of the lock behind her, followed by the rhythmic taps of her high heels down the concrete stairs and across the narrow sidewalk toward the parking lot. Each step grew fainter until the sound faded away completely.

My legs were awake now. I swung them back over the edge of the short couch and lay horizontal again, wondering what time the sun would come up. The apartment was so silent and still, it was a little scary. I didn't like being alone anymore.

Twenty-four

I'd always been an eternal optimist, but my attitude was changing quickly. Watching the Wesson family unravel had had a profound effect on my perspective. Suddenly, everyone else's problems seemed like a cakewalk in comparison.

Young, rich celebrities checking in and out of rehab, the burglary victim I'd interviewed, even my friend who blamed her failed relationships on her parents' divorce—none of them seemed to have it that bad.

I was back in L.A. at the end of May in 2006 for the Season 5 finale of *Idol*. This time, it felt a little different. As I approached the intersection of Hollywood and Highland, I saw hundreds of enthusiastic fans. Making sure my media badge was showing, I pushed my way through the shoulder-to-shoulder crowd. Reporters and photographers from every major radio and TV market in the country were there. Although we all got along well, we were still competitors in the field. We needed the same interviews at the same time, and sometimes, that didn't make for a pretty scene.

Out of the corner of my eye, I saw Randy, Paula, and Simon approaching us. Unfortunately, I wasn't the only one. Like a pack of hyenas, we surrounded the startled trio of celebrities, who were expecting orderly one-on-one interviews, as their PR folks had planned.

A video camera smacked me in the back of the head. When I turned toward the culprit, another camera struck me on the left side of my face. An elbow to my jaw later, I forced myself toward the center and jabbed my microphone as close to the judges' mouths as possible. It was too late to turn back now.

Panicking producers tried to disperse us, yelling, "Back up. You'll all have a chance for interviews. Get in line."

We moved back as a group, and I was still stuck in the rear third. I feared the judges would grow tired and leave before it was my turn. I felt defeated as I watched it play out.

Our society sure has mixed-up priorities. The Wessons are the ones who should be the focus of so much attention. And even worse, I'm a part of the media madness.

I wanted to cry.

My frustration must have been written all over my face. I looked up, and through the waving arms and bobbing heads, I saw Simon staring at me with a compassionate expression, then give me a reassuring wink. I nodded and smiled back. Little did he know, but Simon had become a lifeline out of the emotional muck the Wessons and I had been wading through lately. He was playing the same role for me now as I was engulfed by the madding crowd.

Simon gave me the boost I needed to brace myself for another body thrashing in the crowd. I pushed forward once again and got my interview. Simon had saved the day.

I REGROUPED DURING the drive back to Fresno, feeling that everything was going to be all right. On the trek upstairs to my apartment, I sifted through the mail that had collected in the box during my week away: cell phone bill, bank statement, dry cleaning advertisement, letter from a mass murderer.

I dropped my bags at the doorstep, hearing laughter on the other side of the door and the unmistakable timbre of Kiani's voice. The girls had come for a visit. I didn't want to spoil the mood with the letter, so I tiptoed back down the stairs and around the corner, sank onto the dirty pavement, and leaned against the building to read it.

```
Dear Alysia:
   Well, I can see that we are somewhat
miffed. Realize that misunderstandings
initially are the foundations for last-
ing true friendships. Not withstanding
the need for a cordial first impres-
sion, one should always be honest with
a person. . . . Your first letter con-
veyed clearly your deep concern for my
family and I had already realized; you
are the last one who would want to see
my family hurt again.
```

Marcus told me that he was proud of my relationship with Elizabeth and his children, and that it was "worth bragging about." I pictured him telling the prison guards that a woman on the outside was taking care of his family. He did want to get some information out there, he said, so I hadn't been "misinformed" about that.

Your motives seemed to me of a genu-
ine and sincere nature. . . . I enjoyed
your letter, Alysia. Do not be so sensitive. It seems as though we've gotten
off on the wrong foot. Just as you feel
I have some misperceptions about you, I
feel you have some misperceptions about
me. . . . Well my friend, I do wish you
well. God Bless You, always.
                    Your friend, Marcus Wesson

I sat on the hot concrete for a good five minutes, staring straight ahead. I looked down and saw an ant carrying another ant's carcass along the middle of the sidewalk. When he got near my leg, he stopped, put down his dead friend, and scurried into the grass. I tried to concentrate on the ants, but I couldn't block out his closing words.

Marcus Wesson thinks he is my friend.

I felt a surge of anger. I suddenly wished I was back at *American Idol*, fighting for interviews again. This time, I would have been able to push my way into the front from the start. No one would have messed with me.

I folded the letter and stuffed it into my pocket. With each determined step up the stairs, I cursed Marcus under my breath.

Your friend? You think you're my friend? Ha! Giving me advice about my job! Don't be so sensitive? Me? I'll show you sensitive.

I strapped my heavy bags on my shoulder and turned the doorknob. Everyone turned to look at me. The gang was all there.

"Hi, Alysia," Elizabeth said, excited to see me. "How was your trip?"

"Are you surprised we're here?" Kiani asked, laughing again.

"Yes! Come here," I said, dropping my luggage with a loud thump.

After a round of hugs, I settled onto the couch next to Kiani. Even though I was still irate, I noticed that she was beaming.

"So, Alysia," she said, turning toward me with a smile. "I'm pregnant!"

I abandoned my negative feelings about her father and focused on his beautiful, happy daughter in front of me.

"Congratulations," I said, hugging her again. "Tell me more!"

She said she and her boyfriend were expecting a girl. The father was a friend of Adrian and Dorian. The two had started dating shortly after she moved out of my apartment.

Kiani grew animated and waved her hands when she talked, especially when she was enthusiastic about a story. I saw a flash of gold and realized that she was still wearing the wedding band Marcus had given her. It seemed odd. Despite that, I could tell she had built some hope for the future. She'd gotten a job at a drugstore in Santa Cruz, and she was enjoying working again. I prayed she finally had the life she deserved.

MY PARENTS RAISED me to believe that people are inherently good. I started wondering if I was focusing too much on the evil things I knew about Marcus. Beyond his heinous crimes and distorted beliefs, there had to be *something* good about him. I set out on a mission to find it.

I didn't think I could handle too much at once, so I decided to start small. I approached Elizabeth with resolve.

"Name one good thing about your husband," I said straightforwardly.

"Why?" she asked, obviously startled by my question. In the thirty-eight years since she'd met him, no one had ever asked her about Marcus's good side.

"Because there's no way he can really be as bad as I think he is," I said.

Lost in thought for a minute, Elizabeth bowed her head.

"Alysia, you know, I can't think of anything right now," she said, clearly saddened that nothing had come to mind.

"Come on, Elizabeth. You loved him, didn't you? What did you love?"

"I don't know. I think I loved him because he paid attention to me."

"But not at the end. At the end, he didn't pay attention to you."

"I know. But I didn't care at the end. I was so depressed, and I was only there because I knew he would hurt the kids if I left."

If only she had known he was going to hurt the kids regardless.

THE WESSON CHILDREN were all reexamining their beliefs and upbringing now that Marcus was locked away. Religion, especially, had played an important role in their lives growing up, but it had since become a source of confusion.

Serafino had gotten married since the murders, and he and his new wife decided to explore their faith together at a new, out-of-town church. The anonymity was comforting for the newlyweds, who immersed themselves in Christian teachings there.

Serafino found a role model in the church's pastor. He trusted the man of God and respected what he had to say. But things took a turn for the worse one day at Bible study, when the pastor began preaching about people who abused the Lord's word.

"Here's a good example," he said. "Let's talk about Marcus Wesson."

Sighs and gasps echoed through the room. Serafino held his breath. His wife wanted to speak out to protect her husband's feelings, but Serafino reached over and put his hand on hers before she had the chance.

"It's okay," he said, whispering. "Let him talk."

And talk the pastor did.

"You guys know of Marcus Wesson, do you?" he said, asking for input from his audience.

"That man is going to hell," one of the parishioners said with contempt.

Serafino sat up straighter in his wooden chair, hearing the elderly lady next to him take a deep breath.

"He is Satan himself in the flesh," she said.

"Yes, he is," the pastor said. "There is not an iota of Jesus Christ in Marcus Wesson."

Serafino began to sweat; he could feel his heart beating faster. He couldn't believe this was happening in church. It was the *one* place he had felt safe.

The outbursts continued as other parishioners joined in. Serafino's skin grew hotter and hotter, until he couldn't take it anymore. He jumped up and ran out of the building.

His wife was overcome with empathy. "Do you guys

realize that was Marcus Wesson's son sitting with you?" she asked before running outside to comfort her husband.

Everyone in the small church gasped again as the pastor followed the couple out, concerned.

He approached Serafino, his face pale and his hands outstretched. "I'm sorry, son. I didn't realize—"

"It's okay. I'm used to it," Serafino said, interrupting. "I have to go."

Even in jail, Marcus was still all too close. From then on, the youngest Wesson son continued his spiritual journey at a different church.

GYPSY'S RELATIONSHIP WITH God was always somewhat of a struggle, because she couldn't disassociate God from thoughts of her father. God reminded her of Marcus, praying reminded her of Marcus, and the Bible reminded her of Marcus.

"After all those years of preaching, my dad managed to make me *less* religious," she said. "Everything he did to us, telling us it was for God. I just kept thinking that God is not ugly, this is not the way it should be."

"Do you pray anymore?" I asked.

"Not really. I love God and I want to go to heaven. But when I think about religion, I get a bad feeling. I should get a warm feeling, but instead I associate it with his teachings."

It bothered me that God had never answered her prayers while Gypsy was growing up. She wasn't asking for a new PlayStation or an A in trigonometry, she just wanted her family to be safe from Marcus. But God had done nothing to stop nine of her brothers and sisters from being murdered, and she was left wondering why. Religion had brought only death and destruction to her family, and I felt she had every right to lose her faith.

OVER THE NEXT few months, Rosie came to visit more frequently. Now that she had her own car, she was able to drive to Fresno without Elizabeth's help. Rosie looked healthier, and I almost believed her when she told me she was okay.

Adrian's girlfriend had set her up with a full-time job selling sunglasses at the Port of San Francisco, and although she was socializing occasionally with her coworkers, I didn't like her living alone on the run-down boat. That said, I knew her job forced her to interact with people, which was exactly what she needed to break Marcus's spell over her.

"I'm so proud of you, Rosie," I said. "Are you still thinking about going to school?"

"Yes. I just want to save some money first."

"You know you're always welcome to come back here. We miss you."

"I miss you, too," Rosie said sadly. "I miss going swimming."

Now that the cool December weather had arrived, the pools at my apartment complex were tucked in for winter under a thick plastic blanket. It was even colder in San Francisco, and I hoped Rosie's boat had a heater.

NEW YEAR'S EVE had always been a big thing for Marcus. He believed the family's home for the coming year should be wherever the family was at midnight. If he wanted the family to live on the boat the following year, he would round up the children and drive them there before the clock struck twelve. He believed this would bring good luck.

I had my own beliefs about celebrating the new year. I advocated using the holiday to let go of all the bad stuff that had accumulated over the past 365 days. The Wessons and I had plenty of negativity to get rid of, and I hoped we could do it together as we welcomed in 2007.

Rosie couldn't get off work, so Elizabeth decided to drive to San Francisco to be with her. I went to a crowded party, where I drank champagne and vowed to start anew. For one night, I released my anger toward Marcus, my sadness over the murdered children, and my worry for the Wessons' future. Just before midnight, I thought of Elizabeth and Rosie, picturing them inside the cramped, dark boat, watching the glowing ball drop on TV. I hoped they were warm enough and having fun.

Maybe this is the year when everything will get better.

At the time, I knew nothing about Marcus's tradition, and it would be several years before I learned where Rosie and Elizabeth had spent their special night, holding to their family's old routine—for the second year in a row.

FIVE . . . FOUR . . . THREE . . . two . . . one . . .

"Happy New Year," Elizabeth said quietly, adjusting her seat belt as she glanced up at Rosie.

"Happy New Year," Rosie replied from the driver's seat. "I think we should stay for a few minutes."

"That's fine."

From the parking lot of San Quentin state prison, the two women gazed out at the sprawling concrete complex in front of them. Marcus was in there somewhere, and he knew his two faithful wives were sitting there that night, thinking of him. They wore no party hats and consumed no champagne; they just drank in the guilt that they were free while Marcus was locked up on one of his favorite holidays.

At 12:10 A.M. on January 1, 2007, Elizabeth and Rosie waved good-bye and drove back to Rosie's boat.

THE NEW YEAR had not brought about the drastic change in Rosie and Elizabeth that I had hoped for, but I was happy to see that Gypsy was striving for independence. After she and little Alysia's father broke up, she decided it was time to work toward some of her lifelong goals. She got a job as a caterer again and enrolled in college courses.

When Gypsy asked if she and little Alysia could move in, I didn't hesitate to say yes. Considering our very different backgrounds, Gypsy and I were surprisingly alike. She was already one of my best friends. Not to mention, I loved that little girl like a daughter.

Having the two of them under my roof was comforting. They took over the spare bedroom, and Elizabeth slept on the couch in the living room. Each morning, little Alysia would sneak into my room when no one was looking and wake me up.

"Excuse me, Miss Alysia," I would say in a groggy haze. "What do you think you're doing?"

She'd crack up until her mom or grandma heard her laughing and ran in to retrieve her.

Although Marcus had faded from memory somewhat, remnants of his wrath showed themselves at the most unexpected times. One night, Gypsy and I were at a club, dancing and meeting new people, when some guys started talking to us.

"So, how did you guys meet?" one of them asked.

It was a simple enough question, but it caught us off guard, and we had no idea how to respond. After an uncomfortable silence, I said, "We've been friends for years."

A few minutes later, the topic of conversation shifted to family and marriage.

"Alysia, are your parents still married?"

"Yes, they are."

"How about yours, Gypsy? Are your parents still together?"

"Umm, not really."

"Oh, they're divorced?"

"Well, no."

"What do you mean?"

"It's a long story," I said, motioning for Gypsy to follow me back to the dance floor. "Isn't this your song?"

It dawned on me that Gypsy and the rest of her family would have a lifetime of difficult explanations in store.

Twenty-five

Y ou really *don't* get any stations out here, do you?" I
asked Elizabeth, as I repeatedly hit the car radio's
seek button, only to find fuzzy transmissions of
Spanish and Christian talk stations.

"I told you," she said, laughing. "We're out in the middle
of nowhere."

The two of us were driving from Fresno to the Santa
Cruz Mountains so she could show me the property where
the family had camped in the army tent for three years.

"Are you sure you don't want to visit the boys first?" I
asked, anticipating the daunting journey on the narrow,
winding road ahead of us.

"That's fine. Let me call Adrian."

"Good luck getting phone reception," I said, making a
sharp U-turn and heading toward the freeway again. "Let's
try this again on our way home."

Twenty minutes later, we pulled into Adrian's driveway,
which was across the street from the beach. Adrian lived with
his girlfriend in a modest but comfortable house and was
working as a personal trainer at a gym nearby.

"When is Dorian coming over?" Elizabeth asked after
hugging Adrian.

"He should be here soon."

I had never gotten a chance to spend much time with Dorian and Adrian, both of whom still lived in Santa Cruz. I had so many questions about their lives, questions that had gone unanswered in the trial. I also wondered how they felt about everything a few years later.

It was early afternoon and the sun was hot, but not nearly as hot as it would have been inland, in Fresno. Elizabeth stayed inside to catch up with Adrian's girlfriend while he and I went outside to talk.

Adrian had grown into a handsome man who moved slowly but with purpose. Although he was very muscular, he was so well-mannered and polite that he came off as gentle and unintimidating. He and I settled into a couple of chairs on the patio, which was surrounded by trees and provided an unobstructed view of the shore.

"Thank you so much for taking care of Mom," Adrian said appreciatively.

"We take care of each other," I said, smiling. "It's beautiful out here. I have always dreamed of living near the beach."

"Thanks," he said. "I love it here."

The warm, salty breeze was just strong enough to rustle my hair, and I could almost feel the humidity reviving my natural curls, which I had worked so hard to straighten that morning.

"Adrian, do you mind if I ask you about your father?"

"I know you must have a lot of questions for all of us," he said softly.

"Yes, I do," I said.

I started by acknowledging how hard Marcus had been on him and Dorian.

"That is true," he said. "He told us he would rather see

us dead than to have a bad attitude. As we got older, he saw us as competition for the girls in the family. And to feel that from your own father—it feels funny when you're living in his house."

"You were adults then. Couldn't you leave?"

"It's not that you're not allowed to leave. It's just you don't know how to leave, because that's all you know and you have no education; none whatsoever."

I asked how he felt about Marcus now. I was expecting to hear that Adrian was happy his family was finally safe from his father, so I was surprised at the degree of compassion he expressed for the man.

"This is what life dealt me," he said. "I can either choose to be angry with him or just make the best of it. So I just choose to forgive him."

"Forgive him? I don't understand," I said, feeling the same frustration I had with his sisters about the psychological manipulation Marcus had wielded over them. "How can you forgive him?"

"That was my world, and it's very humbling, especially now that it's exposed. It humbles you a lot, a lot. And it still hurts, but you have to stand tall."

"But you have kids, Adrian. Can you imagine treating them like that?" I asked, referring to his two young children, a boy and girl who lived with their mother.

"I look at my little princess, and I can't even understand. I just can't understand how he even thought about crossing that line. I can't. You have to be insane."

"Is your dad where he belongs?"

"If they were to let him out, I would be afraid. So that answers your question."

"Have you thought about the execution?"

"That's still settling in. To realize someone is actually going to kill your father on purpose, that's hard. I know he deserves it, but at the same time, I don't hate him. I admired him, yet I feared him deeply. I look at myself now, and I would love to go back in time and change things. But if I were to take a different path in life, how would I be? And you know what? I like myself."

"I like you, too," I said, smiling.

Dorian, who had arrived in the meantime, poked his head outside to greet us.

"I'm interrogating your brother," I said, laughing. "And you're next."

Dorian sat down and joined the conversation. Adrian sat through the small talk, then left us alone.

Like his brother, Dorian had an impressive frame. He was a little taller than Adrian, but his appearance had changed significantly since I'd last seen him. Previously, he had plucked his eyebrows until they were fairly thin and worn a hint of black eyeliner on the lower lids, a strong contrast with his large muscles and chiseled jawline. I never understood why he chose to groom himself like that. Now, devoid of the plucking and makeup, he looked like he belonged on the cover of a magazine.

Right after the murders, he told me, he'd decided to use aikido as his stress release. He'd finally saved enough money to take some classes, so he and his girlfriend walked into a dojo in Santa Cruz to sign him up. But it was not to be.

"I'm sorry, Mr. Wesson," one of the workers told him. "We're not comfortable with you joining our club."

"What do you mean?" Dorian asked, confused. "I have the money right here."

"No. We have heard about the murders in Fresno, and we don't think it would be right to allow you here."

Although Dorian was embarrassed, he also felt defensive about his family's history. "But that's my dad, that's not me," he said with tears in his eyes. He knew people had thoughts like this, but this was the first time anyone had ever confronted him.

"I'm sorry. Why don't you try another dojo?"

Dorian left the studio, worried that the rest of his life was going to be like this. So far, it had. As I talked to his brothers and sisters, they all told me that people continued to cast them in a negative light, just because they were related to Marcus.

"It will get better," I said to Dorian, hoping I was right. "I'm just glad you and your brother got away from your father when you did."

Dorian told me that when he and Adrian were first on their own, they felt shell-shocked, thrown into a society they'd never known. "It was really sad, actually. At first, I was like the guy in the movie *Blast from the Past*. I was like, wow, this is what was out there."

The first movie he saw in a theater was *Apollo 13,* and, just like the girls, he thought it was an amazing experience.

"Usually, when you're growing up, you get desensitized," he said, "and me, I was almost twenty-two and I'd never done anything before."

When it came to finding a girlfriend, Dorian said, he didn't have any experience, so he emulated his father, talking down to women and expecting them to wait on him.

"My relationships didn't last long," he said, laughing. "You know, I think my dad's plan backfired. Unless he'd kept us in a bubble our entire lives, we would eventually have seen he was wrong."

Dorian told me he still struggled with self-esteem issues stemming from his father's continuous insults and beat-ings, recalling that Marcus constantly told them they would never amount to anything. I thought of the contrast with *my* parents, who had always told me that the "sky was the limit" and that I could get whatever I wanted if I tried hard enough.

"I was young and I believed him," Dorian said almost apologetically. "I thought that was what a father tells his son. It's damaged me to this day."

Dorian was so much bigger and stronger than his father, I wished he had the emotional strength to stand up to him now. I also wondered why, given what Dorian and Adrian had learned in their aikido classes, they had never fought back against Marcus, a man who undertook as little physical exertion as possible.

"Didn't you guys ever want to go back and beat the shit out of your father?"

"To be honest, I never thought about confronting him. It's strange, but it never crossed my mind."

I didn't tell him how often the thought had crossed *my* mind.

"You know what I realized?" Dorian asked, cocking his head a little.

"What?" I asked.

"My dad is bisexual."

"What?" I squawked, almost jumping off my seat.

"Yeah. Remember how I used to wear makeup?"

"I hadn't noticed," I lied.

"Well, I used to wear powder and eyeliner and pluck my eyebrows."

"Oh. Why?"

"Because of my dad."

He told me about how his father used to put makeup on him for the plays the boys performed for the girls on Friday nights, the same plays in which Marcus wore dresses and lipstick.

"That's a hideous thought, huh?" Dorian asked, chuckling at my look of horror. I couldn't take much more of this, but I knew I needed to ask one more question.

"Dorian, what is going through his head right now?"

He paused for a minute, then looked out at the sea.

"Well, he foretold his own prophecy. He always used to say, 'When they find out what I do, they'll lock me up and throw away the key.' I'm talking ten years before it happened, he said the government would lock him up and never look back. I guess he was right."

I had heard enough. We walked back inside and joined the rest of the family.

After a few hours, Elizabeth and I took a stroll down the beach.

"I can't believe the things your husband said to your children, telling them they were worthless and stupid," I said, still frustrated.

"I didn't know he was saying those things, Alysia," Elizabeth replied, shaking her head.

We sat on a wooden log in the middle of the sand, where she began to cry as I watched a group of children building sand castles ten feet in front of us.

"I just feel so guilty," she said. "I should have known."

"It was all him, Elizabeth. Even if you knew, you couldn't have done anything about it."

She cried for a few more minutes until I pulled her out of it. "Let's go home," I said, putting my sandals back on. "We'll go to the property another time."

WE HAD PLANNED to stop by to see Kiani, but neither of us would have been very good company. So, a couple of weeks later, Kiani came to visit us in Fresno. We sat on my bed and chatted for hours.

Previously, Kiani had told me that she'd thought her childhood was perfect until the murders, but I knew from her testimony that wasn't true. She finally admitted to me that she'd gone through a severe depression when she was twenty-five. She said she'd wanted to go to school, learn how to drive, and start dating, but she'd repressed those feelings, too worried about offending Marcus.

"I went through a time when I didn't want to live any-more," she said.

"What changed?" I asked.

"It all changed when I had Jeva," she said, bursting into tears. She was crying so hard that she couldn't even talk, harder than I've ever seen her cry before. I jumped up to fetch some tissue.

"Thanks, Alysia. I'm sorry," she said, taking the tissue, wiping her eyes, and blowing her nose. "It's just, Jeva gave me a whole new life to live. She was my everything. At that time, I thought about leaving, but I could not leave my baby. Right when I had her, my problems all went away. I woke up each day and I could focus on her."

"She may have saved your life, Kiani," I said, reaching out to hug her.

"I think she definitely did. I can't explain how, but she just made me so happy. And then everything happened."

"Are you mad at your father?" I asked, knowing she'd never admitted it before.

"I think my dad should be where he's at. Being angry is very confusing to me. Growing up and everything I don't remember being mistreated. I know I got *loving*, and it was wrong. But when it happened, I didn't know I was being abused."

I started fighting back tears myself. "When did you realize it was wrong?"

"Never, until everything happened. I'm glad I didn't know it was wrong. That's why it's confusing for me to hate my dad. I'm like, Dad gave me a good life, I wasn't mistreated."

Kiani told me that she wanted to become a model, but she felt her lack of social experience and self-confidence would hold her back.

"It's just, I'm embarrassed. That sounds bad, but I get embarrassed that my name is Wesson. It's too hard to get a job, and it affects me all the time. They say, 'Oh, it's *that* family. There's the girl who had kids with her dad.' "

She said she was so self-conscious about it that she no longer wanted to use her last name. She had decided to use a different one, to make herself more anonymous. I wished that letting go of those six letters would make all of her problems disappear. If only it were that easy.

THE WESSON NAME was affecting all of Marcus's children. Serafino, now the youngest child in the family, was living with his wife in Fresno. His goal was to become a policeman someday. Currently working as a security guard, Serafino told me about a neighborhood watch meeting he'd attended at an apartment complex that had been having problems with crime. His plan was to reassure the residents that they would be safer with him on patrol.

Things were going well until a woman asked his name. He paused, then finally said, "Sergeant Wesson."

This caught everyone's attention, and he knew what question would follow. "You're not related to *Marcus* Wesson, are you?"

He'd always told the truth, but not that day. He knew these people wouldn't trust him to protect them if they knew who he really was.

"No," he lied. "I'm not related to him."

"Thank God," one of the residents said. "He's a sick bastard. I hope they burn him."

"We don't need any people like that around here."

"And the family, oh my God, they're just like him."

Serafino listened to the barrage of insults with a pit in his stomach, but somehow he managed to finish the business at hand.

I thought he looked very professional and put together in his security-guard uniform; I wished Marcus could have seen him. Serafino had grown a little heavier and seemed more mature now that he'd lost the childhood innocence in his face. Of all the boys, he resembled his father the most.

I hadn't talked to him much over the past year, but I noticed he walked with a new air of confidence. I wondered if it had come from the uniform or from his first encounter with fatherhood.

Sitting on the couch together, we inevitably began talking about Marcus. Like his brothers, Serafino said he still had physical scars from his father's abuse.

"When he was hitting you, didn't you hate him?" I asked, wincing with empathy.

"No. It's like young women in abusive relationships. The men beat them and disrespect them, but the women still love them and make excuses. They defend their boyfriends to everyone. That's what we did. We didn't know any better. Somehow, I thought I deserved it."

Elizabeth had brought us coffee from McDonald's, and I could tell Serafino was uncomfortable, because he kept fiddling with the stir stick, swirling it around in his cup every few minutes.

"If you could go back in time, what would you change?" I asked.

"To put it in mild terms, I'd stop it. All it would have taken is *one* phone call. Think about it. Not the way my cousins called the police in the end, because my dad was prepared for that. He had his soldiers. He literally trained soldiers to be on command because he was preparing for that day. I hate thinking about it, but I was one of the soldiers."

Serafino looked down and shook his head, recalling how he'd blocked the doorway the day of the murders, willing to take a bullet for his father. He said an officer pulled his gun halfway out of the holster, but Serafino just stood there.

"For some reason, I finally moved. They rushed in, but, of course, it was too late by then. Standing there with Rosie and Kiani, I was just pushing people out of the way, and without knowing it, we were doing what my dad had trained us to do."

360 | ALYSIA SOFIOS

"Are you mad you stood there now?"

"Of course, I resent it with a passion. It sounds so corny when other people say it, but I really blame myself for what happened. People tell me I was a victim, but I don't know. I just did what I was trained to do."

"Do you think a lot about the last time you saw everyone alive?"

"Oh yes. I saw some things that no one knows. I didn't tell anyone because they didn't ask me the questions. I would not have lied, but they just didn't ask."

I was frozen with shock. So many people had speculated for years about what had happened in that room, and I'd thought Marcus was the only one with the answer. Could Serafino solve the mystery?

"What did you see, Fino?" I asked, scooting closer to him, my elbows on my knees, with rapt attention.

But after a long silence, he shook his head and said nothing. He wasn't ready to talk about the details.

"I will say, those things will haunt me for the rest of my life," Serafino said sadly. "I saw something that wasn't right."

We both drifted off into deep thought. I didn't want to push him any further. I realized for the first time that I might not really want to know what happened in that room.

So I asked another question that still perplexed most everyone who heard about this gruesome story: "If it *was* Sebhrenah who did it, what do you think was going through her mind?"

"I know she had no choice. She was put on a path that she didn't know any better. It's like all my family was born in a dark room. We lived in that dark room, and it was not a good life. Then my dad opened the door and we saw a light.

And we were told to go to the light because it was the only way out. Sebhrenah walked toward the light that day."

Serafino thought for a minute. "You know how I can best describe the way everything went down? It was an invisible gun."

"Invisible gun?" I asked, not understanding his analogy.

"Yeah. All our lives, it was like we had an invisible gun pointing at our heads. My dad put it there when we were born. We spent our lives doing everything with a gun to our heads. At the end, Sebhrenah did what she did because of the invisible gun."

I studied Serafino carefully. "What about now? Is the gun gone?" I asked.

He smirked, turning his head left, then right.

"It's almost gone," he said, reaching up and swiping the air where I'd been looking. "It's finally almost gone."

Twenty-six

I couldn't shake the "invisible gun" theory. Ever since I'd met them, I had been struggling to describe the syndrome afflicting this family, yet Serafino had summed it up flawlessly in just two words. As disturbing as those words were, I felt somewhat relieved. I finally had an explanation for the family's behavior that I could pass on to my friends and family. After all, how could people really know what they would do with guns to their heads?

I knew Marcus's hold was loosening on Elizabeth, Rosie, and the rest, but they weren't free yet. They were still holding on to him, too, and I was determined to find some way to help them break those ties. My quest kept me up at night. They weren't the only ones needing closure, and I wasn't about to wait for Marcus's execution to get it.

There was only one thing left that I hadn't tried, but it came with a price. I could face the monster head-on, and try to get answers to the questions his family was too afraid to ask. What really happened to the kids? Who pulled the trigger? Why wasn't he sorry for all those years of abuse? But even the prospect of sitting face-to-face with him nauseated me.

So first I had to ask *myself* a question. Was I really going to be able to confront Marcus Wesson, the subject of my nightmares, the most evil man I knew in the world? Yes, I could do it—and felt I had to do it—for the survivors I had grown to care so much about.

Settling down to write him another letter, I had to swallow my pride. I knew I had to be nice.

```
Marcus,
   I hope all is well since the last
time we corresponded. I've been quite
busy lately. . . . The weather in
Fresno is beginning to cool off for the
season. The thick fog is rolling in and
blanketing the valley again. I miss the
hot and dry days of summer. Growing up
in Michigan, I'll never take another
blue sky for granted.
   Getting to the point of my letter, I
would like to visit you. As I expressed
earlier, I have many unresolved feelings.
I realize you are not able to answer the
questions I'm left with; however, I know
it would help to meet you face-to-face
(and perhaps talk about the weather some
more). . . . I hope you will oblige my
request. Who knows, it may resolve some
things for you as well. Anyway, please
send me a form to expedite the visita-
tion process. I expect you'll understand
why this is important to me.
              Hope to hear from you soon,
                        Alysia Sofios
```

I wasn't sitting on eggshells waiting for his response, but the thought of meeting him continued to loom over my head like a cold, black cloud.

I CAME HOME one day to find that Elizabeth had rearranged the furniture. Everything seemed a bit out of place, especially the blue couch, which now blocked one wall and had become the unattractive focal point of the room. That made two of us. I had been feeling a bit out of place myself lately.

I heard the girls' familiar footsteps on the path below as they approached the stairs in their high heels. Rosie and Kiani were surprising me with a visit. I knew it was them, but I acted surprised nonetheless.

Elizabeth, Gypsy, and little Alysia walked down the hall to greet them, joining us in the living room. I thought back to the first time they had walked into my apartment, and I marveled at the drastic changes I saw before me now. Everything about them was different—except for the shoes. And they all seemed, well, so *happy*.

While Kiani and my roommates were distracted with giggly conversation, Rosie signaled me to follow her into the bedroom.

"What's going on?" I whispered.

She closed my bedroom door, her face lit up like a sixth-grader's. I had never seen her look so innocent or so over-joyed.

"I have a boyfriend," she whispered back.

I stood there trying to comprehend the magnitude of her news, but I couldn't. I thought I must have misheard her.

"Okay, say that again."

Rosie laughed and repeated that she did, indeed, have a boyfriend.

"It's true, Alysia. You were right."

I could feel a heaviness lift from my shoulders, and I swore I could hear a faint chorus of "Hallelujah." I grabbed Rosie and squeezed her tight.

"Don't tell anyone yet," she said, still whispering. "And don't laugh, but he's a police officer."

Talk about poetic justice. I followed her into the living room in a blissful daze.

It doesn't look so weird in here after all.

All of a sudden, I loved the stuffed blue couch that matched nothing else in the room. I sank into its tired cushions and wondered why they felt more comfortable than ever before. I felt a burst of euphoria even as my eyes welled up with tears.

Turning to look out the window so the others wouldn't see me crying, I shouldn't have been surprised at what I saw: a mourning dove was sitting on the ledge of my balcony, staring at me. We exchanged knowing glances until I regained my composure. Then, the dove spun around, spread its wings, and flew into the sun. I tilted my head, watched as it disappeared in the cloudless blue sky, and mouthed the words "thank you."

"Are you okay, Alysia?" Kiani asked.

I turned back toward the smiling group and froze the image in my head. Elizabeth, holding a book open, was reading to a captivated little Alysia. Kiani and Gypsy were smirking at me in between bites of ice cream from their overflowing bowls. I looked down at Rosie's hand and saw that her wedding band was gone.

"I'm more than okay," I responded with a wink.

FOR THE FIRST time since my accident, I had some downtime. My grandma had just died, so I booked a flight to Florida to be with my family and attend her funeral. Elizabeth, who knew I had a five-hour layover, shoved a manila envelope at me as I ran out the door.

"It's reading material for your wait. I won't be needing it anymore," she said. "Tell your mom I'm thinking of her. Have a safe trip."

She hugged me tightly, and I stuffed the envelope into my carry-on bag without another thought.

I waited until I was sitting in an uncomfortable orange metal chair at the airport to open the mysterious package. I couldn't believe what I saw inside: a thick stack of letters Marcus had written to Elizabeth, filled with the same crazy talk that had controlled his family for so many years. To let go of them was a staggering accomplishment for her. I was thrilled that, at long last, she was ready to take a stab at life on her own terms.

With a bittersweet smile and tears in my eyes, I flipped through the pages and skimmed Marcus's insane demands. Knowing now that they would never be fulfilled, I wanted to share this revelation with my fellow human beings—even the twenty-something guy in the funny striped hat sleeping in the chair across from me. I wanted to run through the crowded airport, shredding Marcus's rambling instructions and screaming, "Take that, Marcus! How do you like me now?"

But figuring that the last thing I needed was to get arrested, I simply raised the envelope to shoulder level and gave it a quick victory shake, inadvertently dumping a small pale object onto the worn carpet below.

It was Elizabeth's beloved seashell.

After she'd kept it so close to her all these years, I was amazed, but gratified, that she was finally able to let it go, too. I knew instantly what to do with it.

That week in Florida was one of sad and somber reflection. Several hours after my grandma's funeral, I walked along the miles of beach near her house, still wearing the flowing blue dress I'd worn to the ceremony. She loved it when I wore blue to match my eyes; black, she said, was too depressing. My grandma and I had made the trek down that stretch of beach together so many times that I could almost picture her footprints next to mine. I found an out-of-the-way spot near an empty lifeguard stand and sank into the warm sand below. Soothed by the sound of the waves crashing, I flashed back to March 12, 2004.

I could still remember every last grim detail. Until that day, I had been in my own selfish world, but that all changed when I met the Wessons.

As I watched the setting sun sparkle across the endless blue ocean, everything seemed to make sense at last. The past few years had been filled with so many ups and downs as I risked everything to help this family right their upside-down world. But I could see now that it had all been part of the bigger picture. We had come together for a reason. I had arrived in Fresno thinking only of my professional growth, but thanks to our symbiotic journey together, my

368 | ALYSIA SOFIOS

development had taken me on a far more personal and spiritual path. I was so thankful that I'd chosen to let down my emotional walls and follow my human instincts. If I hadn't, I never would have realized what I'd missed.

I thought about my dear friend Elizabeth. She was so busy making up for lost time as a parent that she didn't have time to think about herself. Someone always needed her help, or her advice, or a ride somewhere. I was pleased that she finally had the freedom to bond with her grandbabies without having to worry that Marcus would beat them for crying when she left the house.

Over the past few years, I'd seen her struggle through the typical stages of grief and then some. Even now, she still felt so much pain and guilt—emotions that Marcus should have been feeling but wasn't. She was the one stuck explaining her husband's actions to her kids, when really, there was no explanation. But she was stronger now, she had her own voice, and she even spoke louder. I knew she was finally seeing Marcus for the man he really was.

My feelings were raw from losing my grandma, so I felt an even deeper sense of loss than usual for those nine wonderful souls who would never have the chance to realize their potential. I was sad that I would never know Sebhrenah, Lise, Illabelle, Jonathan, Aviv, Ethan, Marshey, Sedona, or Jeva. I gazed up at the puffy white clouds with wet, blurry eyes, then reached into my pocket for Elizabeth's weathered little seashell.

Slowly, I walked waist-deep into the frigid water. I said a prayer for my grandma and the nine children, pulled my arm back like a baseball pitcher, and threw the shell as hard as I could into the crest of a wave. As I watched the purple and orange rays of the sunset fade into the horizon, I felt the overwhelming sense that my grandma was out there somewhere, taking care of those nine Wesson children.

If a fragile seashell could make its way out of the Pacific Ocean and end up in the Atlantic three decades later, anything was possible.

Epilogue

T oday, the survivors of the Wesson mass murder are thriving.

Elizabeth continues to encourage her children to establish the close sibling relationships Marcus never allowed them to form. She no longer blames her nieces Ruby and Sofia for the murders and has apologized to both of them. In May of 2010, Elizabeth was legally divorced from Marcus. She has not written to him in years. She is attending community college in Fresno and has recently qualified for a scholarship based on her 4.0 average.

Rosie and her boyfriend had a baby girl in 2009. The happy family lives in Northern California. She has earned her GED and is taking courses to become a nurse. She continues to rescue and care for stray animals.

All the push-ups and sit-ups paid off for Kiani, who has become a fitness model, showing off her rock-hard abs and toned arms in runway fashion shows and print ads. She works in a pharmacy in Santa Cruz, where she lives with her boyfriend and their daughter.

Gypsy is attending a university in Fresno and is set to graduate with a business degree this fall. She works as an apartment manager and lives on her own with little Alysia.

Alysia just finished kindergarten at a charter school, where she is thriving.

Dorian still lives in Santa Cruz and is pursuing his dream of becoming a martial arts instructor. Casting agents have approached him about becoming a model. Adrian moved to San Francisco. He works as a personal trainer and is taking college courses in nutrition and food science. He loves spending time with his two children.

After earning his GED, Marcus Jr. enrolled and graduated from a fire academy in the Fresno area. In 2010, a local fire department hired him as a firefighter.

Serafino works as a security supervisor in Fresno, where he and his wife are raising their two sons and a daughter. He still hopes to become a police officer someday.

Sofia and Ruby are both integrating themselves back into the family, as the two split factions slowly learn to forgive each other.

The Fresno police detective Doug Reese was honored for his work in the Wesson case. He received a prestigious Investigative Excellence Award from the Robert Presley Institute of Criminal Investigation. Upon accepting the award, Reese said, "It was a big relief that there was closure."

The Wessons' house on Hammond Avenue was sold to a man who demolished it as a community service in July 2006, ridding the city of an unpleasant reminder.

Alysia recently moved to Los Angeles for her reporting career—these days focusing on *American Idol* and other entertainment stories, rather than hard news. She received one more letter from Marcus, giving her his permission for a prison visit if she would call him her friend. She refused and has no intention of responding.

Marcus remains on death row at San Quentin, where he has refused to meet with the defense lawyer handling his appeal. Due to a temporary moratorium on lethal injection in California, no one has been executed in the state since January of 2006.

The Wesson children's physical scars of abuse are still fading, and the whole family, many through therapy, is working to erase the emotional scars. So far, Kiani, Rosie, Gypsy, and Marcus Jr. have changed their last names to disassociate themselves from their past—and Marcus Wesson.

Acknowledgments

Most of the information in this book came out of extensive interviews with the surviving Wesson family members. Special thanks to Elizabeth and Gypsy Wesson, who endured countless hours of relaying emotional details of their traumatic past. They, along with Kiani Wesson and Rosa Solorio, will always be an important part of my life. I am also grateful for my friends Dorian, Adrian, Marcus Jr., and Serafino Wesson for their candid interviews and honest answers, even when my questions were tough. Also for their, along with Almae Wesson's, broadcast interviews early on in the case.

Much of the dialogue in this book was reconstructed based on Marcus Wesson's wife and children's memories of their lives with him. For police interrogations, 911 calls, diary entries, and trial testimony, I used court transcripts and exhibits whenever possible, or cross-checked information with published news reports. I also used portions of Marcus Wesson's letters that he wrote me, as well as letters and songs his family made available to me after the trial.

To protect the privacy of my former coworkers and extended Wesson family members, I used a handful of pseudonyms, which are marked with asterisks so the reader can distinguish them from the others.

This project would not have been possible without the help, cooperation, and support of dozens of people:

To Caitlin Rother, whose stellar research methods, work ethic, and penchant for accuracy are second to none. I am proud of what we have accomplished together.

To my agent Janet Reid, who believed in this story from the start, and made sure we found the best way to tell it. Because of you, and Abby Zidle from Pocket, an inspirational message of hope has come out of this horrible tragedy. Caitlin would also like to thank agent Stephany Evans and Gary Heidt.

To Carol Uchita, who has always been a devoted and trusted friend to me and the Wesson women. We are forever grateful for all you have done.

To my friends and family, for being a lifeline during this process, and helping me fulfill my dream. And to my friends and coworkers at KMPH, especially Lisa Burger, for making sure I go after exclusives.

And to Attorney Phalen "Chuck" Hurewitz, for his valued advice and effort during this process, Kelly Wiefel from the Fresno County Coroner's Office, Sherry Spears from the Fresno County Superior Court, Presiding Judge Hilary A. Chittick, Mary Calderon from the Fresno County Courts.